TREASURES OF ANCIENT AMERICA

TREASURES
OF
ANCIENT AMERICA

THE ARTS OF THE
PRE-COLUMBIAN CIVILIZATIONS
FROM MEXICO TO PERU

TEXT BY

S. K. LOTHROP

of the Institute of Andean Research

SKIRA

CREATED BY ALBERT SKIRA FOR HORIZON MAGAZINE ®

BOOK TRADE DISTRIBUTION IN THE UNITED STATES BY THE WORLD PUBLISHING COMPANY

Book trade distribution in the United States by
THE WORLD PUBLISHING COMPANY
2231 West 110th Street, Cleveland 2, Ohio

★

© 1964 by Editions d'Art Albert Skira, Geneva
Library of Congress Catalog Card Number: 64-23255

PRINTED IN SWITZERLAND

ACKNOWLEDGEMENTS

Our particular thanks are due to the private collectors and curators of museums who have kindly allowed us to reproduce the works in their keeping; the ownership and present location of each work is indicated in the captions accompanying the illustrations.

We should also like to thank the following persons whose co-operation and advice have facilitated the making of this book: Dr. Eduardo Arias Robredo, Dr. Luis Aveleyra Arroyo de Anda, Mr. Charles Balser, Sr. Barbachano Ponce, Dr. Luis Barriga, Dr. Etta Becker-Donner, Dr. Ignacio Bernal, Dr. Junius Bird, Dr. Geoffrey Bushnell, Sr. Dorton Manuel Cassas Mannique, Mr. Adrian Digby, Mrs. Louisa Dresser, Mr. Dudley T. Easby, Dr. Gordon Ekholm, Sr. Julio Espejo Núñez, Dr. Franz Feuchtwanger, Sr. Fernando Gamboa, Dr. René d'Harnoncourt, Sr. Cirilio Huapaya, Dr. Alfred Kidder, Sr. Rafael Larco Hoyle, Dr. Milton Arno Leof, Sr. Toribio Mejía Xesspe, Dr. Alejandro Méndez, Sr. Santiago Morera, Dr. Jorge Muelle, Sr. Miguel Mujica Gallo, Sra. Lola Olmeda de Olvera, Mrs. Jane Rosenthal, Sr. Guillermo Salazar, Dr. Carlos Samayoa, Dr. Doris Stone, Sr. Antonio Tejeda, Sr. Alvaro Vargas, and Dr. Henry Wassén.

Acknowledgement is made to the Hakluyt Society, London, for permission to print the quotations on pages 53, 54, 56 and 60 from "The True History of the Conquest of New Spain" by Bernal Diaz del Castillo, translated by A. P. Maudslay and published by the Hakluyt Society in 1908-1916; to Alfred A. Knopf, Inc., New York, for the illustrations on pages 62, 66 and 127; to the Instituto Nacional de Antropología e Historia de México for the illustrations on pages 40 and 126; to the Fondo de Cultura Económica, Mexico City, for the illustration on page 95; and to Chaski, Órgano de la Asociación Peruana de Arqueología for the illustration on page 194.

A. S.

CONTENTS

LIST OF ILLUSTRATIONS IX

INTRODUCTION 3

1. MEXICO 7

The Pre-Classic 11

Eastern Mexico:
The Olmec Style 16
Remojadas 24
Classical Vera Cruz Sculpture 29
Tajin 34
The Huastec Area 34
Cerro Montoso 36

Central Mexico:
Teotihuacan 39
The Toltec of Tula 49
Chichimec Period 50
The Aztec 51

Western Mexico:
Guerrero 71
Michoacan 72
Nayarit 75
Colima 75

Southern Mexico:
The Zapotec and Monte Alban 76
The Mixtec 82

Chronological Table 90

2. THE MAYA 91

The Toltec of Yucatan 124

3. THE INTERMEDIATE AREA 129

El Salvador and Honduras 133
Nicaragua and Costa Rica 134
Panama 142
Colombia 147

4. PERU 153

Northern Peru:
The Chavin Styles 156
Mochica 164
Recuay 178
Chimu 180

Southern Peru:
Paracas 189
Nazca 201
Tiahuanaco 204
Inca 215

CONCLUSION 225

INDEX OF NAMES AND PLACES 227

LIST OF ILLUSTRATIONS

INTRODUCTION

Hands and Forearms of Beaten Gold with Nails covered with Silver. Provenance Unknown. Chimu Style. Length, 12¾ inches. Width, 5 inches. Collection Miguel Mujica Gallo, Lima, Peru 2

MEXICO

Pottery Figurine from Tlatilco, Mexico City. Middle Pre-Classic Style. Private Collection, Mexico City 8

Pottery Figurines of the Pre-Classic Period. From Mexico. Private Collection 10

Pottery Figurines of the Pre-Classic Period. From Mexico. Private Collection 11

Effigy Bottle from Las Bocas, State of Puebla, Mexico. Middle Pre-Classic. Height, 7 inches. Private Collection 12

Effigy Jars representing a Toucan (left) and a Fish (right). From Tlatilco, Mexico City. Middle Pre-Classic. Height, 5 inches and 5½ inches. Private Collection and Museo Nacional de Antropología, Mexico City 15

Seated Figure of Andesite. Olmec Style. From Sayula, Vera Cruz, Mexico. Height, 48 inches. Museo de Antropología, Vera Cruz University, Jalapa, Mexico 17

Olmec Basalt Head from San Lorenzo, Vera Cruz, Mexico. Height, 9 feet, 4 inches. Museo de Antropología, Vera Cruz University, Jalapa, Mexico 18

The Kunz Anthropomorphic Axe, from Oaxaca, Mexico. Olmec Style. Height, 10¾ inches. American Museum of Natural History, New York 21

An Olmec Ritual Cache from La Venta, Vera Cruz, Mexico. Height, about 8 inches. Museo Nacional de Antropología, Mexico City 22-23

Pottery Statue representing a Woman who has died in Childbirth. Remojadas Style. From Tlalixcoyan, Vera Cruz. Height, 53¾ inches. Museo de Antropología, Vera Cruz University, Jalapa, Mexico . . 25

Pottery Figure of a Smiling Skeleton. Classical Remojadas Style. Height, 14½ inches. From Los Cerros, Tierra Blanca, Vera Cruz. Museo de Antropología, Vera Cruz University, Jalapa, Mexico 26

Laughing Head from a Broken Pottery Figurine. Remojadas Style. From Los Cerros, Tierra Blanca (?), Vera Cruz. Height, 6½ inches. Museo de Antropología, Vera Cruz University, Jalapa, Mexico . . 27

Pottery Head of a Serpent, one of a Pair found in a Cave. From Acatlan de Pérez Figueroa, Oaxaca (near the Vera Cruz Border). Remojadas Style. Height, 31 inches. Museo Nacional de Antropología, Mexico City 28

Stone "Yoke." Classical Vera Cruz Style. Height, 16¼ inches. From the State of Vera Cruz, Mexico. American Museum of Natural History, New York 30

"Palma" of Basalt adorned with Human Hands. Classical Vera Cruz Style. From Tlacolulan, Vera Cruz. Height, 14¼ inches. Museo de Antropología, Vera Cruz University, Jalapa, Mexico 32

"Hacha" representing a Human Head with a Headdress in the Form of a Leaping Dolphin. Classical Vera Cruz Style. From San Andres Tuxtla, State of Vera Cruz. Height, 11¼ inches. Covarrubias Collection, Museo Nacional de Antropología, Mexico City 33

Huastec Statue, front and back. From San Vicente Tancuayalab, San Luis Potosí, Mexico. Height, 62¼ inches. Brooklyn Museum 35

Pottery Jar portraying Centipedes. Cerro Montoso Style marked by Incised Zone Outlines. From Otates, Vera Cruz. Height, 6⅛ inches. Museo Nacional de Antropología, Mexico City 37

Sculptured Façade of the Temple of Quetzalcoatl. Teotihuacan, D.F., Mexico 38

Restored View of the Pyramid of the Sun. Teotihuacan, D.F., Mexico (Drawing by J. A. Gomez Rubio) 40

Idol representing a Temple with a Water Goddess on the Façade. Height, ca. 16 feet. Museo Nacional de Mexico, Mexico City (Drawing by Antonio Tejeda) 41

Stone Stela carved in Four Sections with Peg and Socket Joints. From La Ventilla, Teotihuacan, D.F., Mexico. Height, 82 inches. Museo Nacional de Antropología, Mexico City 42

Statuette representing a Standing Human Figure. Style of Teotihuacan. From the State of Puebla, Mexico. Height, 10¼ inches. Covarrubias Collection, Museo Nacional de Antropología, Mexico City 43

Onyx Marble Mask, formerly with Inlaid Eyes. Classical Teotihuacan Style. Museo Archeologico, Florence, Italy 45

The Rain God Tlaloc. Detail of a Fresco of the Classic Period at Tetitla, Teotihuacan, D.F., Mexico 46

Classical Teotihuacan Bowl. Height, 4½ inches. Diego Rivera Museum, Mexico City 47

Pottery Head of an Animal with a Human Head in the Open Jaws. Toltec Period. Found at Tula, Hidalgo, Mexico. Height, 5⅜ inches. Museo Nacional de Antropología, Mexico City 48

Columns which supported the Roof of a now Fallen Temple. Height of Atlantean Figures, 15 feet. Toltec of Tula, Hidalgo 50

Aztec Pottery Incense Burner recently excavated on a Terrace of the Great Pyramid at Tlateloco. Height, 42 inches. Museo Nacional de Antropología, Mexico City 55

The Calendar Stone of the Aztec. Diameter, nearly 12 feet. Museo Nacional de Antropología, Mexico City (Drawing by Antonio Tejeda). 57

The Aztec Goddess Coatlicue, "Lady of the Serpent Skirt." Height, 8 feet. Museo Nacional de Antropología, Mexico City 59

Aztec Statue representing a Priest of Xipe clad in the Skin of a Sacrificed Victim. Found in Texcoco, Valley of Mexico. Height, 15¾ inches. Museum für Völkerkunde, Basel, Switzerland 61

The Goddess Tlazolteotl clad in the Flayed Skin of a Sacrificed Woman. From an Aztec Manuscript, the Codex Borbonicus, in the Library of the Chamber of Deputies, Paris (Drawing by Miguel Covarrubias) 62

A Grasshopper carved in Red Carnelite. From Chapultec, D.F., Mexico. Museo Nacional de Mexico, Mexico City 63

Wooden Mask encrusted with Mosaic of Turquoise and Colored Shell. Aztec or Mixtec Workmanship. Height, 7¼ inches. Museo Preistorico, Rome 64

Front of a Human Skull adorned with Mosaic of Turquoise and Jet. Height, 7⅞ inches. British Museum, London 65

Aztec Pottery Designs from the Valley of Mexico, from the Interior of Bowls painted in Black on Yellow. Sequent Styles introduced ca. 900, 1200 and 1350 A.D. (Drawing by José Luis Franco) 66

Ceremonial Shield adorned with Featherwork outlined in Gold. Diameter, 27½ inches. Museum für Völkerkunde, Vienna 67

Onyx Jar, found on Isla de Sacrificios, Vera Cruz, Mexico. Height, 9 inches. Museo Nacional de Antropología, Mexico City 68

Pottery Figurine representing an Elaborately Painted Woman. Style of Nayarit. Height, 21 inches. Diego Rivera Museum, Mexico City 70

Pottery Effigy Vessel representing a Dog, wearing a Mask in the Form of a Human Face. Colima Style. Height, 8¼ inches. Museo Nacional de Antropología, Mexico City 72

Pottery Effigy Jar showing a Man seated on a Small Stool. Colima Style. Museo Nacional de Antropología, Mexico City 73

Pottery Model of a Ball Court showing Players and Spectators on Top of the Parallel Walls. Style of Nayarit. Width, 14½ inches. From Western Mexico. Art Museum, Worcester, Mass. 74

Zapotec Urn representing a Jaguar. From Monte Alban, Oaxaca. Period II. Height, 36 inches. Museo Nacional de Antropología, Mexico City 77

Zapotec Urn representing a Maize God. Monte Alban III Style. Height, 20⅜ inches. Lola Olmeda de Olvera Collection, Mexico City. Formerly Sologuren Collection 78

Zapotec Urn representing a seated Deity. From Monte Alban, Oaxaca. Period III. Height, 12¾ inches. Museo Nacional de Antropología, Mexico City 79

Zapotec Mosaic Mask of Jade and Shell representing a Vampire Bat. From Monte Alban, Oaxaca. Period II. Height of head, 6¼ inches. Museo Nacional de Antropología, Mexico City 81

Two of the Danzantes at Monte Alban, Oaxaca, Mexico. Period I, 650-200 B.C. 82

Mixtec Cast Gold Pendant representing Mictlantecutli, the God of Death. From Tomb 7, Monte Alban, Oaxaca. Height, 4¾ inches. Museo Regional de Oaxaca, Mexico 84

Mixtec Cast Gold Pendant representing a Sun Disk. Zaachila, Oaxaca. Height, 4⅝ inches. Museo Nacional de Antropología, Mexico City 85

Mixtec Cast Gold Pendant representing the Aztec Deity Xipe, his Face covered with Flayed Skin. Coixtlahuaca, Oaxaca. Height, 4 inches. Museo Nacional de Antropología, Mexico City 86

Mixtec Vessel from Mihuatlan, Oaxaca, Mexico. Height, 12¼ inches. American Museum of Natural History, New York 88

THE MAYA

Cylindrical Pottery Tube adorned with the Head of the Sun God held in the Jaws of the Earth Monster. Temple of the Cross, **Palenque, Chiapas,** Mexico. Classic Maya. Height, 37⅞ inches. Museo Nacional de Antropología, Mexico City 92

A Classic Maya Date with Numerical Values expressed by the Heads. Stela D, Copan, Honduras (Drawing by Abel Mendoza) 95

A Corner of the Great Plaza at Tikal, Department of El Peten, Guatemala 97

Stucco Head in the Half Round, cut from a Wall at Comalcalco, Tabasco, Mexico. Classic Maya. Height, 17¼ inches. Museo Nacional de Antropología, Mexico City 99

Lintel 24 from a Palace at Yaxchilan, Chiapas, Mexico. Classic Maya, ca. 750 A.D. British Museum, London 100

Lintel from Piedras Negras, Guatemala. Classic Maya, ca. 757 A.D. Width, 49 inches. Museo de Arqueología y Etnología de Guatemala, Guatemala City 101

Stela 12 at Piedras Negras, Guatemala, dated 795 A.D. Height, ca. 10 feet. Museo de Arqueología y Etnología de Guatemala, Guatemala City (After Gordon) 103

Seated Human Figure in the Open Jaws of the Sculptured Monster known as the Great Turtle or Zoomorph P at Quirigua, Guatemala. The Dynamic Phase of Late Classic Maya 104

Stela D and Altar in the Great Plaza at Copan, Honduras. Dated at 736 A.D. Late Classic Maya. Height, 12 feet, 2½ inches 105

Fuchsite Statuette found in an Early Classic Maya Deposit at Uaxactun, Department of El Peten, Guatemala. Height, 10 inches. Museo de Arqueología y Etnología de Guatemala, Guatemala City . . 106

Pottery Figurine, with Head and Shoulders cast from a Mold, the Rest Modeled. Jaina Style, Late Classic Maya. From Campeche, Mexico. Height, 10⅝ inches. Barbachano Ponce Collection, Mexico City . . 108

Pottery Figurine. A Standing Male Figure dressed in a Long Ceremonial Robe. Jaina Style, Late Classic Maya. From Jaina Island. Height, 9 inches. Museo Nacional de Antropología, Mexico City . . . 109

Part of a Battle Episode from a Mural at Bonampak, Chiapas, Mexico (Drawing by Antonio Tejeda) 110

The Judgment of Prisoners, forming Part of a Mural at Bonampak, Chiapas, Mexico (Drawing by Antonio Tejeda) 111

The Leyden Plaque. Found near Puerto Barrios, Guatemala. Height, 8½ inches. Rijksmuseum, Leyden, Holland 112

Jade Mosaic Mask representing an Old Man. From the Ruz Tomb under the Temple of the Inscriptions at Palenque, Chiapas, Mexico. Classic Maya, ca. 700 A.D. Height, 4¾ inches. Museo Nacional de Antropología, Mexico City 114

Jade Death Mask. From the Temple of the Inscriptions at Palenque, Chiapas, Mexico. Museo Nacional de Antropología, Mexico City 115

Jade Pectoral from Nebaj, Department of the Quiché, Guatemala. Late Classic Maya. Width, 5¾ inches. Museo de Arqueología y Etnología de Guatemala, Guatemala City 116

A Polychrome Two-Part Effigy Vessel, perhaps an Incense Burner. From a Tomb under an Early Classic Maya Building at Tikal. Height, 14¾ inches. University of Pennsylvania Museum, Tikal, Guatemala   118

A Two-Part Effigy representing a Hunchback Figure, probably an Incense Burner. From Kaminaljuyú, Guatemala. Height, 8¾ inches. Museo de Arqueología y Etnología de Guatemala, Guatemala City   119

Pottery Incense Burner representing a Mythological Bird with a Human Head. Found in a Cave near Purulhá, Department of Baja Vera Paz, Guatemala. Post-Classic Maya (?). Height, 18½ inches. Museo de Arqueología y Etnología de Guatemala, Guatemala City   121

Painted Panel from a Polychrome Jar. Classic Maya. From Altar de Sacrificios, Guatemala. Height, 6⅝ inches. Museo de Arqueología y Etnología de Guatemala, Guatemala City (Drawing by Antonio Tejeda)   122

Polychrome Jar found in a Tomb at Altar de Sacrificios. Height, 6⅝ inches. Museo de Arqueología y Etnología de Guatemala, Guatemala City   123

Part of a Bas-Relief representing Two Teams of Ball Players. From the East Bench in the Great Ball Court at Chichen Itza, Yucatan, Mexico. Height, ca. 4 feet (Drawing by Miguel Angel Fernandez) . .   126

A Maya Coastal Village with Scattered Houses and Trees. From a Mural in the Temple of the Warriors, Chichen Itza, Yucatan, Mexico. Length, 12½ feet (Drawing by Miguel Covarrubias)   127

THE INTERMEDIATE AREA

Cast Gold Pendant representing a Crocodile God. From La Vaca, Punta Burica, Costa Rica. Height, 4¾ inches. Banco Central de Costa Rica, San José, Costa Rica   130

Carved Marble Jar with Animal Handles. From the Ulua Valley, Honduras. Height, 12 inches. University Museum, Philadelphia   132

Polychrome Effigy Jar representing a Turkey. From Nacasola, Nicoya Peninsula, Costa Rica. Height, 8 inches. Juan Dada Collection, Museo Nacional de Costa Rica, San José, Costa Rica   135

Nicoya Red Ware Effigy representing a Pregnant Woman. From El Panamá (Culebra Bay), Guanacaste, Costa Rica. Height, 11½ inches. Charles Balser Collection, San José, Costa Rica   136

Twin Effigy Vessels representing Lovers, seated on a Bench. From the Vicinity of Guápiles, Costa Rica. Height, 13¼ inches. Private Collection, San José, Costa Rica   137

Light Green Jade Pendant representing a Bat. Ca. 500-700 A.D. Length, 6 inches. From Las Huacas, Nicoya Peninsula, Costa Rica. Carnegie Museum of Pittsburg (Drawing by Miss Symme Burnstein)   138

Jade "Axe God." Guápiles Style but found in the Nicoya Peninsula, Costa Rica. Height, ca. 7 inches. United States National Museum, Washington, D.C. (Drawing by Miss Symme Burnstein) . . .   138

Cast Gold Pendant representing a Crocodile with a Human Figure in its Mouth. From La Vaca, Punta Burica, Costa Rica. Length, 6 inches. Weight, 267.3 grams. Banco Central de Costa Rica, San José, Costa Rica   139

Cast Gold Pendant representing a Mythological Animal. From Puerto Jiménez, Osa Peninsula, Costa Rica. Height, 4⅞ inches. Banco Central de Costa Rica, San José, Costa Rica   140

Cast Gold Pendant representing a Lobster with a Crocodile Mouth. From La Vaca, Punta Burica, Costa Rica. Height, 4⅛ inches. Banco Central de Costa Rica, San José, Costa Rica   141

Embossed Gold Plaque representing a Crocodile God. Late Coclé Style. From Sitio Conte, Coclé Province, Panama. Height, 10¼ inches. Width, 7 inches. University Museum, Philadelphia   143

Coclé Polychrome Plate. Late Style. Diameter, 11½ inches. Museo Nacional de Panama, Panama City   144

Coclé Polychrome Bowl. Early Style. From Cativé, Soná, Veraguas Province, Panama. Museo Nacional de Panama, Panama City   145

Seated Figure of Cast Gold, a Bottle with a Spout on Top of the Head. Quimbaya Style, Colombia. Height, 9 inches. University Museum, Philadelphia   146

Stylized Cast Gold Pendant. Provenance Unknown. "Darien" Style. Height, 6⅝ inches. Weight, 293 grams. Museo de Oro, Banco de la República, Bogotá, Colombia   148

Sheet Gold Pectoral from the Headwaters of the Sinú River. Calima Style (?). Height, 8⅝ inches. Weight, 188 grams. Museo de Oro, Banco de la República, Bogotá, Colombia   149

Cast Tumbaga Pendant from the Vicinity of Popoyan, Colombia. Height, 11 inches. British Museum, London   150

Cast Tumbaga Pectoral from Huaca del Dragón, Caldas, Colombia. Tolima Style. Height, 9¼ inches. Weight, 315 grams. Museo de Oro, Banco de la República, Bogotá, Colombia   151

PERU

A Puma Hide of Hammered Gold. Mochica Style. From the North Coast of Peru. Length, ca. 40 inches. Weight, 510 grams. Collection Miguel Mujica Gallo, Lima, Peru 154

El Lanzon. Height, 15 feet. Chavin de Huántar, Peru (Drawing by Pablo Carrera) 157

Wall Panels from Chavin de Huántar, Peru (Drawing by Pablo Carrera) 158

Black Ware Carved Pottery Jar. Chavin Style. From Chongoyape, Lambayeque Valley, Peru. Height, 8¾ inches. Museo Nacional de Antropología y Arqueología, Lima, Peru 159

The Raimondi Wall Panel from Chavin de Huántar, Peru. The Last Phase of Chavin Sculpture. Museo de Antropología y Arqueología, Lima, Peru (Drawing by Pablo Carrera) 160

Painted and Incised Jar adorned with Puma-Headed Snakes. From Sausal, Chicama Valley, Peru. Height, 9½ inches. Collection Rafael Larco Hoyle, Lima, Peru 161

Puma Head of Hammered Silver. From Pachacamac, Peru. Height, 8 inches. American Museum of Natural History, New York 162

Portrait Jar representing an Aged Wrinkled Face with Shrunken Jaws. Cupisnique Style. From the Chicama Valley, Peru. Collection Rafael Larco Hoyle, Lima, Peru 163

Rectangular Jar surmounted by a Sculptured Dragon holding a Human Head. Mochica Style. Height, 6¾ inches. Museo de América, Madrid 165

Bas-Relief from a Mochica Pottery Jar showing a Chief carried in a Litter (Drawing by Antonio Tejeda) 166

A Group of Typical Mochica Warriors on a Painted Pottery Jar (Drawing by Pablo Carrera) . . . 167

"Mountain Jar." Late Mochica Style. Height, 8¾ inches. Museo Nacional de Antropología y Arqueología, Lima, Peru 168

Mochica Portrait Jar with Stirrup Spout. Museo Nacional de Antropología y Arqueología, Lima, Peru 171

Effigy Vessel representing a Seated Cripple with a Staff. Late Mochica Style. Height, 10½ inches. Collection Rafael Larco Hoyle, Lima, Peru 173

Effigy Vessel representing a Captive Deer-Man. Mochica III. Height, 9¾ inches. Collection Rafael Larco Hoyle, Lima, Peru 174

Bird Effigy Jar from Huancaco, Peru. Mochica Style. Height, 13¼ inches. Length, 12¾ inches. Museo Rafael Larco Herrera, Lima, Peru 175

Ear Disks adorned with Bird-Headed Warriors carrying Shields, Spears and Slings. Mochica Style. Diameter, 4 inches. Museo Rafael Larco Herrera, Lima, Peru 176

Head Ornament of Repoussé Gold representing a Plumed Feline Deity. Mochica Style. Width, 14½ inches. Museo Rafael Larco Herrera, Lima, Peru 177

A Chief or Deity seated on a Low Throne. Recuay Style. Provenance Unknown. Height, 8¾ inches. Collection Rafael Larco Hoyle, Lima, Peru 179

Repoussé Gold Breastplate adorned with Birds and Seven Rows of Human Figures. Width, 24 inches. Chimu Style. Collection Rafael Larco Hoyle, Lima, Peru 181

Ceremonial Chopping Knife of Copper with a Golden Handle representing a Standing Human Figure. From Illima, Department of Lambayeque, Peru. Chimu Style. Height, 16 inches. Collection Miguel Mujica Gallo, Lima, Peru 183

Large Jar of Hammered Silver. Chimu Style. Found at Chanchan, Peru. Height, 27¼ inches. Circumference, 67 inches. Museo Nacional de Antropología y Arqueología, Lima, Peru 184

The Base of a Bowl of Beaten Silver adorned with Small Birds. Chimu Style. Diameter, 6⅞ inches. Collection Rafael Larco Hoyle, Lima, Peru 185

Poncho with Feather Decoration consisting of Birds, Pumas and Fish surrounded by a Geometric Border. Chimu Style. Provenance Unknown. Height, 31 inches. The Art Institute of Chicago 186

Feather Headdress and Poncho decorated with Stylized Owls. From the Coast of Peru. Height, 51 inches. Width, 26 inches. University Museum of Archaeology and Ethnology, Cambridge, England . . 187

Gorget made of Beads of Colored Shell. Chimu Style. From Chanchan on the North Coast of Peru. Height, 17 inches. American Museum of Natural History, New York 188

Bowl decorated with a Jaguar Head and Bird Motifs. Paracas Cavernas Style. From Ocucaje, Ica Valley, Peru. Museo Nacional de Antropología y Arqueología, Lima, Peru 190

XIII

A Mythological Demon carrying a Trophy Head. Paracas Necropolis Embroidery. From the Paracas Peninsula, Peru. Height, 9 inches. Museo Nacional de Antropología y Arqueología, Lima, Peru . . 192

Embroidered Mythological Bird. Paracas Necropolis Style. From the Paracas Peninsula, Peru. Height, 8½ inches. Museo Nacional de Antropología y Arqueología, Lima, Peru 193

Basic Styles of Textile Decoration. Paracas Necropolis 194

Embroidered Figure of a Dancer carrying a Baton and Fan. Paracas Necropolis Style. From the Paracas Peninsula, Peru. Height, 9 inches. Museo Nacional de Antropología y Arqueología, Lima, Peru . . 195

An Embroidered Mythological Figure. Paracas Necropolis Style. From the Paracas Peninsula, Peru. Height, 9¼ inches. Museo Nacional de Antropología y Arqueología, Lima, Peru 196

Detail of Textile composed of Knitted Figures. Paracas Necropolis Style. Etnografiska Museet, Göteborg, Sweden 197

Fabulous Textile composed entirely of Knitted Figures. Paracas Necropolis Style. Height, 20½ inches. Width, 41 inches. Etnografiska Museet, Göteborg, Sweden 198-199

Cylindrical Jar and Jar with Twin Spouts and a Bridge Handle. Late Nazca Style. Height, 6½ inches and 7 inches. Museo Nacional de Antropología y Arqueología, Lima, Peru 202

Ceremonial Effigy Jar adorned with Mythological Figures and Trophy Heads. Nazca Style. Height, 25 inches. Museo Nacional de Antropología y Arqueología, Lima, Peru 203

The Bennett Stela. From Tiahuanaco, Bolivia. Height, nearly 24 feet. Now in La Paz, Bolivia . . . 205

The Gate of the Sun at Tiahuanaco, Bolivia. Height, 10 feet. Width, 12½ feet 206

The Sun God of Tiahuanaco as pictured on the Peruvian Coast. From Fundo Pacheco, Rio Grande de Nazca, Peru. Museo Nacional de Antropología y Arqueología, Lima, Peru (Drawing by Lauro Venturi) 207

One of a Pair of Polychrome Jars. Coastal Tiahuanaco Style. From Cahuachi, Rio Grande de Nazca, Peru. Height, 25 inches. Museo Nacional de Antropología y Arqueología, Lima, Peru 209

Effigy Jar, One of a Group of Eleven. Coastal Tiahuanaco Style. From Fundo Pacheco, Rio Grande de Nazca, Peru. Height, 19½ inches. Museo Nacional de Antropología y Arqueología, Lima, Peru . . 210

Ceremonial Polychrome Jar, One of Eight Used to Store Feather-Decorated Temple Wall Hangings. Rukana Style. From La Victoria, Churunga, Cuenca de Ocoña. Height, 37 inches. Circumference, 74 inches. Museo Nacional de Antropología y Arqueología, Lima, Peru 211

Effigy Vessel representing a Male Llama. From Fundo Pacheco, Rio Grande de Nazca, Peru. Coastal Tiahuanaco Style. Height, 29 inches. Museo Nacional de Antropología y Arqueología, Lima, Peru 212

Detail of Tapestry Poncho. Coastal Tiahuanaco Style. The Art Institute of Chicago 214

Inca Silver Doll from Cerro Plomo, Chile. Height, 7 inches. Museo Nacional de Historia Natural, Santiago de Chile 218

Inca Silver Llama with Gold Appliqué. Height, 9⅛ inches. American Museum of Natural History, New York 219

Inca Vase of Standard Aryballos Shape. Height, 44 inches. University Museum, Philadelphia 220

Inca Plate. Diameter, 9⅜ inches. The Art Institute of Chicago 222

Inca Poncho from the Island of Titicaca, Bolivia. Height, 38 inches. Width, 30 inches. American Museum of Natural History, New York 223

INTRODUCTION

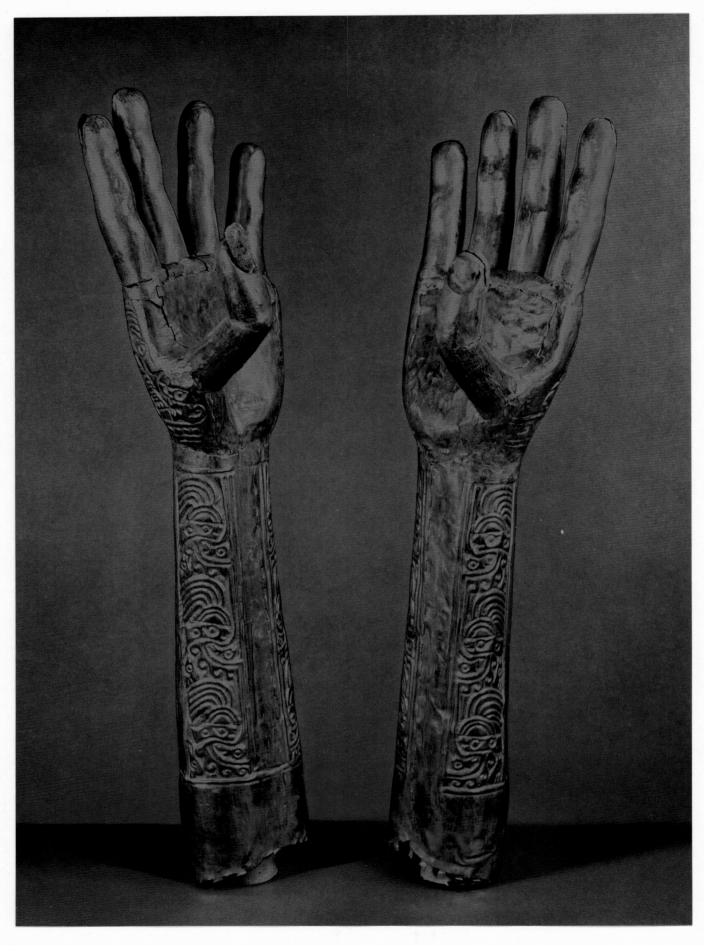

HANDS AND FOREARMS OF BEATEN GOLD WITH NAILS COVERED WITH SILVER. PROVENANCE UNKNOWN. CHIMU STYLE. LENGTH, 12¾″. WIDTH, 5″.
COLLECTION MIGUEL MUJICA GALLO, LIMA, PERU.

INTRODUCTION

It is the purpose of this volume to describe and picture the outstanding arts and crafts of aboriginal America which flourished within the area of highest cultural development. This includes the lands between central Mexico and southern Peru and Bolivia. The entire region lies within the Tropics, but it embraces almost every type of environment from deserts and lowland rain forests to mountain ranges covered by glaciers and perpetual snow. In ancient times the inhabitants were scarcely less diversified than the topography: in their physical appearance and speech, in their technological and social development. The area has never been a political unit, not even as a result of the Spanish Conquest and the subsequent centuries of colonial governments. The period covered is about 2500 years, roughly from 1000 B.C. to 1500 A.D.

The material culture to be discussed is known to us today through European historical sources and archaeological discoveries. Eye-witness accounts of the Conquest are few and only one of the Spanish Royal Historians ever visited the New World. Contemporary descriptions of the Aztec capital have survived but no Spaniard who entered the Inca capital before it was sacked left a written word.

The early voyages of discovery were not outstanding financial successes. To be sure, gold and pearls were secured but the chief profits came from Indian slaves. Columbus himself sold 509 in Seville in 1495; his brother landed another 300 in Cadiz in 1496. No doubt many individuals brought back souvenirs and curiosities but, apart from the loot of Mexico, few native American artifacts dating from the sixteenth century are known to exist. We illustrate some of the surviving Mexican artifacts (pp. 64, 67); everything else we picture is archaeological.

Apart from gold and silver which could be reduced to bullion, Europeans found little use for American manufactures and few regarded them as art. Among the tens of thousands of ruined towns and cities constructed of stone in Mexico and Peru, no great buildings survive today which are complete and functional except one of the Mitla "palaces" in Mexico, at last reports partly church, partly stable and partly pigsty. The great Inca road system was allowed to disintegrate. A minor survival until the eighteenth century was the tapestry vicuña blankets of Peru with incorporated European designs. Philip II is said to have used them on his bed in the Escorial. American jade objects were brought to Europe, not because they were admired but for their reputed medicinal value.

The loot of Mexico, detailed inventories of which still exist, found little favor in Spain and was distributed as curios, chiefly to friends of Charles V and Cortez in Spain, Italy and Austria. Some European artists, however, were at once impressed by its beauty. Among them were Albrecht Dürer and Benvenuto Cellini. Fine craftsmanship must command respect. Wrote Peter Martyr d'Anghiera, the first Royal Historian, "I do not wonder at gold and precious stones. But am astonished to see the workmanship excel the substance." Aesthetic values and standards of beauty change. Green was the ideal color to the Aztec and other Mexicans. Thus the Emperor Montezuma told an incredulous Cortez that the feathers of the quetzal bird or a fine jade pectoral were more precious to him than two loads of gold.

Our appreciation of New World art today is limited by the fact that we do not know the name of a single artist in any region. The techniques developed in the Old World by which anonymous works can be assigned to schools or even to individuals have still to be tried out on a comprehensive scale in the New, as they probably will be in the future. No doubt there always have been critics, but, even in the areas where more or less primitive writing once existed, we have no trace of contemporary appraisals.

Another barrier to understanding is the fact that a large part of what has survived from the centuries before the Conquest bears the stamp of complex religious beliefs and reflects both unknown canons of beauty and the symbolism of long forgotten deities. Skilful interpretations of sixteenth century sources, however, have made it possible to trace the portrayal of individual gods through stylistic changes covering centuries.

The huge sculptures representing the gods of old, by their very size and intricacy, are proof of the esteem in which they were once held. To us today, many can only be described as monstrous. For myself, I cannot believe that any native could regard the Lanzon of Chavin or the Aztec bloodthirsty divinities as a delight to the eye, but, nevertheless, they have a definite majesty and are awe-inspiring even to a non-believer ignorant alike of their functions or the names by which they once were invoked. They definitely belong in a volume of "treasures," together with other artifacts acceptable alike to the aboriginal American and European tastes.

★

Today Alaska and Siberia are separated by Behring Straits, some fifty-six miles in width, but, owing to several islands, the longest stretch of open water is only about twenty-five miles. In winter it is possible to walk across. In summer no knowledge of navigation is needed to cross in small boats. During periods of intense glaciation, when the sea level was lowered, Asia and North America have become a single continent. From 50,000 to 35,000 years ago, the Arctic and Pacific oceans were separated by a plain a thousand miles wide, and an ice-free corridor extended southward through Alaska. Man probably reached the New World at this time, subsisting partly on the giant grazing animals of the Pleistocene, mammoth and elephant, also the American bison, horse, camel and ground sloth. Radiocarbon dates show that man had reached the Straits of Magellan more than 10,000 years ago.

The tool kit of the first migrants seems to have consisted of crude percussion-flaked implements. There developed, however, several types of pressure flaking. This technique, which has been called both a craft and an art, persisted on a very high level in central Mexico, Yucatan and elsewhere until the Conquest. Both in the Maya lowlands and at Teotihuacan during the classical period, not only utilitarian blades but complex effigy forms were shaped by pressure flaking.

In Paleolithic Europe we have definite attempts at representation of men and beasts. Carvings are crude but the paintings seen on the walls of caves have been appraised at a high level. Very little that is comparable has yet been found in the New World on a similar time level. In Mexico a small mammoth bone has been discovered with scratched outlines of bison, tapir and mammoth. A surprising find made nearly a century ago is the sacrum of an extinct llama (camel) carved to represent an animal, perhaps a coyote or dog. This came from the vicinity of Tequixquiac north of Mexico City. It supposedly was found at a depth of forty feet in a geological formation dating from the last glaciation. It must be the oldest attempt at sculpture yet recorded in the New World.

For thousands of years the Paleo-Indians subsisted on the great steaks of the giant beasts they hunted, but they also must have had other food sources, the smaller animals, wild fruits, nuts, grains, etc. When the Pleistocene fauna became extinct, man had to increase his other means of subsistence. This led to the development of agriculture. The need to plant and cultivate called for settled communities.

The domestication of plants was a long drawn out process which took thousands of years. Incipient agriculture has been detected in northeastern Mexico at about 6000 B.C.; the oldest known cultivation in Peru dates from approximately 2000 years later. These early settlements must have been largely dependent upon animal foods and wild plants. Farming, however, became increasingly important with the development of maize as the basic crop. In Mexico maize was known by 3500 B.C.; in Peru maize first appears about 1500 B.C. Present evidence in general is that cultivation of the seed plants originated in Middle America and spread southward. Root crops such as manioc and potatoes probably stem from South America.

No uniform cultural development followed the domestication of food plants and the establishment of permanent settlements. Basic crafts such as basketry, weaving, pottery-making and metallurgy slowly emerged and ultimately led to what may be considered works of art. In the New World, however, primitive farming communities have always existed, just as they do today in Europe, within sight of the palaces and great cathedrals of the major cities. Furthermore, large areas in the Americas never supported centers of population with an enduring architecture but, nevertheless, produced artifacts of such merit that we illustrate them in this volume.

This book is not a history of art. Rather it is a presentation of outstanding objects now in museums and private collections. They are described from north to south, beginning with the most ancient fully developed styles in each area.

1

MEXICO

POTTERY FIGURINE FROM TLATILCO, MEXICO CITY. MIDDLE PRE-CLASSIC STYLE. PRIVATE COLLECTION, MEXICO CITY.

MEXICO

No great historical migration process within human memory has been so fully documented as the European discovery and colonization of the New World, yet never have the various cultures of an entire continent been overwhelmed and obliterated in such a brief period. To be sure, great civic centers such as Carthage had been utterly destroyed and entire provinces had been devastated. In Mexico, however, where the first great military encounter between the Old World and the New took place, the contact between alien civilizations proved most cataclysmic and ruinous.

For this there were several reasons. It must be remembered that it took a papal Bull to establish the humanity of the Americas, to acknowledge the natives as of the seed of Adam and therefore open to redemption. Yet to the invading Spaniards, they were cannibals who practised human sacrifice and worshipped devils. Had the Spaniards encountered centaurs, cyclops or unicorns they could not have been more surprised. The terror inspired among their neighbors by Aztec demands for blood sacrifices to appease their gods brought allies to the aid of Cortez and added to the fury of conflict. New methods of warfare, amphibious attacks and the destruction of the Aztec capital, house by house, led to total defeat.

Thus throughout Mexico the natives saw themselves enslaved, their beliefs discredited and the images of their gods wantonly destroyed. The Spanish triumph caused the elimination of native arts together with the symbolism they expressed. Our examination of ancient art thus becomes an "archaeological autopsy," buttressed by a few eye-witness accounts of the sixteenth century. Delving further into the past, we find that older cultures also were overwhelmed by force and that the Aztec themselves indulged in book burning. Buildings at Tula, the Toltec capital, were torn down. Centuries earlier, Teotihuacan, greatest of all Mexican cities, was destroyed by fire. Yet these native wars could scarcely have been as calamitous culturally as the conflict between two continents.

POTTERY FIGURINES OF THE PRE-CLASSIC PERIOD. FROM MEXICO. PRIVATE COLLECTION.

Hand-made pottery figurines were manufactured in quantity throughout the Pre-Classic period in Mexico. Although there is a bewildering variety of types, intensive study has made it possible to follow the development of stylistic trends, and these small effigies, combined with dates ascertained by radiocarbon tests, have been an important key to development of archaeological knowledge of the far past. In technical publications the various types and subtypes are designated by a complex system of letters and numbers.

The examples illustrated on pages 10 and 11 all are assigned to the middle Pre-Classic period. The subject in all but two cases is a standing female figure with short stubby arms, big hips and thighs, but small feet. Elaborate treatment of the hair is a feature seen on them all but no two have the hair arranged in the same fashion. Of the two male figures in the center of page 10, one wears trousers and the other perhaps is clad in furs. The women all are naked but may be adorned with ear disks and necklaces as well as simple designs painted on the face and body.

All these figurines are from Tlatilco on the outskirts of Mexico City except the two at the right on page 11. The taller type cannot be assigned to a single locality but has been found throughout the Valley of Mexico. Two long braids of hair hang down the sides below the hips but the hair has been cut horizontally across the back at shoulder height. Next to it is an example from Lake Chupícuaro in the State of Guanajuato. Heights range from 3⅜ to 5¾ inches.

POTTERY FIGURINES OF THE PRE-CLASSIC PERIOD. FROM MEXICO. PRIVATE COLLECTION.

THE PRE-CLASSIC

The evolutionary stages between the paleo-Indian hunters and the establishment of permanent agricultural settlements covered several thousand years. Owing to the discovery of normally perishable artifacts in dry areas or protecting caves, intensive archaeological studies are now in progress which will no doubt elucidate the time and place of basic inventions and the spread of cultural traits over wide areas. Attempts to embellish utilitarian artifacts must extend far into the past, but the oldest manifestations of attempted art now known are placed after the invention of pottery.

No one knows where or when clay was first modeled and baked in the New World. In Mexico and northern Central America the event took place probably before 2000 B.C. At any rate, by about 1800 B.C., permanent communities existed in the vicinity of the major lakes in central Mexico, which, although lacking the characteristics of the later Classical cultures, were far from primitive. Furthermore, the same pattern of settlement, with local variants in style, extended over southern Mexico, Guatemala,

EFFIGY BOTTLE FROM LAS BOCAS, STATE OF PUEBLA, MEXICO. MIDDLE PRE-CLASSIC. HEIGHT, 7″. PRIVATE COLLECTION.

El Salvador, eastern Honduras and perhaps parts of Nicaragua. Our observations and illustrations are chiefly from the Valley of Mexico and adjacent territory, not because this area is believed to be the center of invention and development but because it has been the scene of intensive archaeological investigation during the last fifty years and more can be said about it.

The underlying features of this widespread culture include an agriculture based on maize, beans of various kinds and squash. This diet was enlarged by many fruits and vegetables. The discovery of pipes indicates the use of tobacco. In most regions, nothing is known about housing but in central Mexico there were small settlements with rectangular houses. The walls either were of adobe or wattle and daub, both types of construction which are still in use. Among the chief settlements in central Mexico are El Arbolillo, Zacatenco, Tlatilco, Ticoman and Cuicuilco. Each was continuously inhabited for many centuries and produced deep beds of refuse deposited in stratigraph layers. These are the "type sites," for painstaking analysis of the prehistoric swill has produced perhaps the most complex and intricate stylistic sequence now available in the New World.

Except to the professional archaeologist nothing could be duller than the study of fragmentary artifacts which have been discarded. The Pre-Classic settlements, however, have revealed ancient graves, at times containing an abundance of funeral furnishings. These were not walled tombs but merely pits in which the dead were placed. Primary and secondary burials occur, also multiple burials. Bodies may be extended or flexed, face upward or down or on their sides. There is nothing to indicate ceremony or symbolism beyond the fact that articles were deposited with the dead, evidently for use in another world. The physical appearance of these ancient people is known from their bones. They were short in stature and narrow-headed. Morphological studies suggest that they were the ancestors of the present Indians. We are ignorant of their language and cannot even make a guess in view of the thirty-odd languages still spoken in Mexico which are classed as independent. The names assigned to the ancient settlements in all cases are those used currently. The Pre-Classic of central Mexico is arbitrarily divided into lower, middle and upper levels or phases. The sequences and estimated chronology of various ancient settlements are shown on the attached table (p. 90) which is based on some of the first dates obtained by radiocarbon tests. Much more accurate and concise results could and will be reached with improved techniques now available.

Las Bocas is a recently discovered archaeological area, said to have strong stylistic links with Tlatilco. The piece here illustrated, however, is unique. At first glance, it appears to be an eagle mask and it is possible to place it over the face and see through the eyes, but there are no holes for attaching it. Furthermore, the cheeks, chin and forehead form a hollow container and there is an orifice for filling it on top of the head.

The oldest archaeological sites yield artifacts which are relatively simple but by no means primitive. Pottery usually is monochrome: white, black or dark coffee color. Decoration consists principally of incised geometric patterns and hatching. Figurines usually represent women. Earlier types continued into the middle levels but bichrome pottery became common, for example, white on red, red on white, etc. Figurine types changed. Woven textiles and various garments are depicted. Tooth filing, tattooing and head deformation are shown. Male figurines represent ball players, dwarfs, dancers, musicians and acrobats. New pottery types include masks, also flat stamps and roller stamps. Effigy vessels of exotic shapes appear as well as zoomorphic incised motifs. We should also mention the stirrup-shaped spouts, a form rare in Mexico but characteristic of Peruvian pottery (pp. 159, 171, 174). Intrusive traits include the use of negative painting and a fresco technique for decorating pottery. More important is the appearance of Olmec effigy forms in pottery in such unadulterated style at certain sites that an actual shift in population has been suggested. Olmec features found in central Mexico include feline motifs and the well-known "baby faces" (pp. 17-21). Jade appears for the first time but only in small pieces which were not carved in Olmec fashion.

The upper Pre-Classic in Mexico is marked by the introduction of new figurine types and polychrome pottery and other new traits including stone carving. It is most noteworthy, however, because it witnesses the development of the ceremonial center and the settlement pattern surrounding it which became characteristic of the Classic period, not only in central Mexico but to the south and east throughout the Maya area. Comparable structures are found in western South America.

The ceremonial center, as the name implies, was the religious focus of a community. It usually was a great truncated pyramid surmounted by a temple (p. 40). Presumably only a few priests dwelt in it as caretakers but the entire community, scattered through the surrounding countryside, assembled there for the great religious festivals. Often the communal market was nearby where the natives congregated on fixed days, as still is the Indian custom. The very size of these structures indicates a highly organized priesthood backed by governments strong enough to command the necessary labor.

There are two outstanding ceremonial centers in Mexico which date from the end of the Pre-Classic period. The older, now known as Cuicuilco, was a circular, flat-topped mound which was enlarged on various occasions until it reached a diameter of over 400 feet and a height of 80 feet, ascended by a ramp and stairway. On top of this truncated cone was an altar covered by a thatched roof; other lesser edifices surrounded the base. Details are lost today because long ago they were buried by lava from the volcano Xitle. It is obvious that to erect a mound of such size, even though constructed of earth and uncut stone, called for a complex political and religious organization which controlled a large force of workmen. In these days of earth-moving machinery, one forgets how difficult it is to move a cubic foot of soil with a digging stick and a basket.

EFFIGY JARS REPRESENTING A TOUCAN (LEFT) AND A FISH (RIGHT). FROM TLATILCO, MEXICO CITY.
MIDDLE PRE-CLASSIC. HEIGHT, 5″ AND 5½″. PRIVATE COLLECTION AND MUSEO NACIONAL DE ANTROPOLOGÍA, MEXICO CITY.

These vessels represent one of several contemporary Mexican types for which stylistic links with the Chavin culture of Peru have been claimed ever since the discovery of the Tlatilco site. It cannot be denied that there are striking parallels, particularly the presence of the so-called stirrup spout in both regions at ca. 800 B.C. Both in Mexico (p. 15) and in Peru (p. 159) black clay vessels were manufactured with highly burnished areas which are in contrast to cut-out matte surfaces. The examples in this volume, however, represent two distinct techniques. In Mexico, the black definitely is a pigment, present on the outer surface only. In Peru the black is the result of manipulation during firing and runs from wall to wall. In Mexico the stirrup spout soon dropped out of use and did not reappear until late Pre-Classic times; in Peru this form persisted on the north coast until the Spanish conquest.

The most famous of Pre-Classic constructions are now known as the Pyramid of the Sun and the Pyramid of the Moon at the ruins of Teotihuacan. Cuicuilco was abandoned after the volcanic catastrophe but Teotihuacan witnessed the change from Pre-Classic styles. We therefore discuss its growth and expansion elsewhere. Before doing so, however, we shall examine the early art styles which are found to the east in the tropical lowlands facing the Gulf of Mexico. Although contemporaneous with the Pre-Classic, they had reached a stage of artistic development of the highest order.

EASTERN MEXICO

THE OLMEC STYLE

In central Mexico the long stagnation of the Formative or Pre-Classic period came to an end during the first centuries before the Christian era with the growth of the great ceremonial centers (p. 14). Nearly a thousand years earlier, however, certainly by the ninth century B.C., ceremonial centers were constructed in a most unlikely area, the hot, humid swamps in the states of Vera Cruz and Tabasco, facing the Gulf of Mexico. Here appeared an art style with no known antecedents, marked by huge basalt carvings and by delicate workmanship in jade. The oldest evidence of mathematics and written dates are here. Today this complex is called "Olmec," a misnomer, as the Olmec were the historic inhabitants of the area. We have no idea who lived there long ago.

Olmec is the oldest great art in Mexico. The style is particularly appealing to European eyes as it lacks the florid complexity and symbolism of the later classical styles. It combines a sensitive discipline of presentation with a technical mastery of materials. In the later jade carvings of classic styles, such as Maya or Zapotec, it often is obvious that the final form has been influenced by the original shape of the material to be worked (p. 113) and the quality of line has been governed by the tools and techniques employed, for example tubular drills or string sawing. On the contrary, Olmec carvings are so admirably finished that techniques of manufacture have been obliterated.

In ancient times, Olmec products were widely appreciated. Both pottery and jade turn up in many Pre-Classic sites in central Mexico. The archaeologically little-known State of Guerrero has yielded many minor Olmec carvings but no megalithic sculpture. Easily transportable Olmec carvings are on record from Guatemala, Honduras, El Salvador, Costa Rica and Panama. Classic Maya stelae may portray now forgotten rulers adorned with Olmec jades. At Mayapan in Yucatan, a Maya city which flourished in the fifteenth century A.D., the Carnegie Institution of Washington excavated a shrine which contained an Olmec stone head cemented into the walls. This carving, now in the museum in Mérida, Yucatan, must have been cherished as an heirloom for perhaps two thousand years.

Olmec artifacts are so widely scattered in place and time that they afford no certain basis for dating. On the southern coast of the Gulf of Mexico, however, Olmec centers, now dated back to about 900 B.C., have been investigated. These were not cities with concentrated housing but community centers which served the surrounding farm lands for ceremonial gatherings and for market places. This region, until the recent discovery of oil, was one of the most uninviting in the New World, yet, in spite of heat, swamps, floods and difficult access to better favored areas, it once had a great civilization.

SEATED FIGURE OF ANDESITE. OLMEC STYLE. FROM SAYULA, VERA CRUZ, MEXICO. HEIGHT, 48″.
MUSEO DE ANTROPOLOGÍA, VERA CRUZ UNIVERSITY, JALAPA, MEXICO.

OLMEC BASALT HEAD FROM SAN LORENZO, VERA CRUZ, MEXICO. THIS IS THE LARGEST KNOWN EXAMPLE AND MEASURES 9 FEET, 4 INCHES IN HEIGHT. THE MOUTH IS OVER 3 FEET WIDE. MUSEO DE ANTROPOLOGÍA, VERA CRUZ UNIVERSITY, JALAPA, MEXICO.

Today we are ignorant of social and economic pressures which ruled in the distant past. The Aztec, it is known, settled on an island in a swampy lake in order to survive but, when they had become a great power, declared they had done so at the direction of their gods. Olmec carvings in the living rock in southern Mexico, Guatemala and El Salvador suggest the presence of conquering armies, but, apart from the Gulf coast, no Olmec large establishments have been detected.

La Venta, one of the best known Olmec centers, is located on an island in a swamp adjacent to the Rio Tonalá. The chief standing feature is a truncated pyramid of clay, once the substructure of an elevated temple. Today this measures 110 feet in height and the base is 240 by 420 feet. Far larger substructures were erected in later times both in Mexico (p. 39) and Peru, but, when it was built, this probably was the largest edifice erected by man in the New World. Facing the pyramid there was a series of courts enclosed by lesser mounds. Once both the walls and floors were richly painted. Mosaic pavements of serpentine and colored clays added to the brilliance of the scene. Scattered through the plazas were monumental sculptures of basalt, once plastered and painted. Most spectacular are the colossal heads of which four were found at La Venta. Also there were stelae and altars with figures in relief. Some of the heads are eight to nine feet high and estimated weights run up to ten tons. The nearest quarries are eighty miles away and transportation must have been by water. No source of jade is known.

Two other Olmec sites carved colossal heads. One of these is San Lorenzo which extends for about a half a mile along a series of ridges. Unlike the other archaeological centers it appears that there were two periods of aboriginal occupation and that the older population, which had produced the megalithic carvings, abandoned the area for reasons unknown. There are no indications of war. Some time later, a second population settled at San Lorenzo and found the standing monuments not to their taste. They did not mutilate them or break them up for building material but simply got rid of them by rolling them into adjacent ravines. This caused relatively little damage and the San Lorenzo carvings are in better condition than those from other Olmec sites. The big head we illustrate on page 18 was damaged over the right eye but the excavators discovered the broken fragments and cemented them in place. The head has rather negroid features but the eyes and lips are delicately outlined; the pupils of the eyes are indicated by raised circles. San Lorenzo does not contain large mounds such as were found at La Venta.

Another major Olmec center in the State of Vera Cruz is known as Tres Zapotes. A colossal head has been found here but it seems probable that the Olmec style persisted here after the abandonment of other Olmec centers. At La Venta there has been found one of the oldest written New World dates, 31 B.C., carved on a stela in the calendrical system attributed to the Maya.

Olmec sculpture often is in the full round. At times, there is a strong suggestion of individual portraits. Many carvings, both in basalt and jade, are called "baby faces." They have flabby lips with drooping corners. Although usually teeth are not shown, the type evidently represents an anthropomorphic jaguar, identified as a Rain deity. Olmec jades, also carved in the full round, often exhibit the monumental quality of the megalithic sculpture. At times they are embellished with incredibly fine incised motifs which may have been cut with cactus spines and an abrasive such as pumice. The group of standing figures on pages 22-23, although not of individual importance, are representative of a type which includes some of the finest Olmec jades. They are naked except occasionally for a belt and breech clout. The arms are cut free but have not been carefully shaped. Heads are deformed.

In addition to statuettes representing a jaguar deity, the Olmec had an axe cult. Ceremonial deposits of axes laid out in parallel rows have been found. Sometimes these are of stones too soft for practical use. Often they are of the blue-green jade rarely seen except in Olmec artifacts. At times they are adorned with incised motifs or have heads in relief. The "Kunz" anthropomorphic axe, named for the former owner, Dr G. F. Kunz, outstanding expert in precious stones, was published many years before Olmec culture had been defined. It conforms to the "baby face" type of Olmec sculpture with the animal nature of this concept emphasized by broad nostrils and monstrous mouth. The shape of the head, shoulders and arms, however, is definitely human. Details are indicated by fine-line incising. The excised background on cheeks and body is not typical of jade carving but is characteristic of approximately contemporary pottery (p. 15).

The origin of the Olmec style is lost in antiquity. The great centers near the Gulf of Mexico must represent a florescence which may have originated in this area or elsewhere. Most scholars, however, now regard Olmec as a "mother culture" which inspired in part the great Middle American classic civilizations, including Teotihuacan, the Maya and Zapotec. Olmec jades reached Costa Rica where two major jade-working centers existed (p. 138). Although southern styles are local, techniques of this difficult material may well have been derived from the north.

What caused the downfall or abandonment of the Olmec style is scarcely less mysterious than its development. All we can say is that the major centers near the Gulf of Mexico appear to have been conquered by unknown peoples who endeavored to overthrow their monuments and deface them. There followed a shift of major artistic achievement in this area slightly to the north and the development of new styles in ceramics, stone carving and architectural forms. The chronological position and interrelationship of these developments, notwithstanding the number of objects in public and private collections, is little understood because trained observers have had small opportunity to record the circumstances of their finding.

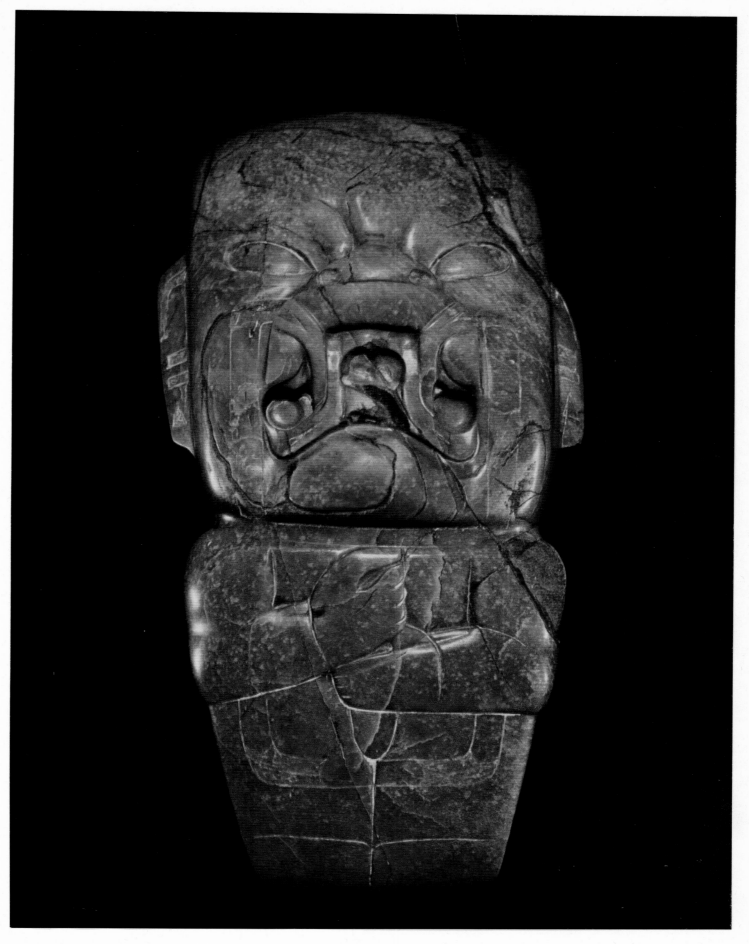

THE KUNZ ANTHROPOMORPHIC AXE, A MASSIVE DIOPSIDE JADEITE CEREMONIAL AXE, SAID TO HAVE COME FROM OAXACA, MEXICO. OLMEC STYLE. HEIGHT, 10¾″. AMERICAN MUSEUM OF NATURAL HISTORY, NEW YORK.

This group was found deeply buried. It consists of a miniature wall of upright jade axe blades. With his back to this is a small figure of coarse stone who confronts fifteen individuals of jade or fine serpentine. It has been suggested that the scene represents a religious ceremony or that it portrays a prisoner about to be sacrificed. Although none of the separate carvings is of top quality, the group as a whole is unique in the Olmec style.

AN OLMEC RITUAL CACHE FROM LA VENTA, VERA CRUZ, MEXICO. HEIGHT, ABOUT 8″. MUSEO NACIONAL DE ANTROPOLOGÍA, MEXICO CITY.

REMOJADAS

At the time of the Spanish Conquest, the southern portion of the Mexican State of Vera Cruz was occupied by peoples known as Olmec, whose name, as we have seen, is now firmly linked with archaeological discoveries of a much more remote era. Farther north in the same state the Spaniards encountered a group called Totonac which name, until recently, was applied to all archaeological finds from their territory, regardless of age. For many years, hollow pottery figurines had come from this region in small quantity and had been eagerly sought by collectors. Some thirty years ago, the search for oil brought outsiders to remote and hitherto isolated parts of Vera Cruz. New and spectacular effigy types began to reach outside markets in considerable quantities. As the Remojadas region proved particularly productive, this name currently is applied to a variety of modeled ceramic styles which now are known to have been manufactured for centuries. They have obvious symbolic and stylistic links with other cultures but still maintain a distinctly local flavor. It is said that local farmers have abandoned all pretense of cultivating their crops in favor of the more lucrative search for antiquities.

The Pre-Classic figurines of Mexico and Central America normally are solid with details added by buttons and fillets of clay or indicated by incising (p. 10). The size is limited by the porosity of the clay which permits the escape of air and other gases when fired. A hollow figurine with thin walls, on the contrary, is shaped by pressure inside and out, which results in a potentially different quality of surface. Provided with vents for the escape of air, the only limit on size is the ability of the potter to fire the entire object at an effective temperature.

Advancement in the arts often is based on technical developments. The discovery or invention of a method for manufacturing hollow figures of clay apparently must be attributed to the Olmec. At any rate, such figurines, in pure Olmec style, appear about 1000 B.C. at Tlatilco and other ancient settlements in the central Mexican plateau, and, concurrently, effigy vessels of purely local types were produced (p. 15). Large hollow pottery figures are more characteristic of Mexico than other parts of the New World. They are typical of western Mexico and of the Zapotec style from Oaxaca. Large pottery effigies are attributed to the Toltec. In later times the Aztec produced huge incense burners.

Remojadas now is a collective term for various ceramic types of various affinities. Best known are the smiling figures of men and women, young and obviously happy (p. 27), perhaps the most successful New World attempt to represent a mood rather than an activity or occupation. Also there are many genre figures, apparently without symbolic significance. They range in subject from couples seated in swings (the ends pierced for suspending cords) to many types of individuals old and young, and even to a seated grinning skeleton (p. 26).

POTTERY STATUE REPRESENTING A WOMAN WHO HAS DIED IN CHILDBIRTH. REMOJADAS STYLE. FROM TLALIXCOYAN, VERA CRUZ. HEIGHT, 53¾".
MUSEO DE ANTROPOLOGÍA, VERA CRUZ UNIVERSITY, JALAPA, MEXICO.

POTTERY FIGURE OF A SMILING SKELETON. CLASSICAL REMOJADAS STYLE. HEIGHT, 14½". FROM LOS CERROS, TIERRA BLANCA, VERA CRUZ. MUSEO DE ANTROPOLOGÍA, VERA CRUZ UNIVERSITY, JALAPA, MEXICO.

LAUGHING HEAD FROM A BROKEN POTTERY FIGURINE. REMOJADAS STYLE. FROM LOS CERROS, TIERRA BLANCA (?), VERA CRUZ. HEIGHT, 6½″. MUSEO DE ANTROPOLOGÍA, VERA CRUZ UNIVERSITY, JALAPA, MEXICO.

Smiling pottery faces from Vera Cruz have been known for many years but were so few in number that many museums only could exhibit casts. Recent Remojadas finds include many complete figures which portray both boys and girls who may be singing and dancing. The Mochica area in Peru at times modeled effigy vessels which express merriment but they are not common.

The pottery figure on the opposite page probably corresponds to the Aztec deity Mictlantecutli, Lord of the Underworld. A Mixtec version of this god, illustrated on p. 84, has a fleshless lower jaw, but the east coast example has lips and cheeks which are grinning and he wears a big hat and a shirt.

POTTERY HEAD OF A SERPENT, ONE OF A PAIR FOUND IN A CAVE. FROM ACATLAN DE PÉREZ FIGUEROA, OAXACA (NEAR THE VERA CRUZ BORDER). REMOJADAS STYLE. HEIGHT, 31″. MUSEO NACIONAL DE ANTROPOLOGÍA, MEXICO CITY.

Also the gods and social orders appear. We know their Aztec names of the sixteenth century. In Pre-Classic times, we find only Huehueteotl, the "Old, Old god," the god of Fire, and Tlaloc, the god of Rain. The complex Aztec pantheon combined deities whose worship came from many peoples and, even if we do not know in what tongue they once were addressed, we can recognize their characteristic portrayals over the centuries. In the Remojadas world we find the Eagle Knights of the Aztec, warriors with helmets shaped like birds with human faces in the open bills. Tlaloc figures and symbols are common. One of the great surviving statues is a half life-size bust of Eecatl with characteristic pouting lips, now in the Museum of Primitive Art in New York. The almost life-size figure on page 25 pictures a dead woman with closed eyes and open mouth, probably a goddess of childbirth and death thereby, similar to the Aztec Cihuacoatl, Serpent Woman. At any rate, the statue has two serpent heads in profile in the headdress.

An important recent discovery in Mexico was a pair of huge pottery serpent heads which were found in a cave near the border between Oaxaca and Vera Cruz (p. 28). They are not the feathered serpents symbolic of Quetzalcoatl or Kukulcan. Their poisonous potential is emphasized by large fangs of which there are two both in the upper and in the lower jaws. The long appendage on top of the nose perhaps is intended to represent a fifth fang. Although found outside the Remojadas area, they definitely must be assigned to that style. A smaller but almost identical head appears as part of the headdress on a pottery statue from central Vera Cruz.

CLASSICAL VERA CRUZ SCULPTURE

This group of carvings has also been called Totonac and Tajin, the latter being a term we use to designate the specific style associated with the thus named ancient city (p. 34). Classical Vera Cruz artifacts until recently were classified as "ceremonial," for their shapes were mysterious and their functions unknown. It has been ascertained, however, that most if not all are associated with the curious ball game known as *tlaxtli* to the Aztec, which combined elements of an athletic contest with a religious cult.

A game played with a massive solid rubber ball was known sporadically from Paraguay throughout lowland South America, the West Indies, Central America, Mexico and even the southwestern United States—no doubt with many local variants. The essential element was that the ball was propelled by the body rather than the hands. Formal courts were known in the West Indies and, on the mainland, from the Maya area northward through central Mexico. From classical times onward, most Maya and Mexican settlements had formal courts with masonry walls which were a prominent architectural feature with the playing field shaped like a capital I. Although the end zones had to be defended, the principal object of the game was to drive the ball through rings set vertically high up on the parallel long walls. The accomplishment of this feat entitled the player to seize all the garments of any spectator he could catch, and the captain of the losing team, as we know from bas-reliefs (p. 126), might be decapitated. The ball itself was so heavy that it could cause serious injury or even death. Hence the players needed protection.

STONE "YOKE." CLASSICAL VERA CRUZ STYLE. HEIGHT, 16¼". FROM THE STATE OF VERA CRUZ, MEXICO. AMERICAN MUSEUM OF NATURAL HISTORY, NEW YORK.

The curious Vera Cruz sculpture seen on page 30 has long been known as a stone "yoke," and many suggestions have been made to explain its use, if any. Some are undecorated but many are elaborately carved in a typical curvilinear style with interlocking scrolls. Some carry abstract geometrical designs, but others clearly represent frogs, owls or men, ingeniously adapted to the peculiar shape to be decorated. Almost invariably they were made from very hard stone of the finest quality, were meticulously carved and have been polished to a high luster. Like other archaeological puzzles, the function of stone yokes was simply ascertained: from figurines and reliefs associated with ball courts. They were body protectors which were slipped on sideways above the hips. Confirmation came from the fact that they actually fit a normally thin individual, do not tend to fall off and permit a surprising ease of mobility although they weigh thirty to sixty pounds.

There can be little doubt that for ordinary use body protectors were made of other materials than stone. Wood and hide or textiles with interior padding come to mind. Basketry is indicated by Toltec frescoes at Chichen Itza. Perhaps stone yokes were for ceremonial occasions only, a kind of dress uniform. On the other hand, once one has actually worn a stone yoke, it does not seem impossible that they were used in competition, for the obviously improved hitting power, like a heavier bat or racket, might compensate for the loss of mobility. Stone yokes have been found in greatest quantity along the Gulf coast of Mexico, but they also turn up in Classical Maya centers as far away as Honduras and El Salvador. In other words, they have the same distribution as the fully developed ball court with rings. Associated with yokes in the ground are two other "problematical" types of carving known as *hachas* and *palmas* (or palmate stones). Both are so notched at the back that evidently they were shaped for attachment to something else. Figurines and sculpture (p. 126) indicated that they were perched on the yokes so that they faced forward from the body of the wearer.

Hachas were originally named from their fancied resemblance to ceremonial axes, for in cross-section they are wedge-shaped. Thus they offer two slightly divergent surfaces for decoration, both carved in relief. A few are thicker which permits carrying the carving from one side to the other but not in the full round. Most hachas represent heads. Some are of animals including bats, monkeys or birds. Human heads predominate, however, often being shown with fantastic headdresses or helmets (p. 33). In a few cases, the outer edge of the hacha serves as a frame for a cut-out interior design which may be a complete human figure. Very rarely the two sides of a hacha were carved differently, for instance with a living face represented on one side and a dead countenance on the other.

Palmas like hachas have a notch on the lower rear corner intended to fit over a yoke. Whereas hachas are narrow from side to side, palmas are flattened from back to front, more on the upper part so that the outline is like an inverted pear. Typically a figure,

"PALMA" OF BASALT ADORNED WITH HUMAN HANDS. CLASSICAL VERA CRUZ STYLE. FROM TLACOLULAN, VERA CRUZ. HEIGHT, 14¼".
MUSEO DE ANTROPOLOGÍA, VERA CRUZ UNIVERSITY, JALAPA, MEXICO.

"HACHA" REPRESENTING A HUMAN HEAD WITH A HEADDRESS IN THE FORM OF A LEAPING DOLPHIN. CLASSICAL VERA CRUZ STYLE. FROM SAN ANDRES TUXTLA, STATE OF VERA CRUZ. HEIGHT, 11¼".
COVARRUBIAS COLLECTION, MUSEO NACIONAL DE ANTROPOLOGÍA, MEXICO CITY.

animal or human, is carved in very high relief on the lower portion and projects against the background of the rounded top, which may be crowded with typical scrolls. A curious aberrant form shows hands and arms extended as if in supplication or prayer (p. 32). We should also mention a human figure bent over backward with an open slit in the chest. This must be one of the oldest records of sacrifice by extracting the still beating heart, a custom which grew to egregious proportions in later centuries.

TAJIN The curious stone carvings described in the previous section have no known center of development and distribution. There are, however, ancient cities which must represent a terminal development of Classical Vera Cruz art. Of these the foremost example is the ruins now known as Tajin. The principal temple, one of the outstanding aboriginal New World edifices, stood on a truncated terraced pyramid rising in six tiers, adorned with niches which number 365 like the days of the year. It is not true, as rumored, that each niche once contained the statue of a deity, but the Tajin architects did not follow the older Mexican tradition of sunken panels and moldings on exterior walls, exemplified by Monte Alban and Teotihuacan. Many of their buildings exhibited walls and columns with carved relief, a type of decoration seen on Classical Maya temples and later Mexican structures erected, for instance, by the Toltec of Tula or the Mixtec at Mitla.

Some of the Tajin bas-reliefs consist of large rectangular wall panels. These retain the characteristic scroll motifs of the Classical Vera Cruz style. They may depict or commemorate, however, fairly complex sacrificial scenes in which several individuals are involved. Thus in substance they recall the Tula Toltec wall reliefs, particularly those seen in the great ball court at Chichen Itza in Yucatan. On the contrary, scroll motifs of Classic Vera Cruz type occur in unadulterated form at Teotihuacan (p. 42) which we know was abandoned centuries before the advent of the Toltec.

THE HUASTEC AREA

The region on the Gulf coast of Mexico embracing parts of the States of Tamaulipas, San Luis Potosí and Vera Cruz is known as the Huasteca, the home for centuries of the Huastec Indians. This is an isolated group of Maya-speaking people, most closely related linguistically to the Maya of Yucatan rather than the Highland Maya of Guatemala. It is conjectured that, in the far past, Maya tribes inhabited the entire shores of the Gulf of Mexico from Yucatan to the west and north as far as the Huasteca area and that, subsequently, the Totonac of Vera Cruz and the little known Nahua-speaking groups farther south in Tabasco detached the Huastec from the main body of the Maya before the characteristic Classical Maya culture had developed.

Excavation of the Huastec area has revealed a long series of pottery types which have been divided into six major periods. Although retaining a distinctly local flavor, the first two periods can be correlated with lowland Maya ceramics of Pre-Classic and with the two earliest Monte Alban styles. The two middle periods suggest a change in outside contacts and relationship with the Mexican highlands dating from the Classical Teotihuacan period. The fifth phase can be correlated with Toltec ascendancy in Central Mexico and Yucatan and the sixth and final period includes the centuries just before the Spanish Conquest.

HUASTEC STATUE, FRONT (LEFT) AND BACK (RIGHT). NOTE THAT THE BACK OF THE HEAD REPRESENTS A SKULL WITH A SKELETON SUSPENDED BELOW IT. FROM SAN VICENTE TANCUAYALAB, SAN LUIS POTOSÍ, MEXICO. HEIGHT, 62¼″. BROOKLYN MUSEUM.

The Huasteca region has produced several characteristic types of sculpture, none of which can be given a definite date. One of the most interesting groups consists of standing human figures, male and female. Both sexes usually wear the same kind of headdress, a square cap topped by a cone with a semicircular fan of feathers at the back. Legs and arms are partly carved in the round, and the latter may be placed asymmetrically. Head and body in most cases are shown full face and the general effect is stiff and lifeless. The style definitely owes nothing to Classical Maya or to the Classical Vera Cruz sculpture found in adjacent territory. A few of the more elaborate statues are carved in the round. From the neck down, body and limbs are completely covered with designs in low relief which must depict motifs which in life were painted or tattooed. The example on page 35 is unique because the front (to judge by the position of the feet) represents a living individual but the back of the head represents a skull below which a skeleton is shown in relief. This skeleton is smaller than the living body and the human foot bones are replaced by the claws of a bird.

The concept of life and death combined in a single being occurs both in pottery and stone but usually is confined to the face, one side of which may be represented as living and the other as dead. The idea, though not common, is an ancient one and widespread. In Mexico, it occurs in Middle Tlatilco and Monte Alban II pottery, also on stone palmas and yokes carved in Classic Vera Cruz style. Variants are known from Colombia and Peru, where an example in Chavin-style pottery has been found. The presence of this life-and-death motif in a carving from the Huastec area suggests that the sculpture should be assigned an earlier date than previously believed. We may add that Huastec men of the sixteenth century shocked the missionary fathers because they wore no loincloths. The statue on page 35, however, wears both a kilt and a loincloth, secured by a belt knotted in front; even the skeleton is modestly supplied with a kilt.

In the preceding pages it has only been possible to touch briefly on some of the highlights of Classical archaeological finds from the lowlands facing the Gulf of Mexico, covering roughly a thousand years before and after the beginning of the Christian era. New discoveries have enhanced the importance of this region in the larger picture of cultural development in Mexico, but much more research will be needed to obtain a better understanding.

CERRO MONTOSO The natives who dwelt on the Gulf coast of Mexico in the sixteenth century called themselves Totonacs, a name formerly applied to all archaeological finds from this area. No one knows how long they had lived there. Architectural remains include ruined and abandoned cities which were seen by the Spaniards. Two types of fine pottery are assigned to the Totonac although little is known about the full range of the styles. A ware named for the Isla de Sacrificios is of a buff clay with linear designs in black, white and red. Cerro Montoso ware has designs in black and red with incised outline. It is known chiefly through a bowl decorated with centipedes (p. 37).

POTTERY JAR PORTRAYING CENTIPEDES. CERRO MONTOSO STYLE MARKED BY INCISED ZONE OUTLINES. FROM OTATES, VERA CRUZ. HEIGHT, 6⅛".
MUSEO NACIONAL DE ANTROPOLOGÍA, MEXICO CITY.

This famous example of Cerro Montoso style found at Otates in the State of Vera Cruz, is decorated with a centipede motif. The style is marked by boldly painted designs in dark red and in black, outlined by incising after the vessel was fired. Although this technique appeared in Pre-Classic wares, the Cerro Montoso style is assigned to the fourteenth and fifteenth centuries.

SCULPTURED FAÇADE OF THE TEMPLE OF QUETZALCOATL. TEOTIHUACAN, D.F., MEXICO.

CENTRAL MEXICO

TEOTIHUACAN

Teotihuacan is a great ruined city situated about thirty miles northeast of the Mexican capital. Abandoned for centuries and its builders forgotten, it was named "Place of the Gods" by the Aztec who believed it was erected by giants, doubtless because of elephant bones left in the vicinity by Paleo-Indian hunters. The name Teotihuacan is also applied to one of the most brilliant of American cultures, notable for its architecture, mural paintings, sculptures and ceramics. Teotihuacan styles spread throughout central and southern Mexico; in slightly modified form, they occur in the Classical Maya cities of lowland and highland Guatemala and even extended into El Salvador.

Teotihuacan today consists of a ceremonial or "down town" area flanking an avenue popularly known as the "Street of the Dead." This terminates in a plaza at the foot of the Pyramid of the Moon and it runs for over a mile south. About fifty yards wide, on either side are literally scores of temples, large and small, standing on terraced substructures. Outside this central group are lesser civic centers, also the houses of the wealthy which deserve the name of "palaces," for they are multi-chambered edifices built around courtyards. Their milk-white walls often are adorned with colorful murals. In addition there are buildings which appear to be apartment houses occupied by many families. The total area of the city can only be determined by future excavations but six square miles now seems a conservative estimate.

Some of the still existing structures call for comment. The largest, now known as the Pyramid of the Sun, is a truncated pyramid on which stood a temple and huge idol, destroyed in the sixteenth century. Set back from the "Avenue of the Dead," it rests on a great paved platform measuring nearly a quarter of a mile on each side. As seen today, the pyramid consists of sloping masonry walls with projecting stone pegs which once supported a thick coating of stucco. As a matter of fact, during "reconstruction" many years ago, a similar outer wall and about twenty feet of hearting were stripped from three sides of the pyramid. Thus reduced in size, the sides of the base now measure 735 feet and it covers an area of 10½ acres. The present height is 210 feet. The Mexican Government has driven two tunnels through the Pyramid of the Sun at ground level. The entire structure is artificial and no natural elevation is involved. Ancient walls were found in the interior and also pottery figurines of styles now called Teotihuacan I and II, definitely related to figurines from Cuicuilco and other Late Pre-Classic sites.

The Pyramid of the Moon is smaller than the Sun Temple and probably represents the original form of the larger structure. The height is 135 feet. The base measures 390 by 490 feet and covers approximately 190,000 square feet. The volume is over

RESTORED VIEW OF THE PYRAMID OF THE SUN. TEOTIHUACAN, D.F., MEXICO.

a quarter of a million cubic meters. This temple, the forecourt, adjacent buildings lining the "Avenue of the Dead," and an area of early settlement nearby are now being excavated and restored. The complex known as the Citadel is on the east side of the Avenue of the Dead near the southern end. It is a massive square with vertical outer walls, measuring about a quarter of a mile on each side, which gives the impression of a fortress. In fact, however, these are not defensive walls but wide platforms on which stand fifteen small temples, three on one side and four on the others. The center of this enclosure is aligned with the center of the platform supporting the Pyramid of the Sun, suggesting a ceremonial relationship.

The most interesting feature of the court was discovered in repairing a terraced pyramid standing east of the center. Buried within the newer structure was a stairway and one face only of an older building profusely decorated with carvings in the round and in relief which still retained a good deal of the original paint. Serpent heads adorn the balustrades. The vertical walls of the terraces, probably once six in number, alternately show large heads in the round portraying the feathered serpent, symbolic of Quetzalcoatl, and Tlaloc heads. These are the Aztec names of deities of the heavens and of rain whose worship was widespread in Mexico until the Conquest (p. 38). Lesser water symbols consist of shells represented in relief.

Apart from this single magnificent façade, large scale sculptures from Teotihuacan are rare. Best known perhaps is the colossal figure on page 41 which is said to represent a Water goddess. This stone was discovered over a century ago amid the fallen temples on the west side of the plaza in front of the Pyramid of the Moon. It lay face down and was known as the "fainting stone" because it was believed that anyone who lay on it was "sure to experience lassitude, or lose animation for a while." In style this statue is far apart from the façade carvings. The great depth is due to the fact that the entire block represents a rectangular temple, complete with moldings on all sides and doorways on back and front. This concept is very clear on the back where the figure of the divine occupant of the temple does not interrupt the architectural lines. Another sculpture of this nature was abandoned unfinished near Texcoco. Its present weight is estimated at 190 tons, which, of course, would have been reduced had it been moved to its final destination. It has been estimated that 2000 men would have been necessary to transport this statue with rollers and ropes.

A totally different type of stone carving was found in 1963 on a farm known as La Ventilla, situated about a kilometer southwest of the Citadel. Although there were no imposing architectural remains above ground, preliminary excavation here revealed complex superimposed constructions which evidently represented a long period of concentrated habitation. The principal discovery was the sectional stela seen on p. 42. This now consists of four separately carved sections, united by peg and socket joints, which probably once stood on a rectangular base. Centuries after Teotihuacan had been abandoned, peg and socket drums for columns were used by the Toltec of Tula, notably in great Atlantean columns which supported the roof of the principal temple (p. 50). Jointed statues, comparable in technique if not in style, are known from the Guatemala highlands and western Salvador.

This is the oldest great idol of the Mexicans. Over sixteen feet high and estimated to weigh more than twenty-two tons, it was carved to represent a rectangular temple with its moldings and doors, front and back, with the figure of a water goddess on the front façade. Found at Teotihuacan, this statue is now in the National Museum in Mexico City.

STONE STELA CARVED IN FOUR SECTIONS WITH PEG AND SOCKET JOINTS. FROM LA VENTILLA, TEOTIHUACAN, D.F., MEXICO. HEIGHT, 82″. MUSEO NACIONAL DE ANTROPOLOGÍA, MEXICO CITY.

The Ventilla stela is topped by a flat disk adorned in a style well known in Teotihuacan. The three lower sections, however, carry the scrolls and volutes characteristic of Classic Vera Cruz sculpture, so faithfully rendered that one suspects the presence of an imported artisan. Similar blending of the two styles occurs on Classic Teotihuacan pottery. Mexican archaeologists have ascertained that the Ventilla stela had a definite function in ancient times. On a hitherto unpublished fragment of the Tepantitla murals two teams engaged in a ball game are shown. The game is not the well-known Middle America type with rings to shoot at; the players all carry massive clubs which suggest a game resembling hockey. At the two ends of the playing field are "markers" closely resembling the Ventilla carving. Their purpose is not wholly clear. They may indicate a goal line; perhaps the circular disks were targets at which the ball was driven.

The smaller sculptures of Teotihuacan style usually are made from stones which will take a high polish, such as basalt, serpentine, onyx or jade. The workmanship is of fine quality and some pieces suggest the portraying of definite individuals. Subjects overburdened with religious symbolism are avoided with the result that Teotihuacan carvings are eagerly sought by collectors. The lesser sculptures fall into two groups. One consists of small human figures, either standing (p. 43) or seated cross-legged. Many of these have come from the State of Guerrero where the Teotihuacan style tends to blend with Olmec. Neither style reached its fullest development in this area and the interrelationships and chronological position of each remain to be determined.

STATUETTE REPRESENTING A STANDING HUMAN FIGURE. STYLE OF TEOTIHUACAN.
FROM THE STATE OF PUEBLA, MEXICO. HEIGHT, 10¼″.
COVARRUBIAS COLLECTION, MUSEO NACIONAL DE ANTROPOLOGÍA, MEXICO CITY.

"Masks" are approximately life-size stone heads. Although hollowed out in the back and pierced for suspension along the rim, they were not intended to be worn as masks by the living as they have no eye holes. Neither were they intended to be worn as breast ornaments because they are too heavy. No example has yet been reported by a trained archaeological observer and it is not known with what they are associated in the ground. Examination of surviving masks makes it clear that an attempt was made to embellish them and make them appear lifelike. In most if not all cases the teeth and eyes were indicated by inlays of shell, obsidian and pyrites. Today such inlays usually have disappeared or are represented only by a stain but there are a few exceptions which retain their original appearance. Almost invariably the ear lobes have been drilled and typical ear disks were attached. In a few cases, cut out areas exist which probably were filled with the colorful mosaics, best known from Aztec or Mixtec examples (p. 64).

Pottery figurines have been found at Teotihuacan in enormous quantities. The oldest types are definitely of Pre-Classic styles and may date from the fourth century before our era. A second phase, also hand-modeled, is noteworthy for vigorous poses and implications of action. These small pottery faces usually have a broad forehead and slender chin which suggest the physical type depicted by the stone masks of the third or Classic stylistic period. Contemporary figurines of this period, however, are radically different because they reflect the symbolism of a complex pantheon and can be identified with definite gods, many of whom were worshipped in later times. Classical figurines were not hand-made but were pressed out in molds, surviving examples of which now insure an ample supply of pseudo-antiques for tourists.

Pottery vessels of Teotihuacan merit a long monograph but we here confine our remarks to certain aspects of the Classic period. Artisans of the greatest technical ability devoted themselves to the manufacture of cylindrical jars set on tripod supports. They often had a conical cover capped by a knob or a small head. Decoration is of several types including brush and negative painting, incising and carving both in rounded relief or with sunken backgrounds (plano-relief). Most spectacular, however, are vessels which have been coated with plaster and painted, reproducing in miniature the subjects represented in the great painted murals (p. 47). This fresco technique first appeared in the Mexican highlands during the middle Pre-Classic and was manufactured until the abandonment of Teotihuacan. It has been found repeatedly in Maya sites of the early Classic period, in greatest quantity at Kaminaljuyú on the edge of the present Guatemala City. Here the painted motifs may stem from Teotihuacan or they may be in the Maya stylistic tradition.

Mural paintings are not among the most durable works of art. It is surprising that so much has survived in a city destroyed by fire so long ago. Colors fade when exposed to the elements and it is fortunate that all archaeologists who worked at Teotihuacan

ONYX MARBLE MASK, FORMERLY WITH INLAID EYES. CLASSICAL TEOTIHUACAN STYLE. MUSEO ARCHEOLOGICO, FLORENCE, ITALY.

THE RAIN GOD TLALOC. DETAIL OF A FRESCO OF THE CLASSIC PERIOD AT TETITLA, TEOTIHUACAN, D.F., MEXICO.

had copies made at once. Full scale reproductions may be seen in the Mexican National Museum; many have been published on a reduced scale. Most murals at Teotihuacan have been found on the walls of buildings classed as "palaces," presumably occupied by rich individuals or high officials. The walls were coated with a very smooth white plaster. Pigments include black, white, light green, light yellow, pink, dark red, light and dark blue. There are no shadows or geometrical perspective. Distance is indicated by placing the more remote higher than the more proximate. The subjects, with few exceptions, are religious. Many gods of the Aztec pantheon are presented in gorgeous raiment, but the gruesome Aztec deities canopied in blood and death are absent. Human sacrifice, however, is suggested by abstract designs showing hearts, blood and sacrificial knives. Symbols of the gods are multitudinous. Associated animals are especially pleasing to European eyes for even the most esoteric are often graceful.

The idea of ceremonial renewal was ingrained in Middle America and called for special rites. Best known perhaps is the Aztec New Fire ceremony, held at the beginning of each 52-year cycle after the destruction of all pottery and household utensils. Architectural rejuvenation might consist of completely filling in an older building and using it as a base for a new edifice. No less than six such superimposed temples have been found in the Valley of Mexico at Tenayuca.

Plaster-coated vessels painted with frescoes appeared in central Mexico during the Middle Pre-Classic. This technique reached its highest development in Teotihuacan III times (see below) and, with that style, spread to the east and south across the Maya area. There is a strong implication that the thus adorned vessels represent ceremonial renewals because the hidden original surfaces often were ornate and because the motifs on the new surfaces reflect in miniature the big contemporary religious murals.

CLASSICAL TEOTIHUACAN BOWL. THE PLASTER-COATED WALLS PICTURE THE DEITY KNOWN TO THE AZTEC AS XOCHIPILLI, LORD OF FLOWERS. HEIGHT, 4½". DIEGO RIVERA MUSEUM, MEXICO CITY.

POTTERY HEAD OF AN ANIMAL WITH A HUMAN HEAD IN THE OPEN JAWS, BOTH COVERED WITH A MOTHER-OF-PEARL MOSAIC. TOLTEC PERIOD. FOUND AT TULA, HIDALGO, MEXICO. HEIGHT, 5⅜". MUSEO NACIONAL DE ANTROPOLOGÍA, MEXICO CITY.

THE TOLTEC OF TULA

Radiocarbon studies now in progress should soon give us an accurate date for the downfall and destruction of Teotihuacan. Its inhabitants settled in other cities such as Azcapotzalco. There followed a period of confusion and disorder with incursions of wild tribes from the north. Among these were the Toltecs. Manuscripts exist in which history begins to emerge from a morass of mythology. We know practically nothing about the newcomers before they established themselves on the Mexican plateau. The Toltec arrived under the leadership of a great chief, Mixcoatl, who in later times was worshipped as a god. They conquered the Valley of Mexico and built their capital on the Hill of the Star in Culhuacan. Here Mixcoatl was murdered by his brother, leaving a widow who died in giving birth to a son. The Toltecs had been worshippers of the god named Tezcatlipoca, but the son Topiltzin was educated in his mother's faith by priests of Quetzalcoatl. On reaching manhood, he killed his uncle and replaced him as the Toltec chief. He then became the high priest of Quetzalcoatl and assumed his name.

For reasons which are not known, Quetzalcoatl decided to move his capital and he founded the city named Tula in the year 980 A.D. There he introduced new arts and crafts and erected a city of fabulous opulence. Later ages picture him as immensely learned, the inventor of agriculture, metalworking, divination, the calendar, writing and books. As the high priest of his namesake god, Quetzalcoatl was opposed to human sacrifice and the bloody rites demanded by Tezcatlipoca, traditional Toltec god. As a result of religious conflict, Quetzalcoatl was forced to leave Tula in 999 and, with a band of faithful followers, he traveled to the Gulf coast and embarked for Yucatan, promising to return someday in the future. This small group of priests and warriors were able to dominate the Maya city of Chichen Itza where they erected great temples in the style of Tula. Toltec chiefs continued to rule there until 1194.

The Toltec did indeed introduce new art styles which combine the symbolism of the two conflicting religious cults. Their architecture features the frequent use of columns and Atlantean supports. Their doorways are divided by columns carved to represent the mythical feathered serpent with heads resting on the floor and with the rattles of the tails upholding the lintels. At Tula the roof of a temple was supported by four fifteen-foot high statues of warriors clad in typical Toltec style. Both at Tula and Chichen Itza there are vast colonnades supported by round or rectangular columns, the latter carved on all four sides. In both cities, bas-reliefs occur as panels or friezes on walls or the sides of benches. These may picture processions of warriors, sometimes engaged in a ritual act (p. 126). They show eagles and jaguars devouring the hearts of sacrificed victims or rows of skulls. Also they picture the symbols of Quetzalcoatl, the Feathered Snake, and occasionally the deified Mixcoatl, whose name means Cloudy Snake.

At Chichen Itza but not at Tula there are a remarkable series of mural paintings. These are not religious pictures like most of the Teotihuacan frescoes but they depict various activities such as battles with scores of warriors fighting, the capture and sacrifice of prisoners, or the humble daily life of a fishing village (p. 127). Excavations at Tula have brought to light the remarkable pottery vessel seen on page 48. It represents a human head wearing a helmet in the form of an animal's head. It is completely covered with a mosaic of mother-of-pearl. Beautiful mosaics dating from the Toltec period have been found at Chichen Itza. Technically they resemble the workmanship attributed to the Aztec and Mixtec (p. 64).

CHICHIMEC PERIOD After the downfall of Tula, central Mexico was invaded by new groups of barbarians from the north, who collectively are known as Chichimecs. These skin-clad hordes attacked the older settlements and fought with each other, but in time they became civilized and sedentary. In the thirteenth century, they settled at Tenayuca and initiated a dynasty which later transferred its capital to Texcoco. During the period of Chichimec supremacy in the Valley of Mexico, the Toltec retained Culhuacan as a stronghold, the locality where they had first placed their capital. They claimed descent from the kings of Tula which gave them great prestige. Newcomers who established themselves in the valley sought wives from the house of Culhuacan and these dynastic alliances made it possible for these Toltecs to survive. In 1367, Culhuacan was destroyed by Azcapotzalco, aided by then humble allies, the Aztec. A few years later, the insignificant Aztecs elected as their ruler a descendant of the deposed kings of Culhuacan. This shrewd move made it possible for them to proclaim themselves heirs of the Toltec.

COLUMNS WHICH SUPPORTED THE ROOF OF A NOW FALLEN TEMPLE. HEIGHT OF ATLANTEAN FIGURES, 15 FEET. TOLTEC OF TULA, HIDALGO.

Toltec carvings often depict warriors, either as Atlantean columns or as bas-reliefs on walls, door jambs or rectangular columns. Their insignia often include the breast ornament seen here, interpreted as a conventionalized bird, and a circular disk was worn over the buttocks. As people adapted to a cool climate, the Toltec made extensive use of fur, even after moving to the tropics. In the carving on page 126, the warriors have both arms adorned with bands of fur. The chief offensive weapon was a dart propelled by a spear thrower. The shaft of the latter usually was encased in fur.

AZTECS

The Aztecs are pre-eminent among New World nations for several reasons. Their capital Tenochtitlan, above which the present Mexico City now stands, was the largest and finest aboriginal metropolis ever seen by Europeans. Its conquest was an outstanding military feat and its loot was the greatest treasure which had reached Europe up to that time. Furthermore, we have eye-witness accounts of Aztec economy as it flourished in aboriginal times, their strange and colorful customs, even their bloody human sacrifices. Descriptions of this exotic civilization and the dramatic story of its downfall soon became available in the principal languages of Europe. Historical research among native sources has revealed the fabulous growth of Aztec power.

The Aztec originally were one of the small nomadic groups which wandered into central Mexico from the north. They were not welcome and, having little military power, were unable to find a permanent home. In the year 1325 A.D. they settled on a swampy island, Tenochtitlan, in what was then Lake Texcoco in the Valley of Mexico. There followed a series of wars, at first with the Aztec as minor allies of more powerful neighbors. From these wars there emerged a confederacy of three cities which later dominated and held tributary most of central and southern Mexico. At first the three partners, Tenochtitlan, Texcoco and Tlacopan, were of equal rank but Aztec leadership was unchallenged when the Spaniards arrived.

The physical growth of the island capital of the Aztec was made possible by the construction of *chinampas*, the so-called "floating islands" which still may be seen in the Xochimilco district today. To make a *chinampa*, mud is scooped up from marsh or lake bottom to form a small island, at first held together by wattles. More mud is added with each planting in order to fertilize and in time tree roots anchor the island solidly to the bottom. As a result of this construction, Tenochtitlan became a city cut by canals. When more living room was needed, it was easy to expand. Eventually Tenochtitlan conquered and engulfed Tlateloco, a neighboring island which had been settled about 1200 A.D. Excavations in this area, now in the heart of Mexico City, recently yielded the great incense burner seen on page 55. It is not here possible to follow the story of growth and conquest in detail. Itzcoatl (1428-1440), the fourth chief of Tenochtitlan, achieved full equality for his people in their alliance. He reformed the religious and governmental structure; he ordered the building of new temples of stone and the great causeways and bridges joining his island to the mainland. Aztec arrogance at this time had become such that Itzcoatl ordered the burning of historical manuscripts of his conquered neighbors with a past more illustrious than his.

The next ruler, Montezuma I (1440-1469) excluded Tlacopan from the triple alliance and pushed his conquests to the east and south outside the Valley of Mexico. He built the aqueduct which brought sweet water to his city from Chapultepec and erected a great dike to prevent floods. His son, Axayacatl (1469-1481), provoked "by the insulting behavior of the Tlatelocan women, who flaunted their backsides at the enraged Tenochan visitors," conquered the neighboring town and suppressed its government. He also sent armies to the southeast as far as Oaxaca and Tehuantepec. Axayacatl is the first ruler we can associate with a work of art for he ordered the carving of the great calendar stone discussed on pages 56-57.

Tizoc (1481-1486) began the rebuilding of the twin temples of the War and Rain gods and he ordered the carving of the so-called Sacrificial Stone. This is shaped like a mill wheel with a hole in the center for burning human hearts. A frieze around the edge depicts the ruler seizing captives for sacrifice. Tizoc, who was said to have died of poison, was succeeded by his brother, Ahuitzotl (1486-1503), who completed the great temples. After two years of war, he held 20,000 prisoners whose hearts were torn out at the dedication, a task he started with his own hands. His conquests extended to Guatemala and northern Vera Cruz. His capital had grown so large that he ordered the construction of a second aqueduct. The city is said to have contained 60,000 houses with an estimated population of 300,000. Montezuma II (1503-1520), fated to be captured by Cortez and lose his empire to the Spaniards, did not add to the conquests of his ancestors but emulated his predecessor in piety by sacrificing 12,000 captives in a single ceremony.

RITUAL Even minor Aztec rituals were accompanied by human sacrifice. Its portrayal and paraphernalia are among their greatest works of art and call for comment. The idea of sacrifice or martyrdom for the good of humanity is found in many religions, past and present, throughout the world. Blood offerings by individuals were practised in Mexico probably as early as Olmec times, for jade spikes are believed to have been used to pierce the tongue and ears. A Classic Maya carving (p. 100) shows a penitent drawing through the tongue a rope with attached cactus spines. Sacrifice by cutting open the chest and tearing out the still beating heart is represented occasionally in Classical Maya and Classical Vera Cruz carvings but does not occur at Teotihuacan, where, however, hearts dripping with blood appear in murals. The big step-up in frequency of human sacrifice seemingly dates from Toltec times. Bas-reliefs showing the consumption of hearts by eagles and jaguars may be seen at Tula and at Chichen Itza. The oldest *tzompantli*, the rack on which the skulls of sacrificial victims were impaled, probably is the example of Toltec date at Chichen Itza.

The Aztec and others believed that, for man to survive, the gods must be made strong and that human blood was their proper nourishment. Furthermore, they believed that the most acceptable blood came from the hearts of warriors, the braver and more noble the better. Slaves, women or children sometimes were slain but were considered inferior to captives taken in battle. Thus a vicious circle was formed: wars provided victims for sacrifice and sacrifice called for wars. As a result of religious demands a most curious custom arose known as the War of the Flowers. When no normal war was in progress, the best warriors of two states met by agreement and fought, both for prestige and to permit the taking of captives. The victors gained renown and the captives died gloriously to feed the gods, being thus assured of an after life in a special heaven.

The Aztec did not consolidate their conquests politically to form a great state. However, they left garrisons and officials to collect tribute which was sent to Tenochtitlan. Tribute rolls of Montezuma survive which list the towns, what each was to provide and indicate the quantity. Thus gold, jade, featherwork, textiles, and local products of all kinds were shipped to Montezuma. Typical listed items include: ten masks of precious stone, twenty bags of cochineal dye, one hundred bags of cacao, four hundred bales of cotton, four hundred jars of honey, eight thousand balls of copal incense. Special officials had charge of the distribution of this wealth. In addition to tribute, Aztec economy depended on trade. They developed a special class of merchants whose goods were transported by slaves. Purchases were facilitated by the use of cacao beans as money in a large part of Mexico and Central America. Trading stations were established as far south as Nicaragua. Fifty years after the conquest of Tenochtitlan, Spanish soldiers who spoke their language were astonished to find a group of Aztec in southern Costa Rica. They explained that they had been sent by Montezuma to collect gold, and, learning of his downfall, had decided not to return home.

TRIBUTE

All Mexican towns contained markets but the largest and most famous was the market in the Tlateloco section of Tenochtitlan. Bernal Diaz, soldier turned historian, thus describes it: "We were astonished at the number of people and the quantity of merchandise that it contained, and at the good order and control that was maintained... Each kind of merchandise was kept by itself and had its fixed place marked out. Let us begin with the dealers in gold, silver, and precious stones, feathers, mantles, and embroidered goods. Then there were other wares consisting of Indian slaves, both men and women; and I say that they bring as many of them to that great market as the Portuguese bring negroes from Guinea; and they brought them along tied to long poles, with collars around their necks so that they could not escape, and others they left free. Next there were other traders who sold great pieces of cloth and cotton, and articles of twisted thread, and there were *cacahuateros* who sold cacao... There were those who sold cloths of henequen and ropes and sandals with which they are shod, and sweet cooked roots and other tubers which they get from this plant, all were kept in one part of the market in the place assigned to them. In another part there were skins of tigers and lions, of otters and jackals, deer and other animals and badgers and mountain cats, some tanned and others untanned, and other classes of merchandise.

MARKETS

"Let us go on and speak of those who sold beans and sage and other vegetables and herbs in another part, and to those who sold fowls, cocks with wattles, rabbits, hares, deer, mallards, young dogs and other things of that sort in their part of the market, and let us mention also the fruiters and the women who sold cooked food, dough and tripe in their part of the market; then every sort of pottery made in a thousand different forms from great water jars to little jugs, these also had a place to themselves; then those who sold honey and honey paste and other dainties like nut paste, and those who sold lumber, boards, cradles, beams, blocks and benches, each article by itself... Paper which in that land is called *Amal*, and reed scented with *liquidambar*, and full of tobacco, and yellow ointments and things of that sort are sold by themselves, and much cochineal is sold under the arcades which are in that great market place, and there are many vendors of herbs and other sorts of trade... I am forgetting those who sell salt, and those who make stone knives, and how they split them off the stone itself... There are for sale axes of brass and copper and tin, and gourds and gaily painted jars made of wood."

TEMPLES   Adjacent to the Tlateloco market was a courtyard, said to have been larger than the plaza of Salamanca, and the huge terraced pyramid supporting the twin temples of Huitzilopochtli and Tezcatlipoca. The incense vessel shown on page 55 was recently found on one of these terraces, buried in the twenty-odd feet of soil which has accumulated since the Conquest. It must have billowed with the smoke of copal or rubber on the day when Bernal Diaz climbed the 114 steps to the summit behind the Emperor Montezuma and Cortez. He was a witness to the dramatic moment when Montezuma took Cortez by the hand and told him to look at his great city and the many others fringing Lake Texcoco. "So we stood looking about us," wrote Diaz, "for that huge and cursed temple stood so high that from it one could see over everything very well."

The Spanish guests of Montezuma asked and received permission to enter the temples and look at his gods. In each of the temples they were sickened by the stench of the walls blackened by the dried blood of sacrificed victims and they were horrified by the fresh blood from the hearts of those who had been killed earlier that day. From this visit, however, we have our best picture of the original appearance of the few surviving major Aztec sculptures such as the monstrous deity on page 59, today stripped of its color and rich adornments.

Again from the pen of Bernal Diaz: "On each altar were two figures, like giants with very tall bodies and very fat, and the first which stood on the right hand they said was the figure of Huichilobos (Huitzilopochtli), their god of War; it had a broad face and monstrous and terrible eyes, and the whole body was covered with precious stones, and gold and pearls, and with seed pearls stuck on with a paste that they make in this country out of a sort of root, and all the body and head were covered with it, and the body was girdled by great snakes made of gold and precious stones, and in one hand he held a bow and in the other some arrows. Another small statue that stood by him, they said was his page, and he held a short lance and shield richly decorated with gold and stones. Huichilobos had around his neck some Indians' faces and other

AZTEC POTTERY INCENSE BURNER RECENTLY EXCAVATED ON A TERRACE OF THE GREAT PYRAMID AT TLATELOCO. HEIGHT, 42″. ONE OF THE FEW ABORIGINAL ACCOUTREMENTS OF THE AZTEC TO BE FOUND IN SITU AND PRACTICALLY INTACT. MUSEO NACIONAL DE ANTROPOLOGÍA, MEXICO CITY.

things like hearts of Indians, the former made of gold and the latter of silver, and many precious blue stones." After commenting on the burning of three newly sacrificed human hearts, Diaz writes of the adjacent image of Tezcatlipoca that he had a face like a bear and eyes made of mirrors and also had a body plastered with precious stones and he added that this deity "was the god of Hell and had charge of the souls of Mexicans and his body was girt with figures like little devils with snakes' tails."

Today we have a few minor artifacts "plastered with precious stones" such as the human skull seen on page 64 and the wooden mask on page 64. These pieces are survivals from the loot of Mexico sent to Spain by Cortez. A few others had been hidden in caves for ritual purposes and have been rediscovered in recent years. Now, for their rich color and beauty, they are cherished as treasures. No doubt that most of the great Aztec gods were adorned with equal or even more opulence and were stripped of any adornments of commercial value before they were cast from their lofty temples and broken up for building stone.

SCULPTURE   The surviving major Aztec sculptures are of stone. They indicate that the Aztecs, who entered the Valley of Mexico as barbarians and whose period of political ascendancy lasted only a century, became great artists in their own right. Our knowledge today is limited by an iconoclasm seldom equaled in world history. Cortez to make his cavalry effective in the capture of Tenochtitlan found it necessary to demolish all buildings and fill in the canals; imposition of a new religion called for the destruction of all temples, all artistic expressions of native beliefs or symbolism and all native manuscripts which might perpetuate the past.

The few existing major sculptures of the Aztec are all archaeological discoveries. Outstanding is the so-called Calendar Stone (p. 57) carved in the year 1479. In 1790, the Spanish viceroy ordered that the Zócalo, the great plaza both in Aztec times and today, be leveled and paved and that an underground aqueduct be built. As a result of the necessary excavation, the monstrous statue of Coatlicue (p. 59) was discovered and later the Calendar Stone, both to the west of the Palace. Both were illustrated two years later in the first archaeological publication to appear in the New World. The Calendar Stone is of basalt which was quarried to the south of Tenochtitlan and must have been transported to the city over the causeway and its bridges. The weight is estimated at twenty-four tons and the diameter of the carved portion is just under twelve feet. In comment, the statue of Chalchihuitlicue found at Teotihuacan (p. 41) weighs about six tons less, but to move it to the National Museum in Mexico City required several months.

The Calendar Stone epitomizes Aztec cosmography. The Aztecs believed that in the past there had been four Suns, each of whom had been destroyed together with a contemporary human race. The present era is that of the fifth Sun, Tonatiuh, who

THE CALENDAR STONE OF THE AZTEC. ESTIMATED TO WEIGH 24 TONS, THE CIRCULAR PANEL IS JUST UNDER
12 FEET IN DIAMETER. ITS SYMBOLS EPITOMIZE AZTEC IDEAS OF THE UNIVERSE. CARVED AT THE ORDER
OF THE EMPEROR AXAYACATL (1469-1481). MUSEO NACIONAL DE ANTROPOLOGÍA, MEXICO CITY.

must be offered human blood to strengthen him for his daily journey. The face of this
Sun appears in the inner circle which is flanked by claws holding human hearts.
In the rectangular panels are the dates when the previous Suns were destroyed.
At the top of the outer band is the date "13 Reed" when the present Sun was born.
The entire central circle together with the loops and squares around it forms a glyph
which records the date "4 Earthquake," the future day on which Tonatiuh must die
and the manner of his destruction. The narrow circular band surrounding the claws
and four dates contains twenty hieroglyphs which name the days of the Aztec calendar.
The next band incorporates eight V-shaped solar rays and glyphs denoting jade or
turquoise, symbolizing blue, the sky and something precious. The final outer band
consists of two great Fire Serpents which meet face to face at the bottom of the disk.

These are charged with carrying the Sun on his daily journey. Originally this sculpture was elaborately painted. Very careful examination has revealed sunken traces of pigment which has made it possible to construct a complete restoration of its original appearance. Colorful as this restoration is, the bare stone, monumental in size, rhythmical in design, obviously intellectual in concept, impresses even a visitor who is ignorant of its symbolism.

On August 13, 1790, the anniversary of the day when the starving Aztec defenders of Tenochtitlan surrendered to the combined might of Spanish arms and their native allies, the most important Aztec statue we now know was discovered by accident in the area which formerly enclosed the major temples of Tenochtitlan. Soon afterwards, the Calendar Stone was found nearby. Neither of these two great survivals of iconoclasm are mentioned in eyewitness accounts of the Conquest nor do they figure in later written descriptions of Tenochtitlan as it once was. They both are so heavy and massive that those who hid them from former worshippers probably did not move them far from their original location.

The statue shown on page 59 represents Coatlicue, "Lady of the Serpent Skirt," mother of the Sun, the Moon and the southern stars, goddess of the earth and of death, also associated with spring. According to legend, Coatlicue, after giving birth to Coyolxauhqui, the Moon, and her 400 brothers, stars of the south, retired to a temple and became a priestess. One day while sweeping, she found a ball of down which she placed in her blouse. The down disappeared but Coatlicue found herself pregnant. This enraged her sons and daughter who came to kill her. At that moment, Huitzilopochtli, god of War and tribal god of the Aztecs, was born. He chased away his brothers, the stars, with a serpent of fire, a solar ray, as he still does every morning. Also he cut off the head of his sister, the Moon. One of the finest Aztec carvings represents this severed head with tears of gold running from the closed eyes.

The statue of Coatlicue we illustrate (p. 59) is the largest of three now in the National Museum of Mexico. Eight feet high, it weighs about twelve tons. No doubt to the Aztec as to us it was awe-inspiring, horrible and monstrous. Unlike the lesser statues there is nothing human about it except the half-concealed pendulous breasts. It is a monument of symbols, skilfully combined and rendered individually with surprising realism.

In other statues Coatlicue has a skull for a head. In this colossal carving the head has been cut off and two streams of blood have replaced it, represented by two big snakes shown in profile. Combined they form a grotesque face. The concept of depicting blood spurting from a decapitated body by means of snakes is much older than the Aztec period. It may be seen in relief carvings of Tajin style on the Gulf coast and also in reliefs in the great ball court of Chichen Itza in Yucatan, dating from the Toltec period (p. 126).

THE AZTEC GODDESS COATLICUE, "LADY OF THE SERPENT SKIRT," MOTHER OF THE WAR GOD, THE MOON, THE SOUTHERN STARS, GODDESS OF THE EARTH AND OF DEATH. HEIGHT, 8 FEET. MUSEO NACIONAL DE ANTROPOLOGÍA, MEXICO CITY.

The goddess wears a gruesome necklace of severed human hands and hearts with a skull in the center. Her feet are clawed. Her hands, when seen from the side, are serpents' heads like those that form her face. The skirt from which she takes her name is a mass of intertwined writhing rattlesnakes. Hanging head downward, they are supported by a belt of snakes, knotted in the front with heads which form tassels. On the base of the statue, hidden when it stands upright, there is carved the froglike figure of Tlaltecuhtli, "Lord of the Earth."

One of the features of Aztec religion were god-impersonators, living individuals clad in the insignia of the deity who, for a time, were reverenced as if they were the actual god. Most picturesque was the ceremony in honor of Tezcatlipoca, whose temple at Tlateloco has been described. Annually a young prisoner with no blemish or physical imperfection was selected to represent the god. For a year he lived in luxury and was feasted as if he were the living deity. As the end drew near he was assigned four beautiful mistresses. Finally however, he mounted the temple steps, breaking the flutes he had played in his carefree past, and his still beating heart was torn out. This ceremony apparently was not commemorated in art, but the much grimmer impersonation of the god Xipe is depicted in statuary, figurines and codices. Xipe Totec, Lord of Flaying, was an Aztec deity with roots in the far past. He was represented in Zapotec, Remojadas and Teotihuacan art. His cult evidently extended to Nicaragua for the Spaniards recorded the fact that the natives had flayed their captives and wore the skins bloody side out in order to terrify the horses. Some years ago, the writer found a wooden mask representing the head of Xipe among the dance paraphernalia in a Salvadorian village on Fonseca Bay. His identity forgotten, he had been modernized by sticking the metal top of a champagne bottle on his forehead. To the Aztec, Xipe Totec symbolized renewal, spring and vegetation. He was the protector of goldsmiths. To him was attributed such disorders of the body as smallpox, boils, scabs and eye diseases.

"They made a very solemn feast to the god called Xipe Totec, and also in honor of Huitzilopochtli. At this feast they killed all the prisoners, men, women and children. The owner of the prisoners handed them over to the priests at the foot of the temple, and they dragged them by the hair, each one his own, up the steps . . . to the block of stone where they were to kill them, and taking from each one his heart, they hurled their bodies down the steps, where other priests flayed them . . . They dismembered them and sent a limb to Montezuma to eat, and the rest they shared among the other chiefs and relatives." The owners of the sacrificed apparently did not eat their own captives.

The god-impersonator might be the victorious warrior but more often was a priest. As the body had been decapitated, a cut was made in the back of the scalp and the flesh peeled off with face intact. This was then placed as a mask over the face of the impersonator and sewn up the back, as seen on page 61. In sculpture, the dead lips frame the living lips.

AZTEC STATUE REPRESENTING A PRIEST OF XIPE CLAD IN THE SKIN OF A SACRIFICED VICTIM. FOUND IN TEXCOCO, VALLEY OF MEXICO. HEIGHT, 15¾".
MUSEUM FÜR VÖLKERKUNDE, BASEL, SWITZERLAND.

The body also was slit up the back and the skin seems to have been peeled off the arms and legs inside out as if pulling off a glove. No attempt was made to retain feet but the hands, severed at the wrists, were left attached to the skin. The slit in the chest through which the heart had been extracted was sewn up, the impersonator pulled on this fresh-cut garment, and the opening in the back was laced tight. As a decorative touch, the edges of the skin at the neck, wrists and ankles might be neatly scalloped. What rites and ceremonies were performed by the impersonator of the god have not been recorded. The role was maintained for twenty days. The skin turned yellow and was called "a garment of gold" but the wearer, it is said, "stank like a dead dog." Xipe Totec was not the only Aztec deity impersonated by a priest clad in the flayed skin of a sacrificed captive but he alone was sculptured in stone. In honor of the earth goddess Tlazolteotl, a woman was sacrificed. In Mexican pictorial manuscripts the goddess regularly is pictured wearing the skin of body and limbs with attached hands as on the Xipe statues but she never has a mask of skin covering the face (p. 62).

Monumental sculpture is rare in Mexico because the introduction of a new religion called for its destruction but smaller carvings have survived in considerable quantity. These may have ritualistic backgrounds but many deities were associated with animals or other aspects of nature which could be portrayed with realism and delicacy. A Maize goddess and a Water goddess, both represented as youthful, were sculptured with directness and simplicity. There are engaging animal figures including rabbits, coyotes, grasshoppers, coiled rattlesnakes, also human heads in the round or half round like the Teotihuacan masks (p. 45). Even the animals with a basin in their backs destined to receive human hearts are carved with a charm which belies their original purpose. Finally, there are surviving wood carvings, many shaped like animals, hollowed out to serve as drums. Few mural paintings attributed to the Aztec exist today. Nothing is known which rivals those of Teotihuacan, the Maya of Bonampak or the Toltec of Chichen Itza.

MOSAICS Among the outstanding skills of Mexico were mosaic incrustations of various objects. Jade, turquoise, malachite, quartz, beryl, garnet, obsidian, gold, tortoise shell, nacre and colored shell were employed for this purpose. The oldest examples, attributed to the Zapotec (p. 81) and Maya (pp. 114-115), are relatively crude in workmanship. Toltec mosaics from Chichen Itza, however, show a refinement in delicacy of technique which reached its peak in the hands of Mixtec artists in the sixteenth century. A display shield, made not for war but for festivals, has a mosaic disk measuring 11½ inches across. The mosaic in this small area is estimated to contain over 14,000 minute elements.

We have already mentioned the mosaic adornment on major Aztec idols. Portable artifacts may have been manufactured by the Aztecs themselves or acquired as tribute.

The goddess Tlazolteotl clad in the flayed skin of a sacrificed woman. From an Aztec manuscript (drawing by Miguel Covarrubias). This deity originally was worshipped by the Huastec but she assumed an important place in the pantheon of the Aztec who regarded her as an earth goddess dedicated to licentious pleasures and carnal sin.

Tlazolteotl was known as the "Eater of Filth" because she consumed the sins of mankind. As the only Aztec deity concerned with individual morals, her priests received confessions and granted absolution. This was permitted only once in a lifetime, so everyone waited until they were old. Her priests also had the important function of casting horoscopes and naming the new-born.

In addition, Tlazolteotl was a goddess of childbirth, as pictured here. Her children were Centeotl, the Maize god, and Xochiquetzal, the goddess of fertility, flowers and weaving.

A GRASSHOPPER CARVED IN RED CARNELITE. FROM CHAPULTEC, D.F., MEXICO. MUSEO NACIONAL DE MEXICO, MEXICO CITY.

The inventories of treasures sent from Mexico to Spain list many examples. Twenty-three of these may be found today in six European museums. We illustrate two of them on pages 64 and 65. During the present century perhaps as many as three dozen more have been found, some by excavation, most of them in dry caves where they had been hidden at the time of the Conquest. They equal the European pieces in technical skill but in most cases the colors are less brilliant.

FEATHERWORK Aztec featherwork, an art now lost, and almost obliterated by time, was a unique achievement. Many people have adorned themselves with feathers or have embellished their persons, their garments and their utensils. The gorgeous feather headdresses of the Classic Maya and other Middle American groups we know only through the cold medium of their sculpture. Outstanding featherwork today includes baskets of the California Indians, garments found archaeologically in the Peruvian deserts and the feather cloaks of Polynesia, chiefly from Hawaii. All are technically alike because, whatever the base material, it was adorned by the attachment of individual feathers.

WOODEN MASK ENCRUSTED WITH MOSAIC OF TURQUOISE AND COLORED SHELL. THE HUMAN FACE WITH TERRACED NOSE ORNAMENT IS FRAMED TOP
AND BOTTOM BY OPEN ANIMAL JAWS AND AT THE SIDES BY STANDING ANIMAL FIGURES. AZTEC OR MIXTEC WORKMANSHIP. HEIGHT, 7¼".
MUSEO PREISTORICO, ROME.

FRONT OF A HUMAN SKULL ADORNED WITH MOSAIC OF TURQUOISE AND JET. THE EYES ARE OF SHELL AND PYRITE.
SAID TO HAVE BEEN A GIFT TO CORTEZ FROM THE AZTEC EMPEROR MONTEZUMA II. HEIGHT, 7⅞".
BRITISH MUSEUM, LONDON.

The Aztec, on the contrary, cut up their feathers in small pieces and, selecting appropriate colors, they used them as pigments which they glued to a base. In fact, however, the process was far from simple, as it called for preliminary designs on paper and involved the use of stencils. As recently as the last century, the skill still existed to "paint" landscapes and other scenes with feathers. At the time of the Conquest, the feather-workers were regarded as such superior artists that they were asked to furnish the designs for the workers in metal. Among the few surviving examples of Mexican featherwork, the ceremonial shield illustrated on page 67 is outstanding. The blue animal it displays has been identified as the fabulous aquatic monster known to the Aztec as *ahuitzotl*. Like the *armes parlantes* in European heraldry this probably is the symbol of the ruler Ahuitzotl. Eyes, claws, teeth, fur and outlines all are thin strips of gold. The rose-red field consists of feathers from the roseate spoon-bill *(Platalea agaja)*, considered by the Aztec to be the "prince of the herons." Originally the shield was adorned with a fringe of quetzal feathers.

METALWORK   Aztec metalwork received high praise from the Spanish invaders but relatively little has been found archaeologically. Most Mexican jewelry now known is in Mixtec style, remarkable for delicate false filigree casting (p. 84). Gold evidently reached Tenochtitlan in tribute, both as nuggets or manufactured articles. The treasure secured by Cortez was valued at 292,000 gold pesos and 500 silver marcs. The bullion value today is just over a million dollars but the purchasing power of gold was very much greater in the sixteenth century.

POTTERY   Aztec pottery ranges from huge incense vessels (p. 55) to ordinary domestic wares for cooking and eating. In general the clay employed is a dull yellow and designs were painted in black (p. 66). Pottery of this type was manufactured in the vicinity of Puebla as early as 900 A.D. before the arrival of the Aztec in the valley of Mexico, probably without a knowledge of pottery. Nevertheless, the style is called Aztec I. A subsequent phase known as Aztec II is dated from 1200-1350 A.D. and is attributed to the

AZTEC POTTERY DESIGNS FROM THE VALLEY OF MEXICO, FROM THE INTERIOR OF BOWLS PAINTED IN BLACK ON YELLOW. SEQUENT STYLES INTRODUCED CA. 900, 1200 AND 1350 A.D. AFTER COVARRUBIAS.

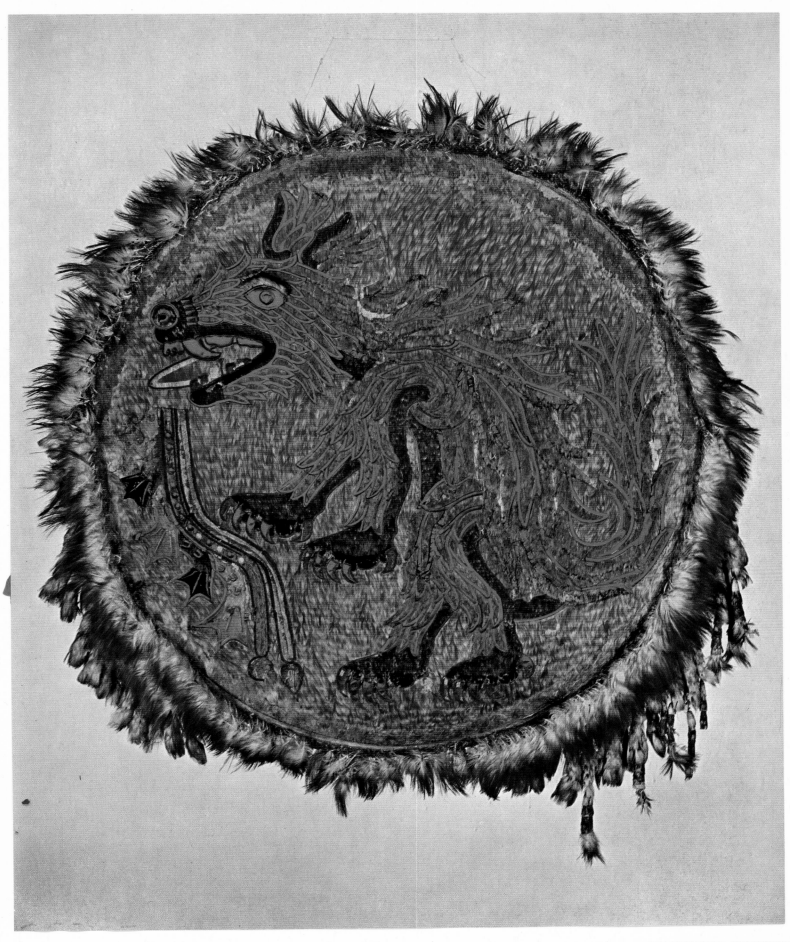

CEREMONIAL SHIELD ADORNED WITH FEATHERWORK OUTLINED IN GOLD. THE ANIMAL IS THE SYMBOL OF THE AZTEC EMPEROR AHUITZOTL
(1486-1503). DIAMETER, 27½″. MUSEUM FÜR VÖLKERKUNDE, VIENNA.

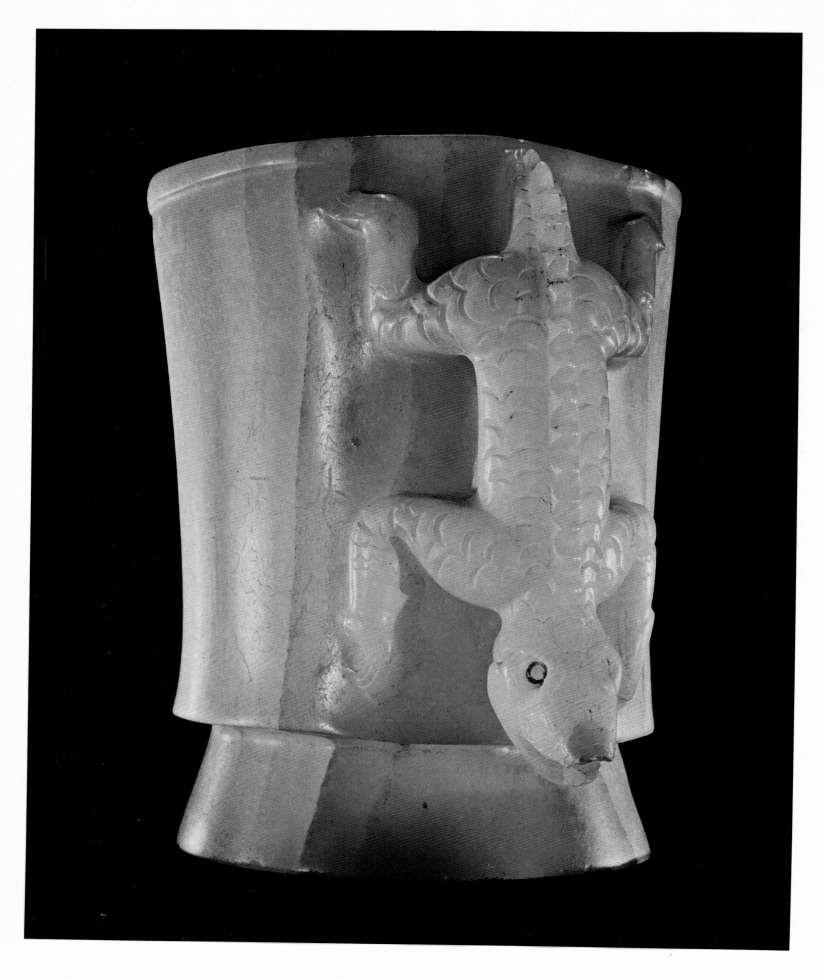

ONYX JAR, FOUND ON ISLA DE SACRIFICIOS, VERA CRUZ, MEXICO. HEIGHT, 9″. MUSEO NACIONAL DE ANTROPOLOGÍA, MEXICO CITY.

Chichimecs of Tenayuca. After settling in Tenochtitlan, the Aztec took over the local pottery types (or acquired women who could produce them) and manufactured the phases known as Aztec III and IV. This entire ceramic sequence is a complex covering about six centuries with Aztec participation in the last two centuries. The motifs during the first two phases consist chiefly of stylized serpent heads, at times reduced to abstract geometric forms. With Aztec participation there was a switch to more realistic themes including birds and fish. Just before the Conquest, grim religious motifs appear such as skulls and cross-bones.

In the description of the great market at Tlateloco, Bernal Diaz wrote that he saw a thousand different forms of pottery. The Aztec themselves manufactured other domestic wares including bowls of highly burnished clay with black designs painted on red or on white. It cannot be said, however, that the Aztec ever produced very distinguished pottery. For this there is a logical explanation, for the Aztec imported the wares manufactured by their neighbors, and they valued highly the beautiful polychrome Mixteca-Puebla ceramics, also known as Cholula ware (p. 88). This unquestionably was the finest pottery of the period produced in Mexico, and the Emperor Montezuma used it for his table. In part these vessels must have reached the markets of Tenochtitlan by trade. At the time of the Conquest, however, most of the Mixtec area had been overrun and paid tribute in the arts and crafts for which these people were famous.

During the period of Aztec expansion, certain artifacts of rare materials or outstanding **LAPIDARIES** workmanship became distributed sporadically and cannot be assigned to any single group. Among these were vessels and carvings of crystal, obsidian and onyx. Two almost life-size crystal skulls, now in England, are outstanding examples. An obsidian jar in the form of a monkey is treasured in Mexico. The first Spanish expedition to reach Mexico in 1518 under Juan de Grijalva, secured "two jars of alabaster, worthy of being presented to the Emperor" when they landed on the Isla de Sacrificios, where the example on page 68 was found in 1827.

Onyx, a fine-grained form of marble, has been confused with alabaster which is a softer stone. It was mined chiefly in the States of Puebla and Oaxaca in Mexico. The Aztec name *tecali* comes from the district where the finest quality is found which has a slightly green tinge. A few Teotihuacan masks are made of it. Onyx vessels usually are white in color. They are so rare that shapes are limited. Tall fluted jars occur, also effigy vessels representing men, monkeys and rabbits. The example on page 68 with a lizard carved as a handle is unique. The technique of manufacture is known through unfinished specimens. The exterior was first shaped by abrasion. To hollow out the interior, it was pierced with tubular drills, thus forming small columns which could be broken off. Working space was thus gained for smoothing the interior walls. The finest examples are incredibly thin and highly polished.

POTTERY FIGURINE REPRESENTING AN ELABORATELY PAINTED WOMAN. STYLE OF NAYARIT. HEIGHT, 21″.
DIEGO RIVERA MUSEUM, MEXICO CITY.

WESTERN MEXICO

The archaeological area described as western Mexico includes the states from Sinaloa in the north to Guerrero in the south. In general it may be stated that there is a great deal of material above ground but very little is known about the circumstances under which it was found. Except for Guerrero, few pieces of sculpture have been discovered. The pottery includes many large figurines and effigy vessels which may have been inspired by Pre-Classic styles. There obviously are many local styles which were traded about so that exact provenance is uncertain. The symbolism of central Mexico usually is lacking but many aspects of daily life are represented including details of dress and ornaments. Group scenes record such ceremonies as ball games, dances, religious processions and burial rites. Sites which can be dated are few except for late Post-Classic or historic groups. El Opeño in Michoacan and Chupícuaro in Guanajuato yield material which is assigned to the middle Pre-Classic (ca. 800 B.C.). The figurine next to the right on page 10 is an example.

The State of Guerrero is noteworthy for the large number and excellence of small stone carvings which have been found within its borders. The archaeological picture suggests that at various times this area has been in close touch with others, but our present knowledge is based on haphazard discoveries and much research is called for to explain these contacts.

GUERRERO

Olmec carvings of small size occur in quantity; it has been suggested that the Olmec style may have originated here, spread to the east coast and there developed its final form. No megalithic Olmec sculptures have been found in Guerrero, however, nor any settlements which can be assigned to the Olmec. A second type of small stone carving in Guerrero reflects the style of Teotihuacan. Similar statuettes have been found in other parts of Mexico but Teotihuacan pottery styles seemingly are absent, although they either were exported to or influenced the Maya potters to the south and east. The third group of Guerrero carvings is known as Mezcala from the region where examples in a fine quality of stone have been found. Here we are fortunate in having a date, for associated pottery types can be placed as late Classic, about 900 A.D. Many of the Mezcala statuettes appear to be reworked stone celts, always carefully polished. The essence of the style is that eyes, arms, legs and other features, whenever possible, are indicated by straight lines cut with a saw. Solid drills sometimes were used but not the ubiquitous tubular drill. The result is a modernistic simplicity.

We should add that small carvings shaped in identical fashion but made of inferior stone have a wide distribution. They occur in quantity as far south as the Department of the Quiché in Guatemala where they are known as *alxiks*. Some of them have been boiled in green-dyed paraffine and sold to unsuspecting tourists as jade.

MICHOACAN "The Kingdom of Michoacan," as the Spaniards first called it, must have been one of the great civilized states of aboriginal Mexico. We know little about it except that their artists were never equaled in certain fields. The people are named Tarascans. We do not know the extent of their sovereignty, but we do know that the Aztec armies suffered such a disastrous defeat that they never attempted to invade them again. The Tarascans appear late in history and, according to their own documents, their territorial expansion dated from the fourteenth and fifteenth centuries.

Tzinzuntzan, the Tarascan capital, is not of great architectural importance but rich burials have been found there. Among the pottery vessels, examples of stirrup-spout handles occur. This device was used in central Mexico two thousand years earlier in the middle Pre-Classic and was characteristic of the north coast of Peru throughout

POTTERY EFFIGY VESSEL REPRESENTING A DOG WEARING A MASK IN THE FORM OF A HUMAN FACE. COLIMA STYLE. HEIGHT, 8¼″.
MUSEO NACIONAL DE ANTROPOLOGÍA, MEXICO CITY.

POTTERY EFFIGY JAR SHOWING A MAN SEATED ON A SMALL STOOL. COLIMA STYLE. MUSEO NACIONAL DE ANTROPOLOGÍA, MEXICO CITY.

POTTERY MODEL OF A BALL COURT SHOWING PLAYERS AND SPECTATORS ON TOP OF THE PARALLEL WALLS. STYLE OF NAYARIT. WIDTH, 14½". FROM WESTERN MEXICO. ART MUSEUM, WORCESTER, MASS.

most of its ceramic history. The Tarascans were excellent metalworkers. Most of the surviving pieces are of copper. They also were outstanding jewelers and were noted for their ability to shape obsidian and crystal. It is probable that many of the labrets and paper-thin ear spools now labeled "Aztec" were the handiwork of Tarascan artists. In addition they were famed for their featherwork but there are no surviving examples. Until recently, almost all archaeological finds from western Mexico were automatically labeled "Tarascan," just as the east coast types were called "Totonac." It is now beginning to be possible to isolate certain pottery types by area and period.

The State of Nayarit has produced two distinct types of effigies. The large hollow figures are much coarser than those of Colima. They often are badly fired, and the surface is rough. Birds and animals are not represented; men and women appear to be caricatures, often with grossly enlarged legs and feet (p. 70). On the other hand, details of dress and ornament are shown both by modeling and by painting. Bracelets, necklaces and nose pendants are modeled. Ears were pierced by a number of holes along the rim through which a series of loops was run. It is not clear what material was used in Nayarit. In Ecuador, however, very similar ear ornaments consisted of spiral gold wires, examples of which are known. Cast gold figures from Colombia and Panama may depict this type of ear adornment. Painted detail is common. If clothes are worn, textile patterns are indicated on skirts, huipiles or headbands. On nude figures, the entire body often is elaborately decorated. Hair frequently is represented by incised parallel lines.

A second form of Nayarit effigy consists of small solid figures grouped together on a solid base. This may be a house with the family as well as their dogs and parrots assembled for a meal. Temples are shown with religious rites in progress. Also there are large outdoor assemblies such as ball courts with players and throngs of spectators, groups of dancers and musicians, a funeral procession with corpse and mourners. These miniature models of large assemblies are not very carefully fashioned. Their charm lies in their spontaneity and the fact that they have caught the spirit of the occasion they represent.

Colima is famous for its highly polished red pottery which probably dates from the Classic period. This includes fluted bowls set on tripods and jars of varied and eccentric shapes. Large hollow effigy vessels are typical. Probably this is a plebeian art, for the human body is shown with little or no clothing. The elaborate headdresses and other paraphernalia of rank displayed in other areas are lacking. The gods and their symbolism are not pictured. Many figures are seated in graceful poses and the only occupation frequently represented is the carrying of water jars on the back or shoulders. In spite of the simplicity of the style, however, facial expressions are varied and create an impression of individuality. Colima potters are generally recognized as the ablest in western Mexico.

Colima large effigies often represent birds and animals with pleasing realism. Depicted are parrots, ducks, aigrets, pelicans, armadillos and dogs. The dogs probably were the variety known to the Aztec as *xoloitzcuintli* which were fattened for eating. Usually they appear enormously fat but they are not necessarily pregnant and in some cases they are definitely males. They are pictured sitting, standing and lying down. Many are smiling; some are howling; a pair are fighting. On page 72 we illustrate a dog with a mask representing a human head. As is often the case, the tail of this dog forms a tubular spout.

SOUTHERN MEXICO

The southern portion of Mexico, the States of Chiapas and Oaxaca, is a cultural and linguistic mosaic, for there are many small tribal groups, each with their own language, but the archaeological picture is dominated by three outstanding cultures and art styles. Maya groups settled in Chiapas in the far past. Oaxaca was occupied for many centuries by the Zapotec, builders of Monte Alban, one of the most picturesque of all aboriginal American cities. Mixtec groups, drifting down from the north, gradually took over and introduced their own cultural pattern. At the time of the Spanish invasion in the sixteenth century, the Aztecs had conquered the entire region. Excavations at Monte Alban have produced a long stylistic sequence which has been placed chronologically by radiocarbon dates. It is not known who first settled Monte Alban. The oldest remains, both in sculpture and in pottery, show strong Olmec influence. This was followed by a period of southern contacts with changes in architecture and pottery types. The Classical Zapotec styles were contemporaneous with Classical Maya but began earlier and lasted longer. Monte Alban had been abandoned before the Mixtec became dominant.

THE ZAPOTEC AND MONTE ALBAN

The ruins of Monte Alban cover an entire mountain top which has been completely reshaped by human hands until no trace of the original contours remains. There is a vast central plaza over 1000 feet long and 650 feet wide and an astonishing succession of levels on which stand great masonry pyramids ascended by broad stairways. Most of the buildings have fallen but the architecture recalls Teotihuacan with sloping lower walls surmounted by upper walls with sunken panels. Originally the temples must have been plastered and painted. Many of the masonry tombs are elaborately decorated with colorful murals.

Zapotec art is best known through the so-called "funeral" urns which were manufactured throughout the entire occupation of the city. These are cylindrical vessels which serve as a base to sustain effigies, often of bewildering complexity. Some have been found in tombs but others were temple offerings or were placed in niches over doorways. Usually they are empty and none have been noted which contained human bones or ashes. The subjects represented change with the period. The majority portray the prodigious succession of deities worshipped by successive generations or perhaps the priests impersonating their gods. Some can be identified by their Zapotec name, such as Cocijo, the god of Rain, whose likeness appears in the first period (650-200 B.C.). The urn on page 79 has been tentatively identified as the Zapotec Yopi, known as Xipe among the Aztecs. He may have been worshipped as early as the first period

ZAPOTEC URN REPRESENTING A JAGUAR. MONTE ALBAN, OAXACA. PERIOD II. HEIGHT, 36″. MUSEO NACIONAL DE ANTROPOLOGÍA, MEXICO CITY.

ZAPOTEC URN REPRESENTING A MAIZE GOD. MONTE ALBAN III STYLE. HEIGHT, 20⅜″. LOLA OLMEDA DE OLVERA COLLECTION, MEXICO CITY. FORMERLY SOLOGUREN COLLECTION.

ZAPOTEC URN REPRESENTING A SEATED DEITY. MONTE ALBAN, OAXACA. PERIOD III. HEIGHT, 12¾″.
MUSEO NACIONAL DE ANTROPOLOGÍA, MEXICO CITY.

under a calendric name but has not been definitely identified until the period III B (700-1000 A.D.). The example illustrated (above) has tattooed volutes below the eyes. The headdress is adorned with a large glyph which has not been identified. A glance at our illustrations clearly indicates that the capacity of Zapotec urns as containers was subordinate to their function as a framework for sculpture. They obviously were not fashioned for eating and drinking. We cannot estimate the number now above ground but it must run into the thousands. Many museums have such large collections that only a small part is on public display.

The urn on page 78 must represent a Maize god, perhaps the Pitao Cozobi of the Zapotec. He is identified by the two cobs flanking his pectoral which probably were molded from actual maize. In the center of the headdress is the head of a bat with two incisor teeth. The body of the bat is surrounded by flowers. Many of the deities portrayed on urns are identified only by associated glyphs and numerals. The meaning of some glyphs is understood and we have calendric names such as god "5 Turquoise" or goddess "11 Death." In addition to urns which represent the gods, there is a much simpler group known as *acompañantes*, the attendants. They may be male or female. They are seated cross-legged, usually with the hands on the knees. Often they wear a cylindrical headdress with flaps on the sides which fall to the shoulders. A special type of attendant wears a headdress which incorporates glyph "C". This also appears as the headdress of the bat on page 78. Another group of urns represents the jaguar or parts of the jaguar, such as the head or a foot with claws. The big example on page 77 dates from period II (200 B.C. – 200 A.D.) and is said to be the oldest jaguar from Monte Alban. It was not found in a tomb but in a refuse bed. The animal is seated and wears a large scarf knotted around its throat. The piece was painted all over and is unusual because one of the colors is green, which rarely is seen on New World pottery except as a pigment applied after firing.

The period known as Monte Alban I is dated from 650 to 200 B.C. It corresponds in time to the late Pre-Classic of central Mexico and produced comparable pottery figurines, usually representing women. It also is contemporary with the great Olmec development on the Gulf coast. Both pottery effigy urns and stone carvings reflect the Olmec style. It is noteworthy that the first settlers at Monte Alban brought with them a primitive form of writing and the use of bar and dot numerals, which imply the use of a calendar.

During the Monte Alban II era (200 B.C. – 200 A.D.) new influences reached the city. At this time, the great styles of Teotihuacan and the Maya area were about to flower suddenly in full development. Mexican archaeologists think that Monte Alban was stimulated by similar influences, particularly from the Maya developments in Chiapas and Guatemala. At any rate, new styles in temples, tombs and pottery appeared. The great urns of this period display a simplicity and monumental quality (p. 77) which contrasts with the riotous extravagance of the full Classic Zapotec style.

One of the outstanding finds at Monte Alban was the head seen on page 81. It is a mosaic of 25 pieces of jade and 6 of shell which represents a vampire bat. From the associated pottery it may be assigned to period II. The technique of manufacture is similar to Classic Maya heads found at Palenque (pp. 114, 115) which must date from several centuries later. The bat was an important art motif at Monte Alban, a fact which suggests contacts with the Maya. One of the Maya days was named "Bat" and this animal appears as a Maya glyph and also is represented pictorially. The bat is not found in the early styles of eastern and central Mexico.

ZAPOTEC MOSAIC MASK OF JADE AND SHELL REPRESENTING A VAMPIRE BAT. MONTE ALBAN, OAXACA. PERIOD II. HEIGHT OF HEAD, 6¼″.
MUSEO NACIONAL DE ANTROPOLOGÍA, MEXICO CITY.

TWO OF THE DANZANTES AT MONTE ALBAN, OAXACA, MEXICO. PERIOD I, 650-200 B.C.

The oldest carvings consist of big stone slabs on which almost life-size human figures have been outlined by incising or sculptured in low relief. There are dozens of them. Their rubbery bodies and contorted positions have earned them the name of *danzantes* (dancers). All are naked males, many with their sex emphasized. Some with closed eyes and open mouths obviously are dead. In many parts of the world, the first act to denigrate a captured enemy is to strip him of his clothes. The *danzantes* of Monte Alban may record victories of its first inhabitants over unknown foes. In style and in concept they are comparable to contemporary Peruvian carvings from Cerro Sechin. Rough treatment of prisoners often is pictured on Peruvian pottery of the Mochica period.

THE MIXTEC

The Mixtec civilization seems to have developed in northwestern Oaxaca and among the adjacent Nahua tribes in the State of Puebla. Hence the art styles usually are designated Mixteca-Puebla. The famous ruins at Mitla with their intricate mural mosaics are said to have been designed by Mixtec architects, but the Mixtec left no megalithic sculpture. They are best known for more delicate arts: beautifully illuminated manuscripts and polychrome pottery with similar adornment; carvings in shell, bone, and semi-precious stones; mosaic turquoise inlays; gold jewelry unsurpassed in the Americas both in design and technical excellence.

In the centuries before the Conquest, Mixtecs and Zapotecs both attempted to dominate the Valley of Oaxaca. Monte Alban had been abandoned by this time but there is no evidence that the Mixtec ever occupied it permanently. They did, however, bury their dead within the city limits, and in some cases they made use of the beautifully painted Zapotec tombs of an earlier period. Such a burial, known as Tomb 7, proved to be one of the most spectacular finds in New World archaeology. When Tomb 7 was opened, it revealed nine bodies, one of them a woman. With them were found over five hundred objects, counting the many necklaces with scores of gold beads and bells as a single item. Also there were gold crowns, bracelets, finger rings and pectorals. There were carvings in bone, jade, shell, onyx and rock crystal. In short, this fabulous cache contained jewelry and ceremonial utensils made of every kind of precious material known to the natives.

Metalworking was not an early art in Mexico and the techniques were introduced from the south about 900 A.D. Sheet gold disks found in Yucatan (where there is no gold) evidently had been imported, but embossed designs were applied locally. These reflect a blending of Toltec and Classical Maya motifs. Cast artifacts of Maya style are almost non-existent and imports were not numerous.

In central Mexico and the states facing the Pacific, metalworking develops in a different fashion with casting and false filigree as the dominant techniques. As revealed by archaeology, copper was the principal metal in the Valley of Mexico and the Tarascan region but gold predominated in the artifacts from Oaxaca and from Chiapas which are attributed to the Mixtec smiths.

A feature shared by the three pendants here discussed are the angular plaques at the bottom of each. These may reflect their southern ancestry for basal plaques are characteristic of gold pendants from Costa Rica, Panama and Colombia (pp. 140-141). Rectangular plaques are constantly associated with frog pendants from the Isthmus. Cast filigree is an ancient technique. It appears in the oldest known Panamanian jewelry, developed to an intricacy scarcely surpassed by Mixtec artisans of later centuries.

Mixtec polychrome pottery, no less than the metalwork, is generally regarded as the finest produced in Post-Classic times in Mexico. This is not only the judgment of modern students but also of aboriginal contemporaries. Montezuma II is said to have used Mixtec pottery as his tableware. Mixtec ceramic influence has been detected from Sinaloa in western Mexico to the Nicoya peninsula in Costa Rica (p. 135) and Mixtec stylistic features have been noted in Maya frescoes at Tulum in Yucatan and at Santa Rita in British Honduras.

When and where the Mixtec culture originated has not yet been determined by archaeologists. Probably there were various developmental centers with differing local styles which tended to amalgamate. At the time of the Conquest, however, Cholula, a city occupied since Pre-Classic times, was the great artistic center and here was produced the splendid Mixtec vessels, often called Cholula ware.

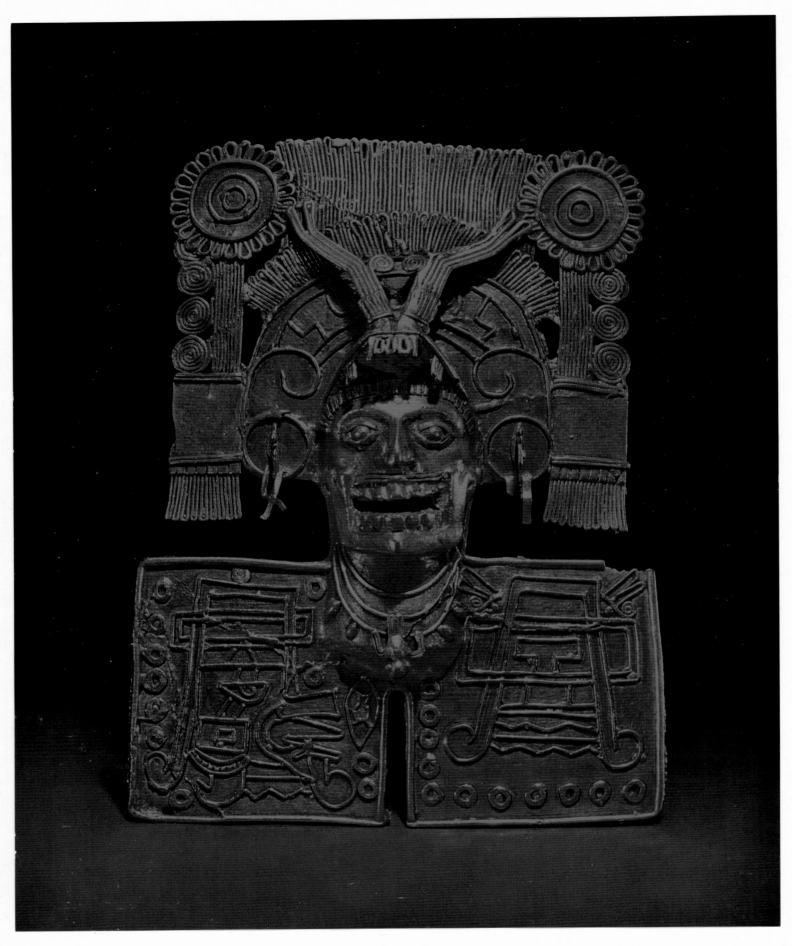

MIXTEC CAST GOLD PENDANT REPRESENTING MICTLANTECUTLI, THE GOD OF DEATH. FROM TOMB 7, MONTE ALBAN, OAXACA. HEIGHT, 4¾″.
MUSEO REGIONAL DE OAXACA, MEXICO.

We illustrate on pages 84-86 three Mixtec pendants from three different localities. On page 84 the god of Death and Darkness appears, known to the Aztec as Mictlantecutli. The big headdress with its many details as well as the head and square plaques below were built up in wax, encased in a mold and cast in a single flow of metal. The left-hand plaque records the day "2 flint knife" in the year "11 Wind." On the right is the so-called "Year Sign," shared by Teotihuacan, Classic Maya, Zapotec, Mixtec and other peoples.

On page 85 is a pendant recently found by Sr. Roberto Gallegos in a tomb at Zaachila, some nine miles from the city of Oaxaca. Like Tomb 7 at Monte Alban, this had been built by the Zapotec and reused by the Mixtec, who deposited not only gold but artifacts of jade and elaborate pottery. There were three bodies in the antechamber and twelve in the tomb itself, as well as the bones of the first occupants which had been placed in niches in the side walls.

The pendant we illustrate consists of a sun disk with a central opening in which is a seated figure whose globular body forms a bell. He wears an elaborate headdress, nose rod, ear disks and necklace. The entire piece was cast as a unit but a crack developed between the sun disk and one of the L-shaped plaques below it. This was repaired not by solder nor by welding but by drilling two pairs of holes and lacing them together with gold wire. "Crack lacing" is an old technique for repairing pottery and gourds, perhaps most highly developed on the west coast of South America.

The Mixtec pendant on page 86 represents the Aztec god Xipe, god of Spring and Vegetation, also patron of goldsmiths. He wears as a mask the flayed skin from the head of a sacrificed victim who possessed a well developed but disorderly beard. The headdress closely resembles the Monte Alban headdress on page 84, but the two pieces came from different localities and there are no data on their relative ages.

MIXTEC CAST GOLD PENDANT REPRESENTING THE AZTEC DEITY XIPE, HIS FACE COVERED WITH FLAYED SKIN. COIXTLAHUACA, OAXACA. HEIGHT, 4″. MUSEO NACIONAL DE ANTROPOLOGÍA, MEXICO CITY.

MIXTEC CAST GOLD PENDANT REPRESENTING A SUN DISK. THE SEATED FIGURE IN THE CENTER IS HOLLOW AND FORMS A BELL. ZAACHILA, OAXACA.
HEIGHT, 4⅝″. MUSEO NACIONAL DE ANTROPOLOGÍA, MEXICO CITY.

MIXTEC VESSEL FROM MIHUATLAN, OAXACA, MEXICO. HEIGHT, 12¼″. AMERICAN MUSEUM OF NATURAL HISTORY, NEW YORK.

This luxury ware was painted in cream, yellow, red, ochre, burned sienna, gray and black, the same colors found in the codices except that there was no blue or green which could be fired. The common shapes include globular jars set on slender tripod legs and topped by cylindrical necks, hemispheral bowls on pedestal bases, also flat plates. Painted decoration may be geometric or symbolic but often the figures of gods, men and animals are pictured in the styles found in the codices.

Some of the most important surviving Mexican manuscripts were produced by the Mixtec. These are pictorial records of military conquests, dynastic histories and ceremonial occasions extending as far back as the seventh century. Dr Alfonso Caso, brilliant Mexican scholar who has contributed so greatly to our knowledge of Oaxaca, places the earliest Mixtec date in the year "5 Flint," which corresponds to 692 A.D. in our system.

A unique Mixtec vessel is illustrated on page 88. It combines the common tripod jar with a modeled figure representing the Aztec Macuilxochitl (Five Flowers), the god of Pleasure, Feasting and Frivolity. A turquoise bead, its color symbolic of something precious, has been set in the left breast over the heart.

CHRONOLOGY OF PRE-CLASSIC CULTURES IN MEXICO AND GUATEMALA

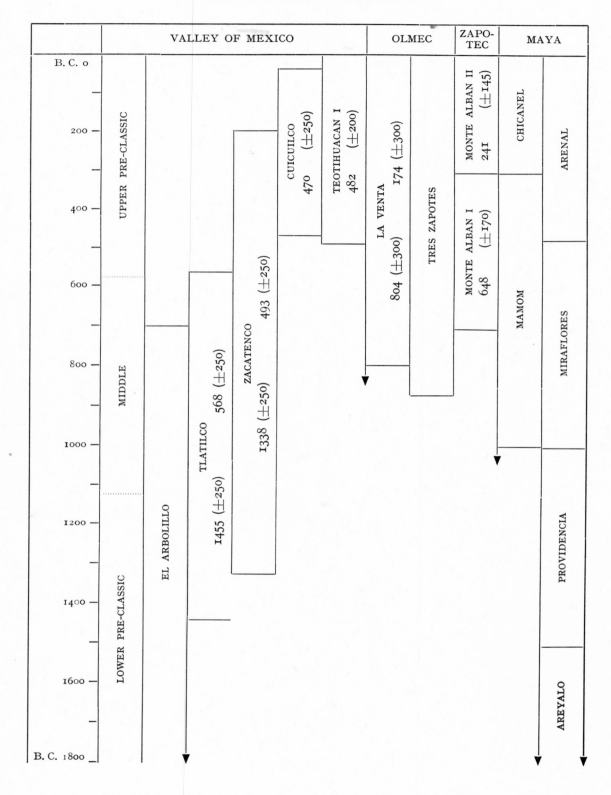

2

THE MAYA

CYLINDRICAL POTTERY TUBE ADORNED WITH THE HEAD OF THE SUN GOD HELD IN THE JAWS OF THE EARTH MONSTER, SURROUNDED BY SHELLS, FISH AND A BIRD. TEMPLE OF THE CROSS, PALENQUE, CHIAPAS, MEXICO. CLASSIC MAYA. HEIGHT, 37⅜″. MUSEO NACIONAL DE ANTROPOLOGÍA, MEXICO CITY.

THE MAYA

The Maya occupy a unique and glamorous place in American archaeology. In part this is due to publicity, for investigation of their ancient cities began in the eighteenth century and illustrated volumes had appeared before the middle of the nineteenth. More time, effort and money probably have been devoted to research in the Maya area than to the entire South American continent. The Maya have not shrunk in stature as a result, but it is no longer argued that theirs was the genius which inspired all the higher cultures of Mexico and Central America. Archaeology has shown that the Pre-Classic stage of Maya development lasted for centuries and that basic innovations must be credited to other groups.

This does not detract from Maya achievements. Still-standing buildings in their great civic centers testify to the enduring nature of their architecture. Their monumental stelae, their jewelry of jade, their murals—all are esteemed of high artistic merit. Others may have invented a calendar and writing but the Maya perfected them. In the fields of astronomy and mathematics they were outstanding. Many of their records have survived because they were carved in stone.

Maya territory falls into three geographical divisions. In the south, from Chiapas through Guatemala to El Salvador, there are high mountains fringed by a narrow coastal plain fronting on the Pacific. Owing to the altitude in the interior, the climate is temperate. This is a region of volcanoes, so the soil is unusually fertile. Rainfall is seasonal but adequate for native crops. Woods such as cedar, oak or pine are abundant. Stone for buildings and for tools was easily available. Yet this mountain area, apparently so well supplied with all the essentials of aboriginal life, although densely populated, contributed little to the growth of Maya culture. In the highlands, many typical features of Maya culture are scarce or absent. There are no great masonry buildings with sculptured façades. Only a few corbelled vaults are known apart from tombs. In Classic times, no great stelae with carved hieroglyphic texts were erected (p. 105).

GEOGRAPHICAL DIVISIONS

93

The central Maya region comprises the Department of El Peten in northern Guatemala and adjacent parts of British Honduras and Mexico, including the Usumacintla drainage. It contains a great tropical jungle with trees reaching a height of 150 feet. It may rain as much as ten feet a year. The shallow soil covers a limestone formation which provided good material for building and for sculpture. Agriculture involved the felling of giant trees with fire and stone axes. To be sure, crops grow with great rapidity, but so do weeds. Shallow soil soon becomes exhausted and the whole process must be repeated.

This is a forbidding land as those who have traveled in it well know. Today, were it not for the chewing gum industry, mahogany cutters where logs can be brought out and the camps of oil prospectors, the area would have few if any inhabitants. Yet this is the region where the Classic Maya culture had, if not its origin, its finest florescence. Here are found many of the largest and most magnificent cities of the Maya: Tikal with its tall temples still soaring over 200 feet into the air; Uaxactun, famous for the finest now known Pre-Classic edifice and its elaborate pottery; Holmul, also renowned for beautiful polychrome ceramics; Palenque, first Maya city to be investigated, noted for its bas-reliefs in stucco and stone, where the most sumptuous of all Maya tombs has recently been discovered (pp. 114-115). In this area there is a concentration of carved stelae with hieroglyphic texts and dates. Here astronomy and mathematics reached their highest development in the New World.

The third division of Maya territory consists of the Yucatan peninsula. This is a dryer area than El Peten and not so productive. It also is a limestone country but so porous that there are no rivers. Life is only possible because there is access to the underground flow of water, either in *cenotes*, places where the surface crust has broken down, or through artificial wells. This is the best known part of the Maya area. The missionary fathers have left written accounts of local Maya institutions. The three surviving Maya manuscripts originated in Yucatan. It also is the tourist section because of its accessibility and the still-standing architectural remains.

THE CALENDAR   To understand the Maya, one must know something of their concept of the universe and time. There was no end to what they could tackle mathematically. To an educated Maya it would have been possible to figure the day on which Easter would fall either a thousand or a million days or years from now. This fundamental interest in time was responsible for the so-called stelae, great shafts of stone with hieroglyphic inscriptions accompanying a carved figure or group. Decipherment of the dates was a romantic accomplishment because scholars in California and Germany achieved it independently. Today we have progressed far beyond that. We know that the Maya usually erected stelae at five, ten or twenty year intervals, that they also recorded celestial information about the stars and moon. Most recently we have learned that the names of cities and individual rulers are recorded. It is hoped that further decipherment will produce written history.

The Maya employed several types of calendar. The simplest, used for divination, was a sequence of twenty names for twenty days combined with numbers running from 1 to 13, each repeated continuously. The combination of name and number was a unit "meaningless without the other as a telephone number is without the name of the exchange." As 20 and 13 have no common factor, the same combination cannot recur until a cycle of 260 days has been completed. Each of these days had a presiding deity and its own potential for good or evil. These cycles were not grouped in larger units for counting time.

The Maya year contained 18 months of 20 days each, plus an added 5 very unlucky days. The least common multiple of 260 and 365 is 18,980. This is called a Calendar Round, a period of about 52 years. It was the longest time period known to the Aztec.

Numbers under 20 were written by the Maya with bars and dots, the bar indicating 5, the dot is one. Thus 8 is a combination of a bar and three dots; 16 is expressed by one dot and three bars. Another system indicates numbers by heads thought to represent gods or their attributes. The heads for 14 to 19 are the same as 4 to 9 combined with a fleshless lower jaw like our "fourteen," "fifteen," etc. In a few texts, numbers are expressed by heads with full bodies attached, a method which gave the sculptor full freedom to use his imagination (p. 95).

A CLASSIC MAYA DATE WITH NUMERICAL VALUES
EXPRESSED BY THE HEADS.
STELA D, COPAN, HONDURAS.

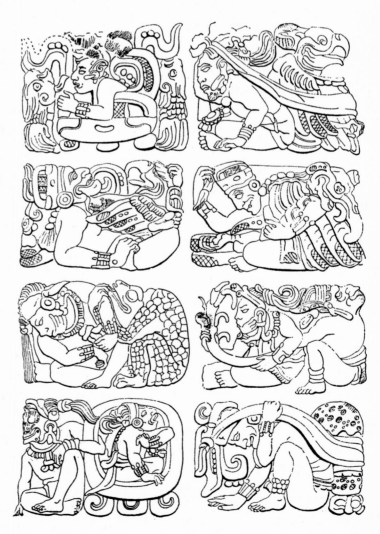

The top glyph at the left has no numeric al value. At the right, the human figure supports a burden representing the number 144,000, which must be multiplied by the value of the human face, which is 9. In the second row, 7,200 is multiplied by 15, and 360 by 5. The third row expresses 0 times 20 and 0 times one. All these numbers added together amount to 1,405,800. This is the number of days which must be counted forward from the beginning of the Maya calendar in the year 3113 B.C. The result is a day and month in the year 736 A.D.

All heads necessarily are in profile to allow the additions indicating the numbers, such as dots on the chin, a hand on the chin, a fleshless lower jaw or a stylized headdress. Otherwise the artist has had complete liberty to picture the body and limbs in poses of his own choosing.

Larger numbers than 20 were indicated by positional notation and the use of zero, just as we write 10, 100, etc., but in the Maya system the progression is by 20's except for the second unit where it is 18, resulting in 360 or an approximate year. Each unit has a written name, like "tens," "thousands," etc. All the higher counts are multiples of the *tun* or 360-day unit and, in recording a date, the size of the unit is indicated both by its position and by a glyph. The largest known period glyph records 64,000,000 *tuns*. We may summarize by stating that the Maya kept track of time by a vigesimal count of *tuns*.

Maya dates are a count of *tuns* plus additional days reckoned from a day and month which occurred in 3113 B.C., long before they developed their Classic culture. The starting point may represent some astronomical event of which we are ignorant. Within their own system, Maya dates are absolute, but, for many years, there was controversy about the correlation of their calendar and our own. This has at last been settled by radiocarbon evidence. The Great or Classic period of the Maya runs from approximately 300-900 A.D.

Archaeological research has repeatedly revealed evidence of Pre-Classic communities in the Maya area. The earliest settlements seem to have been in Yucatan, Chiapas and in western Guatemala. The aboriginal site now called Kaminaljuyú has produced a ceramic sequence beginning around 2000 B.C. Tombs dated towards the close of the Pre-Classic are so grandiose and richly furnished that they obviously were made for individuals who governed large and well organized communities. The daily digging here of new house foundations has recently brought to light dozens of pieces of broken sculpture. These do not have inscribed texts like the Classical Maya carvings, but in style and in picturing complex ritual they seem ancestral to the Classic sculptures. Their shattered condition suggests a catastrophe, an invasion which might have caused a shifting of developing Maya civilization to the lowlands of Guatemala.

EXTERIOR ARCHITECTURAL SCULPTURE In these lowlands, the present Department of the Peten, nothing has been found earlier than middle Pre-Classic, ca. 1000 B.C. The architecture of this era is unknown except for the extraordinary pyramid at Uaxactun, adorned with huge masks inspired by Olmec style and, very recently, a "masonry" of shells laid in mud mortar in neat rows.

Classic and Post-Classic Maya buildings, like the Gothic cathedrals of Europe, are covered with carvings. The local limestone of the Peten and Yucatan supplied the necessary material for sculpture and for construction and also was the source of lime mortar. They did not employ the true arch but the corbel vault, each half of which has inherent stability with the central opening closed by capstones. This device also is found in the highlands of Peru. Its weakness is that it cannot roof wide rooms without the walls

A CORNER OF THE GREAT PLAZA AT TIKAL, DEPARTMENT OF EL PETEN, GUATEMALA. TEMPLE I IN THE BACKGROUND, PARTIALLY RESTORED, HAS A TYPICAL MAYA ROOF COMB AND IS 160 FEET HIGH.

becoming excessively heavy. Roofs also were constructed of massive beams covered with small cross-beams and capped with lime mortar. All Maya buildings stood on substructures the height of which depended on their function. The multichambered edifices popularly known as palaces rest on low platforms, but one of the Tikal temples tops a terraced substructure over 115 feet high. Maya pyramids are steep and do not approach in bulk the huge Mexican constructions of Cholula or Teotihuacan.

Façades usually are divided in half by a medial molding which encircles the building and a similar molding forms a cornice at the summit. The decorated upper zone often is perpendicular but may slope backward, a characteristic feature of Palenque architecture. In eastern Yucatan, upper zones may be terraced.

To make their buildings more impressive, the Maya invented two non-functional methods of adding to their height and the area carrying sculpture. One, known as a roof comb, is a central wall built above the roof for the entire length of the building, which it often equals in height. There may be a single solid wall or there may be two walls slanting together like the letter A in order to support each other. These elongated steeples must have been a delight to the architects who designed them, for, by cut-out areas, harmonious proportions and sculptured relief decoration on both sides, they enhanced the entire edifice. The tallest existing roof comb is Temple IV at Tikal. Its top now fallen, it still stands about 220 feet high. A roof comb impresses from whatever angle it is viewed.

The so-called flying façade consists of building up an exterior wall so that, seen from in front, it suggests a non-existent second story. In the United States today, many one-story commercial buildings hide the ends of gabled roofs with this device. To the Maya artist, however, the flying façade presented an added area which could be decorated. There are standing examples in Yucatan where both roof comb and flying façade may be seen on a single building.

For the Maya, sculpture was the handmaiden of architecture. Favorite fields for decoration were the upper zones of façades and roof combs. Styles and techniques varied from city to city. At Copan much of this carving was in the full round but statues were made in sections with projecting tenons which held them against the walls. At Palenque and Comalcalco in the west, stucco replaced stone in late Classic times. A large bearded stucco head from Comalcalco appears on page 99. In Yucatan, late Classic buildings are profusely decorated. At Uxmal, the House of the Governors is 320 feet long, 40 feet wide and 26 feet high. It is surrounded by a mosaic frieze 11½ feet wide estimated to contain 20,000 stones, each carved to fit its place and carry its share of the design. At Hochob and elsewhere, entire façades were built to represent grotesque dragons with the central doorway indicating an open mouth. A roof comb of this city contains human figures carved in the round with one row standing on the shoulders of the others.

Copan is celebrated for its three decorated stairways. The Jaguar Stairway is flanked by a pair of huge rampant jaguars which once had inset spots, perhaps of obsidian. The stairway of the Reviewing Stand is adorned by two crouching human figures holding torches and the top step carries a carved text. The Hieroglyphic Stairway is unique. Thirty-three feet wide including the carved balustrades, it gave access about eighty-five feet above the ground to a now completely fallen temple. The entire width of the

STUCCO HEAD IN THE HALF ROUND, CUT FROM A WALL AT COMALCALCO, TABASCO, MEXICO. CLASSIC MAYA. HEIGHT, 17¼″.
MUSEO NACIONAL DE ANTROPOLOGÍA, MEXICO CITY.

LINTEL 24 FROM A PALACE AT YAXCHILAN, CHIAPAS, MEXICO. A KNEELING PENITENT MAKES A BLOOD OFFERING BY DRAWING A ROPE WITH
ATTACHED CACTUS SPINES THROUGH A HOLE IN HIS TONGUE. CLASSIC MAYA, CA. 750 A.D. BRITISH MUSEUM, LONDON.

risers was carved with a hieroglyphic text which had a total length of over half a mile. Each of the approximately 2000 individual glyphs is an artistic masterpiece in itself. Further adornment consisted of five over life-size statues representing lavishly garbed dignitaries who appear to be seated on the steps. At the base of the stairway are two big zoomorphic altars and a stela.

Interior sculpture is less common but is of several types and, owing to protection from the weather, it includes many outstanding examples. In the central part of the Peten and in the Usumacintla basin, the Maya often carved the under side of the lintels spanning doors. Those in the major temples at Tikal were cut in wooden beams. On page 100 we illustrate a lintel in high relief which comes from a palace at Yaxchilan, dated at about 750 A.D. The scene represents a kneeling penitent who makes a blood offering by drawing a rope with attached cactus spines through a hole in his tongue. Below is a basket filled with paper to catch the blood. The kneeling figure must be a personage of importance for he wears a richly adorned ceremonial robe, a big headdress and massive jewelry, presumably of jade. Baskets of the type shown are still in use with the incurved wall resting against the hip.

INTERIOR SCULPTURE

LINTEL FROM PIEDRAS NEGRAS, GUATEMALA. A CHIEF KNEELING ON AN ALTAR OR THRONE IS SURROUNDED BY ATTENDANTS. CLASSIC MAYA, CA. 757 A.D. WIDTH, 49". MUSEO DE ARQUEOLOGÍA Y ETNOLOGÍA DE GUATEMALA, GUATEMALA CITY.

The lintel on page 101 is one of three extracted from the rubble of a collapsed Piedras Negras building. Both in harmonious composition and execution it is generally considered one of the finest of Maya carvings. The center of the scene is filled by a throne or altar with a dignitary kneeling on a spotted jaguar skin. At the right there is a group of four individuals, two of whom are children. To the left are three standing figures, their arms crossed as a gesture of submission or reverence. Below the throne there are seven seated individuals who hold various objects in their hands. These various groups are framed by panels adorned with 158 hieroglyphs.

Another form of interior adornment consists of carved slabs built into the walls. These are characteristic of Palenque as is the delicate low relief style. Although not abandoning formal religious symbolism nor the intense Maya interest in details of dress and adornment, these sculptures are a markedly local development.

One of the great archaeological discoveries of the century was the presence of a vaulted tomb at the base of one of the Palenque pyramids, reached by stairs from the temple floor 75 feet above. This is of prime interest not only for the rich funeral furnishings (pp. 114-115) but also for the magnificent relief sculpture both in lime plaster and stone.

STELAE
AND ALTARS

Maya artists and sculptors obviously devoted vast amounts of time to the adornment of their civil and religious edifices, but they also created two types of free-standing megalithic carvings which were displayed adjacent to their buildings in harmony with their civic planning. What are called stelae consist of tall rectangular shafts of stone set upright in the ground. Not all but many are carved, back, front and sides, with richly adorned personages and hieroglyphic texts. Often but not always, altars stand in front of stelae. In shape they range from simple utilitarian drums or squares to fantastically complex beasts.

We know from the recorded dates that stelae often were set up at intervals of five, ten or twenty years. We have no idea why. We know that they record astronomical calculations, doubtless of even less interest to most of the Classic Maya world than to the general public today. Recently, the names of towns and rulers have been identified in their writing. Some history may emerge but not much. Stelae were erected for about six centuries but their importance had faded so long before the Conquest that there is no full explanation of their function.

The stela-altar cult apparently began in the Tikal region in the center of El Peten, where University of Pennsylvania archaeologists keep recording ever earlier dates. The stela style is repeated on the Leyden Plaque (p. 112), a jade slab with a figure on one side and on the other what until very recently was the oldest known Maya date (320 A.D.). Both contemporary pottery and newly found sculpture indicate that, at the moment when the Classic Maya was emerging, strong waves of Teotihuacan styles permeated Tikal. The Leyden Plaque shows that the Maya entered their Classical period wearing fantastic regalia and with the custom of mistreating their captured enemies.

In carving the human figure, the Maya did not attempt to make large statues in the round. Everything is shown in relief but there developed marked local and chronological styles. In general, the eastern cities such as Copan and Quirigua tend towards frontal presentations cut in high relief with ever increasing elaboration in detail of ornament (p. 105). If a second figure is represented, it is on the opposite side of the shaft. The general effect is formal and stately. Realism is limited to face and hands and to details of the extraordinarily complex ceremonial accoutrements. We have no knowledge of how these were constructed for they were made of perishable materials.

In the central and western Classic cities, side presentation was more common than frontal in the early Classic. Later, however, body and legs may be pictured frontally with arms and head in profile, thus breaking the lateral symmetry. Three quarter views appear, also dancing poses which suggest motion. An interesting development is the picturing of group scenes composed to fit the narrow decorative field afforded by a stela. The example on page 103 presents twelve individuals so placed that there is a suggestion of distance if not of perspective.

This scene, carved in relatively low relief, contains twelve figures composed to fill the narrow decorative field afforded by the side of a stela. It represents the questioning of prisoners by a chief with two attendants. Distance is suggested by relative height. All heads are in profile but some of the bodies are viewed diagonally. The awkward position of some of the bodies is due to the Maya custom of lashing one or both arms of prisoners across the back in obviously painful positions.

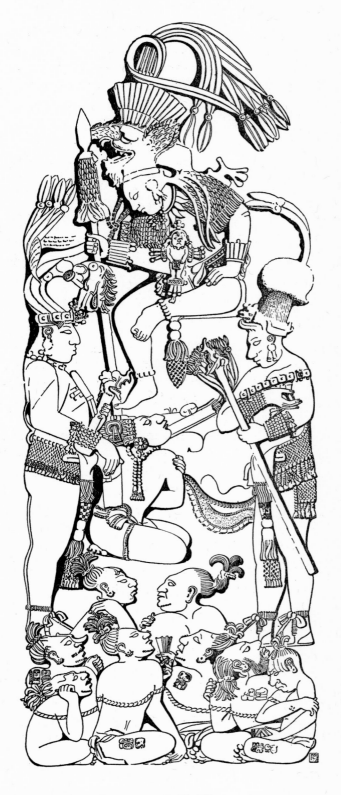

STELA 12 AT PIEDRAS NEGRAS, GUATEMALA, DATED 795 A.D. HEIGHT, ABOUT 10 FEET. MUSEO DE ARQUEOLOGÍA Y ETNOLOGÍA DE GUATEMALA, GUATEMALA CITY.

The complexity and damaged condition today of Maya stelae make their study difficult. In ancient times, they were painted, probably in contrasting colors which facilitated understanding. Examples have been found in over a hundred cities and over a hundred have been discovered in a single city. The largest recorded stela is at Quirigua, dated 771 A.D. It is 35 feet long and weighs approximately 65 tons, but the average stela is eight to ten feet high.

Altars which accompany stelae may be square or circular, carved on the sides or tops. At Copan, there are a number of eccentric-shape altars which represent various forms of mythological dragons. At Quirigua for a short period, greatly enlarged versions of such beasts, usually referred to as zoomorphs, were set up at calendric intervals in place of stelae. The largest, sometimes called the Great Turtle, is a crouching monster with a magnificently carved seated human figure in the open jaws (below). The stone measures 9 feet, 8 inches by 11 feet, 6 inches and is 7 feet, 3 inches high. The date is 695 A.D. (9.18.5.0.0.).

This piece has been called the finest example of existing ancient American sculpture. It certainly represents the peak of complexity in Maya symbolism. The body of the dragon is smothered in elaborate scrolls which are presented on two interlocking planes. Interspaced are panels with hieroglyphs, many of the full figure type. The seated figure is the first head at Quirigua to be represented *without* a beard after a period of forty years.

SEATED HUMAN FIGURE IN THE OPEN JAWS OF THE SCULPTURED MONSTER KNOWN AS THE GREAT TURTLE
OR ZOOMORPH P AT QUIRIGUA, GUATEMALA. THE DYNAMIC PHASE OF LATE CLASSIC MAYA.

STELA D AND ALTAR IN THE GREAT PLAZA AT COPAN, HONDURAS. DATED AT 736 A.D. (9.15.5.0.0 IN THE MAYA CALENDAR), THIS CARVING REPRESENTS THE FULL FLOWERING OF THE LATE CLASSIC MAYA STYLE. HEIGHT, 12′, 2½″. PART OF THE CARVED TEXT ON THE OPPOSITE SIDE IS SHOWN ON PAGE 95.

FUCHSITE STATUETTE FOUND IN AN EARLY CLASSIC MAYA DEPOSIT AT UAXACTUN, DEPARTMENT OF EL PETEN, GUATEMALA. THE STYLE HAS OLMEC TRAITS AND IS INTRUSIVE IN THE MAYA AREA. HEIGHT, 10″. MUSEO DE ARQUEOLOGÍA Y ETNOLOGÍA DE GUATEMALA, GUATEMALA CITY.

MINOR SCULPTURES The non-monumental Classic Maya sculpture consists of stone and pottery statuettes, and articles of personal adornment, often of jade. The little fuchsite statuette on page 106 was found in an early Classic deposit, dated at 350 A.D., but it clearly is an heirloom. It exhibits Olmec traits such as the bare head, naked body, incised eyebrows, hands and cheek ornaments. The face, however, definitely is not in Olmec style. This little piece was once gaily adorned for it was drilled with fifteen pairs of small conical holes which meet at an angle. They permit the attachment of colored decorations from the top of the head to the soles of the feet. When found, the eyes and mouth were colored with red oxide of iron.

Pottery figurines first appeared in the Pre-Classic, dropped out of fashion, then re-appeared in the late Classic in certain restricted areas. Large numbers are known from highland Guatemala and the Lubaantun region, also the lower Usumacintla drainage, coastal Campeche and the adjacent Jaina island. The pair illustrated on pages 108 and 109 are characteristic of the Campeche-Jaina types. Their charm today is due not only to their originality but to the fact that the often-incomprehensible symbolism of Maya religion is absent.

Jaina figures are small, rarely more than eight inches high. Some are hand-modeled, some are molded in whole or in part. Both men and women are represented, sometimes in pairs, sometimes with an animal. Hollow examples may have interior pellets which rattle or, by the addition of a mouth piece, may serve as whistles or ocarinas.

Except for mural paintings, Jaina figurines give us our best picture of Maya life in late Classic times, from 700-900 A.D., but they portray the aristocrats. They record ideals of physical beauty and also the innate Maya love of finery and display. Many types of dress are seen, also jewelry including bracelets, necklaces and ear ornaments, presumably of jade. Hair styles, tooth-filing and tattooing are represented in minute detail. The towering headdresses are modeled, unfortunately without color which might afford a clue to their construction.

Classic mural paintings were few and rarely have survived. The most famous, at **MURALS** Bonampak in the State of Chiapas, can be reached only with difficulty and can hardly be seen owing to the darkness of the rooms and lime drip which covers the walls. Fortunately, two experienced artists have made copies which have been published and the Mexican government has built a full scale reconstruction of the three painted chambers.

Owing to the absence of defensive walls or fortresses in Classical Maya cities, it has been held that the Maya pursued a peaceful existence. From the beginning of the Classical era, however, the treading of victors on captives is represented (p. 112) and such scenes carved in stone increase in number and complexity with the passage of time (p. 103). Bonampak, never a major community, recorded a triumphal campaign in great detail. Preparation for war is shown, including the councils and ceremonies. There is a tremendous battle, probably with the exploits of individuals depicted. Prisoners are haled before the winners and in some cases tortured. Finally there is a great victory celebration for which everybody puts on their best finery. A dance is held around a terraced pyramid, and the captain of the losers is sacrificed. All this sequence was recorded with such detail that we imagine it was an unusual occasion.

POTTERY FIGURINE, WITH HEAD AND SHOULDERS CAST FROM A MOLD, THE REST MODELED. THE COSTUME IS A SHIRT WITH SLEEVES EXTENDING TO THE ELBOWS AND A LONG SKIRT. THE COMPLEX HEADDRESS APPARENTLY INCLUDES SHELLS AND FLOWERS. A BOWL PROBABLY HOLDS COPAL INCENSE. JAINA STYLE, LATE CLASSIC MAYA. FROM CAMPECHE, MEXICO. HEIGHT, 10⅝". BARBACHANO PONCE COLLECTION, MEXICO CITY.

POTTERY FIGURINE. A STANDING MALE FIGURE DRESSED IN A LONG CEREMONIAL ROBE. THE RIGHT FIST APPARENTLY IS COVERED BY A KNUCKLE DUSTER. THE LEFT HAND HOLDS A TWISTED FABRIC TERMINATING IN A TASSEL. JAINA STYLE, LATE CLASSIC MAYA. FROM JAINA ISLAND. HEIGHT, 9″. MUSEO NACIONAL DE ANTROPOLOGÍA, MEXICO CITY.

Part of a battle episode from a mural at Bonampak (above). A commander in chief, marked by his jaguar-skin poncho and sandals, has taken a prisoner whom he grasps by the hair. The entire scene embraces scores of warriors in combat and covers three sides of a room, including the vertical walls and most of the vault above.

The judgment of prisoners (opposite page), forming part of a mural at Bonampak. The head chieftain still wears his jaguar-skin insignia but has changed his headdress and has put on various ornaments of jade. Facing the chief is another high official and between is a naked prisoner pleading for his life. Below is the superbly drawn body of a warrior relaxed in death with a decapitated head at his feet. On either side are other captives, two with bleeding finger nails which indicate they have been tortured. This scene appears over a doorway and is flanked by some thirty other figures including two high officers and their wives, other richly clad officials of lesser rank, more prisoners and armed guards. The standing figures are approximately 45 inches high.

It will be many years before the complexities of Bonampak murals are fully analyzed. We may note the animation, the rhythm seen in the assemblage of large groups, the skill with which contorted positions are handled by foreshortening (p. 110). There is no attempt to indicate contours by shading, however. Distance is not created by perspective but by partly obscuring the more distant figures with the nearer and by placing the more remote higher on the painted walls (p. 111). Individuality has been suggested by the many differing details of costume. The arrogance of victorious warriors can be judged by their poses. The fear and sufferings of the captives are very evident.

The Bonampak murals, painted at the end of the eighth century, have no rivals in the Americas, North or South. Their animation and fluidity were not surpassed in contemporary Europe. With artists of such mature talent available, why did not other Maya communities employ them? From very late buildings in Yucatan we know that sometimes outer walls were frescoed. It seems possible that the flat zones on Classic Maya edifices once were brilliantly painted but torrential tropical rains have removed all evidence.

JEWELRY AND ORNAMENTS The smaller carvings of the Classic Maya are mostly objects of jade used for personal adornment. No sources of jade were known in the entire Maya area until the recent discovery of jade in a mountain in highland Guatemala, which, from its quality, may have been worked in Post-Classic times. The lowlands of Guatemala and Yucatan consist of limestone. Hence all jade was imported. The Leyden Plaque (below), the oldest Maya dated jade object, is a flawless oval disk, which on stylistic grounds is thought to have been manufactured near Tikal in the center of El Peten. The ability to shape and engrave such a refractory material suggests a long acquaintance with it.

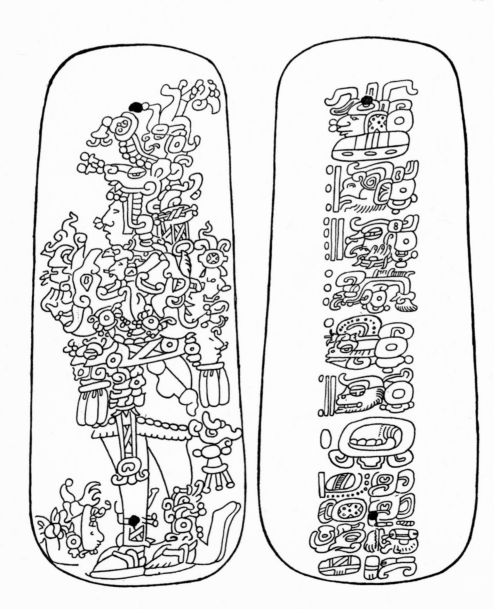

THE LEYDEN PLAQUE. A THIN JADE PLATE, ON ONE SIDE INCISED WITH AN EARLY DATE (8.14.3.1.12 = 320 A.D.); THE OTHER SIDE SHOWS AN ELABORATELY CLAD MAYA PERSONAGE TREADING ON A CAPTIVE. FOUND NEAR PUERTO BARRIOS, GUATEMALA, TOGETHER WITH COPPER BELLS, INDICATING THAT IT HAD BEEN AN HEIRLOOM FOR MANY CENTURIES. HEIGHT, 8½″. RIJKSMUSEUM, LEYDEN, HOLLAND.

The elaborate necklaces, ear ornaments, pectorals, bracelets, etc., pictured on Classic Maya statues and figurines evidently represent jade. Dredging the Sacred Cenote at Chichen Itza, over half a century ago, produced varieties of jade objects, all fragmentary because they had been "killed" ceremonially. With the great discovery of the Ruz tomb at Palenque, archaeologists at last could study jade funeral furnishings and personal adornments as actually placed on the body.

We here discuss two of the outstanding Palenque finds, a pair of jade heads, each constructed by fitting together individually carved pieces. Like the Zapotec jade head on page 81, it is probable that no single block of jade of sufficient size to complete the carving could be found. In all three examples, however, except for eyes or teeth of shell, it was the purpose of the artist to match the color of individual stones. In Middle America regardless of culture, be it remembered, jade was considered the most precious of all substances and its color was a symbol of beauty.

My impression is that both Palenque heads are attempted portraits. They are not masks because there are no eye holes. They are not drilled for attachment to some background like the Teotihuacan "masks." In technique they are unlike the mosaics of Aztec or Mixtec workmanship, constructed of multicolored small fragments to show symbolic patterns (p. 64).

The smaller Palenque head (p. 114), when we were kindly allowed to photograph it, at once produced an impression of individuality. The shape and curious treatment of the eyes, the bulging forehead, the thick nose with a wide bridge—all seemed foreign to the stylized Palenque concept of beauty. When turned in the hands, it becomes apparent that this is the head of an old man with lined face and shrunken jaws. Age is pictured in this fashion elsewhere in Palenque art. The physical type obviously is distinct from that seen on the other head.

The second Palenque head (p. 115) is life-size, a death mask worn by the great chief for whom the tomb was built. To find jades of matching quality probably was not easy and over two hundred pieces were required for its construction, presumably over a plaster base. In style it contrasts with the other head. Pupils and eyes of shell are shown, also the typical Classic hair cut, trimmed in terraces beside the cheeks. The bridge of the nose is represented in typical Palenque fashion by a narrow ridge carried up past the brow ridges on the forehead, a convention extending to other Maya settlements. A peculiar characteristic of this face is the tapering outline and pointed chin. A glance at our illustrations will indicate that most Maya faces are more nearly rectangular with the width across the eyes and across the mouth being approximately equal. We do not think the restoration can be questioned because the burial contained very similar stucco heads of great beauty. All these heads can best be explained as portraits of the same individual.

JADE MOSAIC MASK REPRESENTING AN OLD MAN. FROM THE RUZ TOMB UNDER THE TEMPLE OF THE INSCRIPTIONS AT PALENQUE, CHIAPAS, MEXICO. CLASSIC MAYA, CA. 700 A.D. HEIGHT, 4¾″. MUSEO NACIONAL DE ANTROPOLOGÍA, MEXICO CITY.

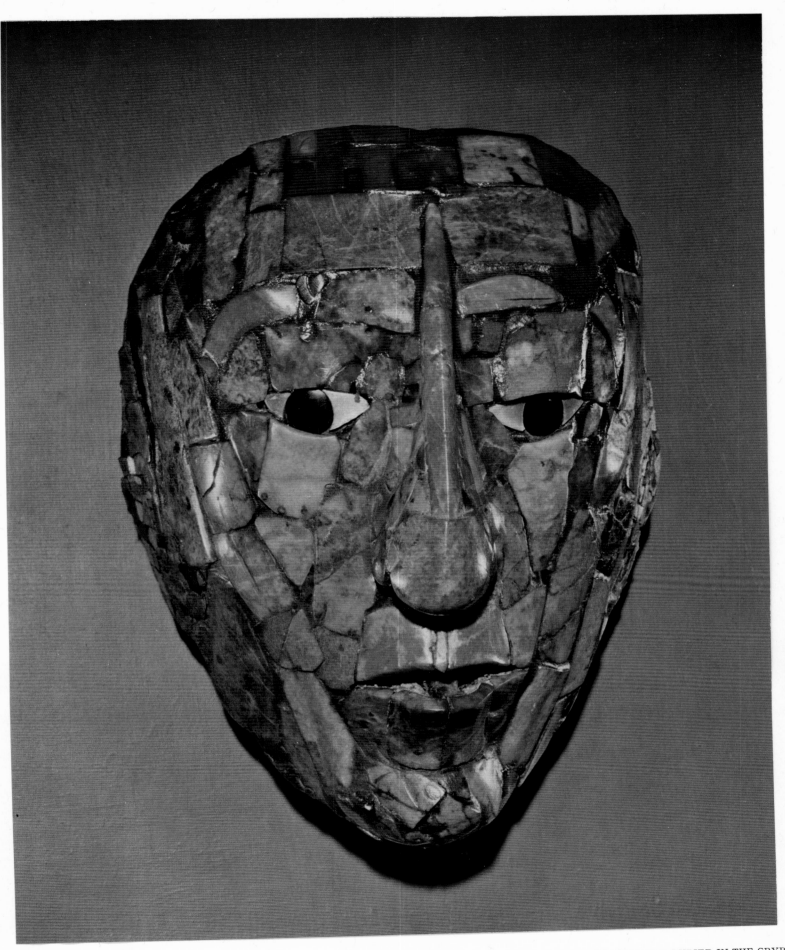

JADE DEATH MASK WITH SHELL EYES AND OBSIDIAN PUPILS. THIS HAD BEEN PLACED OVER THE FACE OF THE PERSONAGE BURIED IN THE CRYPT
UNDER THE TEMPLE OF THE INSCRIPTIONS AT PALENQUE, CHIAPAS, MEXICO. MUSEO NACIONAL DE ANTROPOLOGÍA, MEXICO CITY.

PLAQUE FROM NEBAJ, DEPARTMENT OF THE QUICHÉ, GUATEMALA. LATE CLASSIC MAYA. WIDTH, 5¾".
MUSEO DE ARQUEOLOGÍA Y ETNOLOGÍA DE GUATEMALA, GUATEMALA CITY.

This plaque is one of a small group, all marked by fine composition and the technical excellence of the carving. We note that the plaques are irregular in shape, which suggests that in late Classic times the Maya had difficulty in securing large pieces of jade and preferred to sacrifice symmetry rather than lose any part of such precious material. It is believed probable that the entire group of pectorals, although found in scattered localities, was made in a restricted area. On stylistic grounds, this is placed near Piedras Negras in the Usumacintla valley.

A completely different type of Classic Maya carving in jade is shown on page 116. This is a pectoral drilled horizontally for suspension at the height of the shoulders of the principal figure. It is a plaque of irregular outline, plain on the back but superbly carved on the front. The jade is of fine quality but partly stained by corrosion from pyrite mirrors.

The principal personage is seated cross-legged on a throne with the torso shown from the front and the head in profile. His body is inclined to his right and he appears to be addressing a small dwarf-like attendant. The front of the throne is adorned by three faces, repeated on the yoke worn by its occupant, and the back of the throne is carved to suggest the body of a serpent. This central scene is emphasized by deep vertical cutting around the principal figure and by scrolls and a pair of heads which flank it on either side.

The Maya were ceramic experts who worked in many styles. We have already mentioned their clay figurines (p. 108) which rank with the major stone carvings in quality. We here discuss only ceremonial vessels and polychrome types which are outstanding.   **POTTERY**

Incense has always had an important role in Maya ritual. Even today, certain Maya groups make special vessels for religious purposes, which, like more ancient types, may be effigy forms. A curious group of incense burners apparently was devised in early Classic times in highland Guatemala and was either traded to or copied in cities of El Peten. They are seated or squatting effigies made in two parts with the torso and head forming a cover. The example on page 119 represents a hunchback whose hands and grotesque but smiling face suggest that he is applauding. Slits in the eyes, mouth and back of the head permit the smoke of incense to pour forth.

Another two-part effigy recently found at Tikal (p. 118) definitely is of Early Classic date. It pictures a human figure seated on a tripod of human bones. Arms, legs and belt are elaborately adorned but the face is grotesque with huge nose and lips. A small human head is held in the hands.

A more common type of incense burner, which was in use from Pre-Classic to Post-Classic eras, consists of a cylindrical vessel with modeled effigy forms built up on the outer walls. In concept these recall the Zapotec urns (p. 78) but the Maya styles, of which there are many, are very much their own.

The complex example on page 121 is of uncertain date. The body is that of a plump bird with the feathers shown individually like overlapping rows of shingles but the face is distinctly human except that the nose has been replaced by the hooked beak of a bird. In the center of the crown there is a small bird facing downward. At the base there is a projecting fence on which two birds are perched. On either side of this vessel three

A POLYCHROME TWO-PART EFFIGY VESSEL, PERHAPS AN INCENSE BURNER. IT REPRESENTS A GROTESQUE HUMAN FIGURE HOLDING A HEAD,
SEATED ON A TRIPOD FORMED BY HUMAN FEMORA. FROM A TOMB UNDER AN EARLY CLASSIC MAYA BUILDING AT TIKAL. HEIGHT, 14¾″.
UNIVERSITY OF PENNSYLVANIA MUSEUM, TIKAL, GUATEMALA.

A TWO-PART EFFIGY REPRESENTING A HUNCHBACK FIGURE, PROBABLY AN INCENSE BURNER.
FROM KAMINALJUYÚ, GUATEMALA. HEIGHT, 8¾″.
MUSEO DE ARQUEOLOGÍA Y ETNOLOGÍA DE GUATEMALA, GUATEMALA CITY.

superimposed flat rings form flanges. A curious parallel to this incense burner, shown on page 92, consists of three-foot high tubes with flanking flanges, profusely decorated in relief. They are not incense burners as the tubes are open at both ends and their function is unknown. Five of these, stylistically much alike, were found in one of the temple substructures at Palenque. The principal head is that of the Maya Sun god with superimposed symbolic elements including a bird with a long bill.

Polychrome pottery first appears in the central Maya area in late Pre-Classic times, about the beginning of the Christian era. No local antecedents have been detected. As well as a new technique of decoration, new motifs and new vessel forms turn up. It has been suggested that innovations were due to a shift in population which may have introduced new ceramic types and even might have triggered the flowering of the Classical Maya civilization. This is an intriguing hypothesis with definite factual support but still lacking proof. What is fully accepted, however, is the influence of Teotihuacan ceramics during the early Classic period. This is recognized at the great lowland centers such as Tikal and is even more evident in the Guatemalan highlands, particularly at Kaminaljuyú.

In the late Classic period, human and animal figures are pictured on painted pottery with increasing frequency. In El Salvador and Honduras, the eastern portion of Maya territory, the style is stiff and ritualistic. If glyphs appear on pottery, they are decorative rather than functional. In the central lowlands, however, life forms were depicted with increasing realism, which, if it did not attain the vigor of Bonampak murals, compares favorably with the surviving Maya manuscripts. Glyphs definitely are functional. Texts obviously refer to what is pictured, and, in some cases, record the dates.

A masterpiece of this type was found in the grave of a young woman during 1962 by the Harvard expedition working at Altar de Sacrificios. Six human figures, two of them erect and the others seated in pairs, evidently are involved in some ceremony. The text encircling the rim is unique. The opening glyph is painted red like an illuminated initial in a European manuscript and the date of the ceremony is placed in 754 A.D. Three additional groups of glyphs are placed vertically between the figures.

The principal celebrant probably is the dancing figure on page 122 who is placed under the beginning of the text. He wears trousers of spotted jaguar skin, gauntlets of jaguar paws and a jaguar headdress with plumes. The head, one arm and one leg are in profile. The body, the other arm and leg are pictured diagonally in perspective.

Facing the dancer are two seated individuals placed one above the other. The upper figure wears a headdress of jaguar skin. Both hands and feet are covered by jaguar legs with claws. There is a scroll representing speech or song in front of the face. The lower figure wears no jaguar or serpent symbols. It has been suggested that he is about to be sacrificed.

POTTERY INCENSE BURNER REPRESENTING A MYTHOLOGICAL BIRD WITH A HUMAN HEAD. FOUND IN A CAVE NEAR PURULHÁ, DEPARTMENT OF BAJA VERA PAZ, GUATEMALA. POST-CLASSIC MAYA (?). HEIGHT, 18½″. MUSEO DE ARQUEOLOGÍA Y ETNOLOGÍA DE GUATEMALA, GUATEMALA CITY.

PAINTED PANEL FROM A POLYCHROME JAR PICTURING A DANCING MAN WEARING JAGUAR PARAPHERNALIA. FACING ARE TWO SEATED FIGURES. MAYA GLYPHS DATE AND ELUCIDATE THE CEREMONY. CLASSIC MAYA. FROM ALTAR DE SACRIFICIOS, GUATEMALA. HEIGHT, 6⅝".
MUSEO DE ARQUEOLOGÍA Y ETNOLOGÍA DE GUATEMALA, GUATEMALA CITY.

The second standing figure (p. 123) is bald and fat. His trousers are of snake skin. His closed eyes and open mouth cannot represent death but may indicate singing or ecstasy. His bent arm holds a snake by the tail, which, with no other support, forms an arch over his head and down the front of the body. This evidently is some species of boa.

Two seated figures again face the dancer. The legs of the upper individual suggest that he is seated on a bench or throne. Beneath is a cross-legged seated figure with jaguar gauntlets and a curious long-nosed mask which may represent a shrimp. A peculiar feature of the composition is that obviously the figures were painted before the glyphs. Two of the heads and an upraised arm occupy space intended for glyphs which had to be placed around them.

POLYCHROME JAR SHOWING A MAN WITH A SNAKE DANCING IN FRONT OF TWO SEATED FIGURES (NOT SHOWN). RECENTLY FOUND IN A TOMB AT ALTAR DE SACRIFICIOS BY A HARVARD UNIVERSITY EXPEDITION. HEIGHT, 6⅝″. MUSEO DE ARQUEOLOGÍA Y ETNOLOGÍA DE GUATEMALA, GUATEMALA CITY.

MANUSCRIPTS Three Maya manuscripts reached Europe at the time of the Conquest. They are now in Dresden, Madrid and Paris. They are long strips of bark paper, painted on both sides and folded like a screen. It is known that the Maya wrote history. The surviving codices record astronomical data, methods of divination and ritual. A fourth codex was excavated by archaeologists. Only the outside is visible but someday a means may be found for separating the other pages without destroying the text.

In conclusion we quote Bishop de Landa: "These people (of Yucatan) also made use of certain characters or letters, with which they wrote in their books their ancient affairs and their sciences, and with these and drawings and with certain signs in their drawings, they understood their affairs and made others understand them and taught them. We found a great number of books in these characters, and, as they contained nothing in which there was not to be seen superstition and lies of the devil, we burned them all, which they regretted to an amazing degree and caused them affliction."

THE TOLTEC OF YUCATAN

Both archaeological evidence and legendary history indicate that intrusions from Mexico at times strongly influenced Maya art. The oldest of these is most evident in pottery from Early Classic Maya settlements where vessels are found which must have come from Teotihuacan in the Valley of Mexico. These include typical shapes such as cylindrical tripod jars and also decorative techniques such as plaster coating and fresco painting (p. 47). Mythological motifs and deities are pictured as in the murals of Teotihuacan. There are even such Mexican features represented as spear throwers with fur-encased shafts and darts guided by a single large feather lashed beside the shaft. Also there is pottery of Teotihuacan forms painted in Mayan style, pottery of Maya type adorned in mixed styles, etc. This Mexican intrusion, as now known, is most marked at Kaminaljuyú in the Guatemalan highlands, to a lesser extent at Zacualpa and elsewhere. In the lowlands of the Department of El Peten, Mexican traits have been noted at Tikal, Holmul and Uaxactun, the three sites which have been extensively excavated.

A second Mexican penetration of the Maya area took place shortly after the breakdown of Classical Maya culture. We have already mentioned the migration of a Toltec group from Tula towards Yucatan under a chief who called himself Quetzalcoatl (p. 49). At approximately the same period we learn from Maya sources that foreigners named Itza took over a city thereafter called Chichen Itza under the leadership of Kukulcan, a Maya name which like Quetzalcoatl means Feathered Snake. Although historical evidence is vague and does not concern us here, standing edifices today testify to the fact that the newcomers proceeded to erect a city largely in the image of Tula but retaining certain Maya features.

It is many hundreds of miles from Tula, which is north of Mexico City, to Chichen Itza in Yucatan; road and rail connections have only recently been completed. Aboriginal travelers had to face mountains, jungles, swamps and probably hostile tribes. Part of the journey might have been by sea or lagoon in dugout canoes. Nevertheless, the Tula-Toltec style emerges at Chichen Itza so unadulterated that we must suppose that Tula-trained architects, engineers and artists supervised the new constructions and trained their successors. Furthermore, the religious symbolism of Tula arrived intact.

The new temples were placed on terraced pyramids with stairs on four sides, flanked by balustrades terminating in serpent heads. Façades were divided by a medial molding in Maya style but the roof combs and flying façades were replaced by merlons fringing the roof. The Maya corbelled vault was retained but the great Atlantean columns supporting the flat roofs of Tula (p. 50) were not needed; the serpent columns in doorways with heads on the ground and tails supporting the lintels continued in fashion and were copied in other centers such as Tulum on the east coast.

Classical Maya buildings characteristically have thick walls in relation to floor space and doors which admitted little light, especially to interior rooms. Eventually more doors were added to the front façade until door and wall space became approximately equal. This trend reached its fullest development in the lower Usumacintla region at such cities as Piedras Negras and Palenque. In Yucatan the number of doorways multiplied and door width was increased, notably at Sayil, by introducing round columns. In both regions, however, the interior walls continued to be massive and doors small.

At Tula there are edifices which may be described as colonnades with flat roofs supported by beams set on rows of columns. This type of building became popular along the east coast of Yucatan, usually with back and end walls of masonry, sometimes entirely without walls. At Chichen Itza the Toltec architects were more daring. The columns are not monoliths but consist of superimposed blocks of stone which lack the peg and socket joints characteristic of Tula (p. 50). Wooden beams were run along the lines of columns and, on this not-too-stable base, massive masonry vaults of Maya type were constructed. The North Colonnade at Chichen Itza, over 400 feet in length, was probably the most sumptuous edifice of this type. The roof consisted of five parallel masonry vaults supported by a back wall and five rows of columns. Needless to say, all such vaulted roofs have fallen.

Toltec artists developed new styles, chiefly in painted bas-reliefs and murals, and new fields for decoration such as door jambs and the sides of square columns. The chief innovation, however, was the carving of bas-relief bands which typically encircle the entire substructure of a building or three walls of large platforms inside the colonnades. In several cases the entire inner walls of rooms were sculptured, not with the freedom of Bonampak frescoes, but with the figures placed in superimposed horizontal bands. In the Great Ball Court on the sloping base of the walls there are six sculptured panels each about 40 feet long. All portray the same subject: the decapitation of the leader of the defeated team (p. 126).

The subjects portrayed are both religious and secular but in either case consist of a procession of independent figures. Religious motifs, which are decidedly Mexican in concept, include representations of Kukulcan, the Feathered Serpent, rarely found in Classical Maya art. Also pictured are eagles and jaguars, Mexican symbols of warrior castes, with bleeding human hearts in their claws. The base of the *tzompantli* where the skulls of the sacrificed were preserved is appropriately adorned with superimposed skulls shown in profile. Occasionally priests and sorcerers are seen but the great majority of human figures are warriors. Some are Mayas, most are Toltecs, and the two are readily distinguished by their clothing, weapons and accoutrements. A rough check-up some years ago revealed that we personally know of nearly 900 such figures. Stiffly posed in identical fashion, these processional groups show little more individuality than modern armies in uniform.

The Classic Maya rarely carved statues in the round. The Toltec of Chichen Itza filled their doorways with Atlantean columns and adorned their balustrades with monstrous heads of feathered serpents. Groups of smaller Atlantean figures were carved

Both teams are wearing Toltec insignia such as fur sleeves on their arms. In the center is a disk adorned with a skull. To the left stands the victorious leader with a knife in one hand and the decapitated head of his opponent in the other. The defeated captain kneels on one knee. Seven columns of blood spurt from the severed neck and either end in serpent heads—like the great Aztec statue on page 59—or turn into serpentine plant forms.

PART OF A BAS-RELIEF REPRESENTING TWO TEAMS OF BALL PLAYERS.
FROM THE EAST BENCH IN THE GREAT BALL COURT AT CHICHEN ITZA, YUCATAN, MEXICO. HEIGHT, CA. 4 FEET.

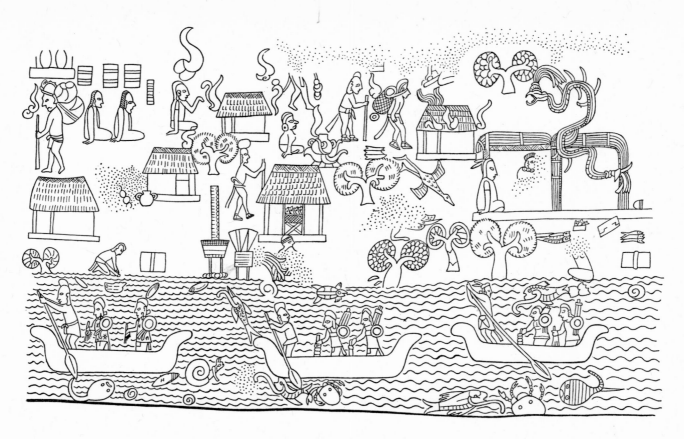

A MAYA COASTAL VILLAGE WITH SCATTERED HOUSES AND TREES.
FROM A MURAL IN THE TEMPLE OF THE WARRIORS, CHICHEN ITZA, YUCATAN, MEXICO. LENGTH, 12½ FEET.

Men and women are peacefully occupied but Toltec domination is implied by the feathered serpent at the right and by the circular shields of the warriors in the canoes. In the water are turtles, crabs, shellfish and fish of various kinds. In the lower right corner a stingray is clearly pictured. Hence the village is located on the sea rather than a lake or river.

to support table-like altars or thrones. On the platforms in front of their temples they placed seated statues with hands designed to support the shafts of banners. The curious reclining figures known as Chacmool are common at Chichen Itza. Also there are jaguar thrones. The finest is painted bright red with globular eyes of jade and teeth of white stones. The spots on the body are indicated by 80 inset disks of jade, each as big as a silver dollar.

Mural painting was highly developed at Chichen Itza during the Toltec period. For the most part purely secular subjects are represented and the various battle scenes, at times involving scores of warriors, may record historical events. Also pictured are aspects of domestic life. In one case a seaside village is represented, its inhabitants engaged in daily tasks around their houses or propelling their canoes. Trees, birds, fish, shellfish, crabs and turtles are also shown (p. 127).

These Toltec frescoes, like the Bonampak murals, are descriptive and often may suggest motion. The human body usually is shown in profile with little or no attempt at anatomical accuracy or foreshortening. The murals at Teotihuacan representing Tlalocan, the earthly paradise, perhaps are ancestral to this style of painting.

Also dating from the Toltec period at Chichen Itza are a number of finely embossed gold disks. In a central panel they picture the exploits of individual Toltec warriors at the expense of their Maya enemies. The major theme is framed by motifs in typical Classic Maya style.

Toltec ascendancy at Chichen Itza lasted a couple of centuries, roughly from 1000-1200 A.D. It had relatively little effect elsewhere in Yucatan except on the east coast where it influenced the local architecture. In the succeeding centuries, Maya populations have continued to live in the lands they occupied in Classical times but their cultural continuity was broken and they never again reached artistic heights. Today the last remnant of fine craftsmanship combined with a sense of color and design is represented by the hand-woven textiles from highland Guatemala—an industry which the machine loom has brought close to extinction.

3

THE INTERMEDIATE AREA

CAST GOLD PENDANT REPRESENTING A CROCODILE GOD. SMALL EAGLE GODS ARE PERCHED ON THE HANDS AND A TWIN-TAILED MONKEY TOPS
THE HEAD. THE DOUBLE TONGUES END IN SERPENT HEADS. FROM LA VACA, PUNTA BURICA, COSTA RICA. HEIGHT, 4¾″.
BANCO CENTRAL DE COSTA RICA, SAN JOSÉ, COSTA RICA.

THE INTERMEDIATE AREA

It is unfortunate that modern geographical usage does not lend itself more readily to archaeological areas of the past. Between the southeastern frontier of the Maya and the northern borders of the Inca empire lie most of Central America, Colombia and part of Ecuador. In recent years archaeologists, for lack of a precise term, have called it "intermediate."

The Intermediate Area is best characterized by its disunity. Its inhabitants were of varied physical types and spoke a great many languages and mutually unintelligible dialects. Communities were small and lacked permanent masonry buildings. Although social classes might be strictly segregated and chieftains might exercise despotic power, political units remained small. Terms defining stages of cultural development in Mexico and Peru, such as Pre-Classic, Classic, etc., are meaningless here. Yet the area was not one of cultural stagnation and desuetude. Artisans working in various local styles created objects of great beauty which deserve a place in this volume and many more might be added were there available space.

In view of the known antiquity of ceramics in Mexico and Peru, one would expect that the basic invention took place in either or both areas. Repeated radiocarbon tests, however, indicate that well made pottery was produced in Ecuador as early as 2400 B.C., including figurines with elaborate hair styles, obviously of artistic merit. Almost as old is some of the Venezuelan pottery and the Monagrillo ware of Panama. The place of these early ceramic types in the over-all New World picture is controversial.

The higher metallurgical skills, including the use of alloys, precision casting from wax models, surface enrichment, etc., make their earliest appearance in the Intermediate Area and spread both north and south. When or where these inventions took place is not yet known. We also should mention the sporadic appearance of megalithic statues, in Nicaragua, Costa Rica, Panama, Colombia and Ecuador, each with local styles.

CARVED MARBLE JAR WITH ANIMAL HANDLES. FROM THE ULUA VALLEY, HONDURAS. HEIGHT, 12″. UNIVERSITY MUSEUM, PHILADELPHIA.

EL SALVADOR AND HONDURAS

El Salvador and Honduras mark the final extension to the east and south of Classic Maya art, limited to a narrow band along the Guatemalan border. Copan, one of the greatest of Maya cities, is in this area (pp. 95 and 105). Settlements with typical Maya sculpture, masonry vaulted buildings, and also a Maya stela with a date of 780 A.D. have been found to the north in the upper Chamelecon valley. Beyond the lands actually occupied by the Maya, beautiful polychrome pottery evidently of Maya inspiration is found as far to the east as Nicaragua, chiefly in territory occupied by Lenca tribes in the sixteenth century. Variant styles are known as Ulua polychrome, Yojoa polychrome and Copador, the last being a term compounded from Copan and Salvador. Underlying the painted ceramics are older monochrome types which belong with the Pre-Classic styles of Guatemala and Mexico.

The outstanding contribution of Honduras beyond the Maya periphery to New World art consists of a group of exquisitely carved marble vessels (p. 132). The characteristic shape is cylindrical. Jars such as we illustrate have a pair of handles shaped like animals. Shallower bowls may have a long single handle. Both types have the outer walls adorned with scrolls which usually frame or are incorporated in a human face. Also scrolls are paired to form conventionalized reptilian heads in profile. In the example illustrated a vaguely human face occupies the central part of the upper walls. Profile serpent heads flank this. Below are a pair of profile serpent heads joined nose to nose. As seen from the front, they form a face comparable to that of the Aztec deity on page 59.

For many years, these marble vessels were known only from the lower part of the Ulua valley in northwestern Honduras and this name is used to designate the style. More recently examples have been excavated in the Comayagua valley in central Honduras. Altogether only a few dozen pieces are known, so few, in fact, that it has been suggested that all were manufactured by a single artist and his family within a couple of generations. The discovery of an example above the floor of an abandoned Classical Maya building dates the entire group as Post-Classic.

At first glance, Ulua marble jars appear to be an offshoot of the Classical Vera Cruz style. This is improbable because of the separation in time. Also, when closely examined, the scrolls are unlike. Those from Honduras are all in the same plane and terminate in a button whereas the Vera Cruz scrolls typically run over and under each other (p. 30). Furthermore, the marble jars of Honduras are refinements of a well-known pottery type found on the north coast of Honduras. It also has been argued that the Ulua jars were inspired by Chinese bronzes of the Shang (1766-1122 B.C.) and Chou (1122-249 B.C.) dynasties. The dates obviously rule out this hypothesis and the fleeting similarity of scroll types breaks down under close scrutiny.

NICARAGUA AND COSTA RICA

Lower Central America is the meeting ground of Middle and South America, linguistically, historically and archaeologically. It is not possible to draw firm boundary lines on a map because for centuries there has been culture borrowing and trade, also migration and wars. Nevertheless, certain regions may be discussed as units.

Western Nicaragua, the lands lying between the great lakes and the Pacific, and northwestern Costa Rica, the Nicoya peninsula and adjacent mainland, are regarded as part of Middle America. In the sixteenth century, the three principal languages were related to tongues spoken in Mexico but not to each other. Historical accounts often fail to localize specific cultural traits but there was much of Mexican origin. Thus the Nicarao pantheon had deities known by name in Mexico; the days of their calendar are similar to those of the Aztec and there is evidence that they knew the 52-year calendar round. Cyclical feasts called for human sacrifice. Both the voladores and Xipe rites were practised. The breeding of turkeys and the use of cacao for money came from Mexico.

The archaeological picture is different. The oldest known pottery, a zone-incised bichrome, is dated at the beginning of the Christian era. The style is distinctly local. Motifs on the oldest polychrome are of southern affiliation. Northern contacts, however, are established with the middle polychrome which was partly inspired by Classic Maya. Actual examples from the south have been found in northern Central America with Post-Classical material. The last polychrome period produced several new ceramic types. The group known as Luna ware, very popular both in Costa Rica and Nicaragua, is completely free of northern symbolism. In contrast, there are two pottery types on which Mexican deities who can be identified by name are pictured. An example of one of these styles, on page 135, has a large turkey head modeled in high relief with painted details. Crude legs and stylized wings and tail are painted on the body of the vessel. On the neck are three human figures with bent knees, associated with a two-headed snake. Below are a band of human heads in profile and a row of conventionalized birds. On the under body there are two dancing crocodiles.

Local pottery styles include monochrome vessels and figurines, with incised decoration, often of considerable complexity. The pregnant lady on page 136 is typical. The face characteristically has little modeling but is built up by clay nubbins.

The vicinity of Guápiles on the northeastern plain of Costa Rica is important archaeologically. This was a great trade center. Veraguas and Chiriquí gold were imported, also polychrome pottery from Nicoya and occasional artifacts from Honduras. Pottery was manufactured locally. The example on page 137 shows a man and woman seated on a bench. Between them they have only three legs. He holds a rattle in one hand; she is beating a drum; both appear to be singing.

POLYCHROME EFFIGY JAR REPRESENTING A TURKEY. FROM NACASOLA, NICOYA PENINSULA, COSTA RICA. HEIGHT, 8″.
JUAN DADA COLLECTION, MUSEO NACIONAL DE COSTA RICA, SAN JOSÉ, COSTA RICA.

NICOYA RED WARE EFFIGY REPRESENTING A PREGNANT WOMAN. FROM EL PANAMÁ (CULEBRA BAY), GUANACASTE, COSTA RICA. HEIGHT, 11½".
CHARLES BALSER COLLECTION, SAN JOSÉ, COSTA RICA.

Costa Rica is famous for its jades. There were two manufacturing centers, one in the Nicoya area in the northwest, the other near Guápiles in the northeast. Each had its own styles but there was trade between them. Nicoya specialized in "Axe gods," small figures which seem to be reworked celts of jade. Guápiles jades tend to be of finer quality and are technically superior. The Guápiles jewelers had mastered the art of string sawing, a process which enabled them to cut curved interior lines. They also added engraved details with lines of incredible fineness, equaled only by the best of Olmec workmanship.

A few Olmec jades have been found in the Nicoya area and it has been suggested that the Costa Rican jades may have been inspired by the Olmec. There is no stylistic resemblance. String sawing was known to both Olmec and Classical Maya artists but was rarely employed. The chief technical link between Mexico and Costa Rica is the

TWIN EFFIGY VESSELS REPRESENTING LOVERS SEATED ON A BENCH. FROM THE VICINITY OF GUÁPILES, COSTA RICA. HEIGHT, 13¼". PRIVATE COLLECTION, SAN JOSÉ, COSTA RICA.

LIGHT GREEN JADE PENDANT REPRESENTING A BAT. CA. 500-700 A.D.
LENGTH, 6″. FROM LAS HUACAS, NICOYA PENINSULA, COSTA RICA.
COLLECTION CARNEGIE MUSEUM OF PITTSBURG.

JADE "AXE GOD." GUÁPILES STYLE BUT FOUND IN THE NICOYA PENINSULA,
COSTA RICA. HEIGHT, CA. 7″. COLLECTION UNITED STATES NATIONAL
MUSEUM, WASHINGTON, D.C.

fine-line incising. We do not know what tools were used.
In the deep drilling of jade Guápiles workmanship was
unsurpassed, for tubular beads over fifteen inches in length
have been found.

Costa Rica, as its name implies, is a land where aboriginal goldwork flourished. The
first Spanish expedition to march from Panama to Nicaragua kept a meticulous record
of the gold secured in each village. Large amounts were obtained from the chiefs in
Nicoya and western Nicaragua. This must have reached the area by trade because
almost no metal has been found in graves. Gold was worked along the Atlantic
watershed of Costa Rica but the big finds have been in the south near the Pacific,
in the Diquís delta and, more recently, near Punta Burica.

The gold we illustrate came from a single site and most of it must have been manufactured to be placed with the dead, for only in a few instances do these pieces show
signs of use. They all are pendants, cast with open backs by the *cire perdue* process,
and they all have loops for suspension. In style, they may be compared with Panamanian jewelry from the Provinces of Chiriquí and Veraguas, which usually is smaller
and less intricate than the Burica group. As is often the case in Isthmian art, each piece
usually combines the aspects of two or more beasts.

The standing figure on page 130 we have called a Crocodile god, identified by his curled
snout and the triangular scales on his arms. These are standard crocodile features,
seen also on Coclé polychrome vessels (p. 145). The gold pendant has upraised arms
and huge hands, on each of which are small Eagle gods. On top of the head there is a
small seated monkey with two tails. Two rope-like tongues issue from the saurian
mouth and terminate in triangular serpent heads. Body and legs seem human but the
feet are greatly enlarged.

On page 141 there is a pendant representing a lobster. Its slender legs, claws and feelers have been designed to facilitate the flow of metal. The mouth, which is underneath and cannot be seen, is that of a crocodile. The flat tail of the lobster represents two crocodile heads, pictured upside down.

The pendant on page 140 has been variously identified as a scorpion, a centipede and a shark. The triangular head usually is associated with frogs, also the elaborate scrolls representing two tongues. They are fringed with crocodile scales and are supported by a pair of arms with small hands. On top of the body there are three erect dorsal fins and ten lateral fins flank it. The bifurcated and curved tail is associated with crocodiles in the art of Coclé.

The crocodile pendant on page 139 has little bells for eyes, a characteristic of Veraguas castings. There is a small human figure in the mouth. This is a subject found in Coclé goldwork. In Veraguas, dogs or jaguars are represented with an ear of maize or a human forearm in the mouth.

CAST GOLD PENDANT REPRESENTING A CROCODILE WITH A HUMAN FIGURE IN ITS MOUTH. FROM LA VACA, PUNTA BURICA, COSTA RICA. LENGTH, 6″. WEIGHT, 267.3 GRAMS. BANCO CENTRAL DE COSTA RICA, SAN JOSÉ, COSTA RICA.

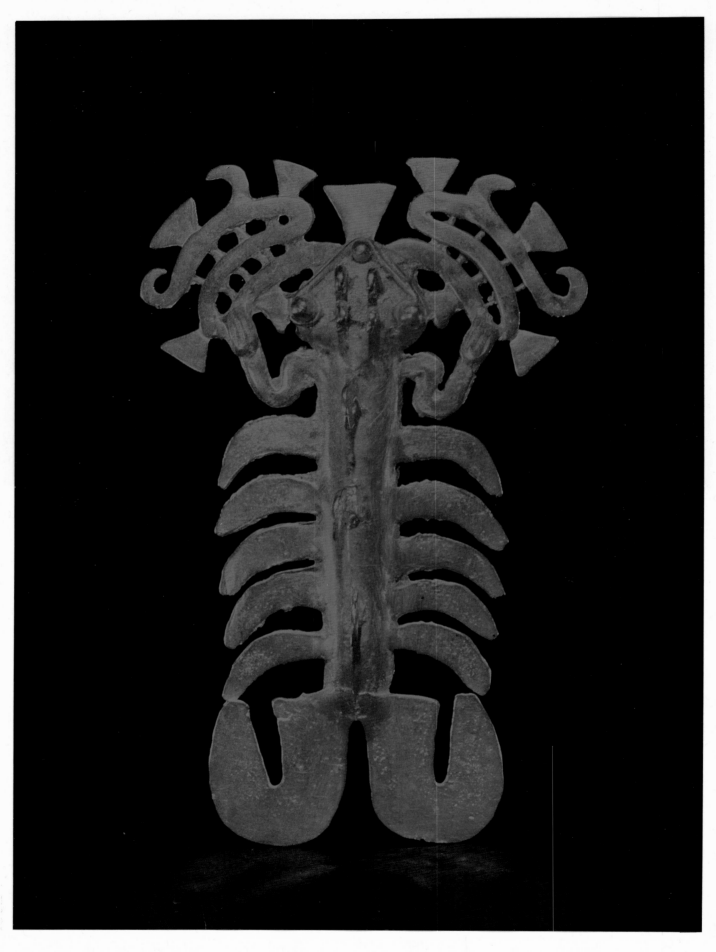

CAST GOLD PENDANT REPRESENTING A MYTHOLOGICAL ANIMAL. FROM PUERTO JIMÉNEZ, OSA PENINSULA, COSTA RICA. HEIGHT, 4⅞".
BANCO CENTRAL DE COSTA RICA, SAN JOSÉ, COSTA RICA.

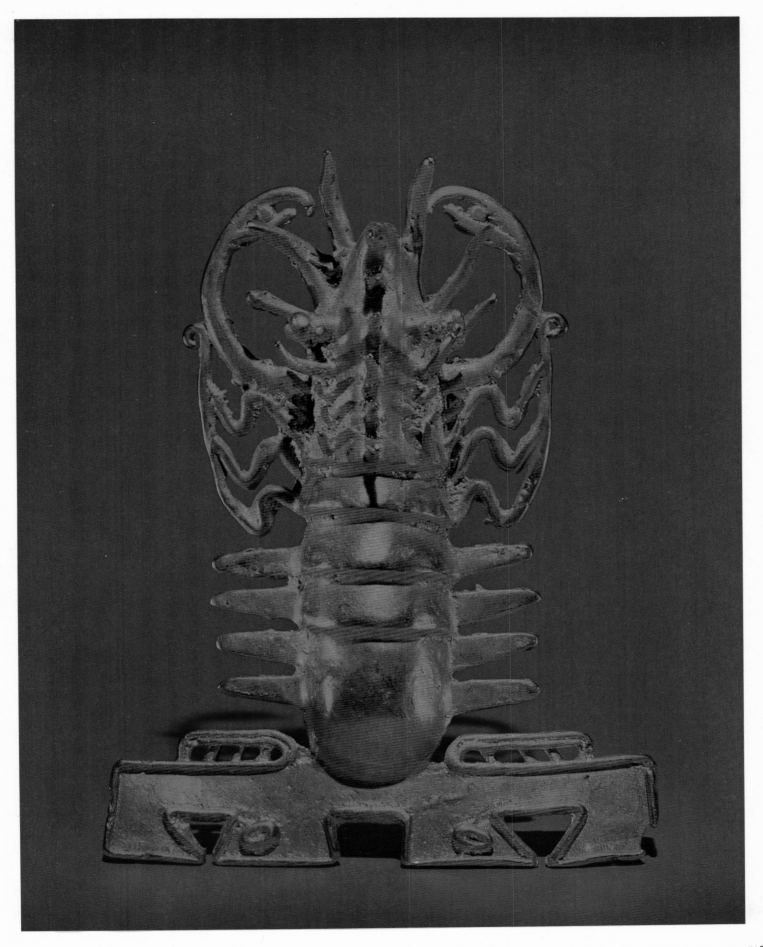

CAST GOLD PENDANT REPRESENTING A LOBSTER WITH A CROCODILE MOUTH. FROM LA VACA, PUNTA BURICA, COSTA RICA. HEIGHT, 4⅛″.
BANCO CENTRAL DE COSTA RICA, SAN JOSÉ, COSTA RICA.

PANAMA

The present Republic of Panama has been famed for its aboriginal gold since the voyage of Columbus in 1502 along the Atlantic coast. Although the first big shipment of bullion was lost at sea in 1511, such wealth came to Spain that the country was officially named Castilla del Oro, "Golden Castile." Spanish raiders scoured the land in search of gold and slaves. Of the surviving official accounts, the most dramatic describes a dead chieftain prepared for burial. On his head was "a great basin of gold like a casque." Around his neck were four or five golden necklaces, his arms and legs were cased in tubes of gold, his chest and shoulders were covered with plates and medals of gold, around his waist was a golden belt from which hung bells of the same metal. He appeared to wear "a golden coat of mail." Beside the chief were the bodies of two women and two men, destined to accompany him to another world. They had been adorned in a scarcely less opulent manner. The weight of the metal the Spaniards carried away was 355 pounds. This account is no flight of fancy. All the ornaments listed are known archaeologically. For more than a century graves have been looted systematically in Panama. Much of this work has been done in secret but finds of over a hundred pounds of gold in a single grave have occurred.

The archaeological styles in Panama are many and their development covered a long period. We picture only the art of the Province of Coclé, evidently esteemed in aboriginal times, as both jewelry and pottery were traded to other areas. The embossed gold plaque on page 143 pictures an anthropomorphic Crocodile god. The body and limbs appear to be human, also the eyes and square teeth. Saurian features include the clawed hands and feet, as well as the head crests which are flanked by conventionalized crocodile scales. In Coclé this deity may wear a belt adorned by tassels in the form of animals which hang beside the legs. This is an ancient religious symbol, the oldest known examples of which appear in the art of southern Peru (p. 196). In the present instance the belt has been omitted but the streaming tassels entirely fill the lower half of the plaque. They represent a pair of crocodiles attached to the human body by their tails.

Coclé polychrome pottery is prized for its quality of line and bright colors. The dominating motif is the crocodile or Crocodile god but there also are birds of various kinds, turtles, deer, monkeys, bats, snakes, crabs, lobsters, sharks and stingrays. The Coclé potter must have lived in a strange and fanciful world abounding in dragons. Rarely is any beast or bird depicted as in nature but usually elements of several are combined. Thus we have two-headed snakes with legs (p. 144), birds with crocodile scales and with crocodile jaws instead of beaks (p. 145) and many other strange blendings. A curious characteristic of Coclé art is that basically it is a happy one. The open crocodile jaws do not threaten but, more often than not, appear good-humored or even smiling. Both birds and beasts are represented as dancing.

EMBOSSED GOLD PLAQUE REPRESENTING A CROCODILE GOD. LATE COCLÉ STYLE. FROM SITIO CONTE, COCLÉ PROVINCE, PANAMA.
HEIGHT, 10¼″. WIDTH, 7″. UNIVERSITY MUSEUM, PHILADELPHIA.

Another characteristic of Coclé pottery is that commonly used geometric motifs—frets, interlocking frets, interlocking triangles, etc.—are almost totally lacking with the exception of a few zigzag patterns. They are replaced by a bewildering variety of scrolls, several dozen in fact, which have been cleverly adapted to fit decorated fields of different sizes and shapes. Scrolls often are the sole or principal decoration but there are many of eccentric shape inserted to fill blank spaces and to balance the major decoration.

COCLÉ POLYCHROME PLATE. LATE STYLE. TWIN CROCODILE HEADS SET ON A COILED SERPENT BODY. DIAMETER, 11½″.
MUSEO NACIONAL DE PANAMA, PANAMA CITY.

At first glance, Coclé scrolls seem so complex that only the most expert potter could be expected to execute them from memory with controlled quality of line. The secret is that each scroll has a simple base line which determines its proportions and that the pattern can be completed by simple and standard additions. On flat plates it was easy to lay out the base line. When a continuous scroll had to encircle a jar, it was not so easy to make the ends meet. No less than seven methods of repairing mistakes have been noted, so cleverly devised that it takes a keen eye to detect them.

COCLÉ POLYCHROME BOWL. EARLY STYLE. A COMPOSITE MONSTER COMBINING BIRD AND CROCODILE ELEMENTS. FROM CATIVÉ, SONÁ, VERAGUAS PROVINCE, PANAMA. MUSEO NACIONAL DE PANAMA, PANAMA CITY.

SEATED FIGURE OF CAST GOLD, A BOTTLE WITH A SPOUT ON TOP OF THE HEAD.
QUIMBAYA STYLE, COLOMBIA. HEIGHT, 9″. UNIVERSITY MUSEUM, PHILADELPHIA.

COLOMBIA

"If the gold in the provinces near the great river of Santa Marta, from the city of Popoyan to the town of Mampox, had been in the power of a single lord, as it was in Peru, the wealth would have been greater than that of Cuzco." Thus wrote a Spanish traveler in 1547, and the great gold collection now in the Bank of the Republic in Bogotá goes far to confirm this opinion. Colombian goldwork is outstanding for its technical excellence, its variety and the large size of individual pieces.

It is currently held that metalworking in aboriginal America started independently in at least four centers. By far the oldest is the copper industry in the Great Lakes region in the United States. Goldwork in Chavin style in Peru must date from the first millennium B.C. The Titicaca basin in Bolivia and southern Peru specialized in copper and may have discovered bronze. Colombia probably developed the art of casting in molds, the copper-gold alloy known as tumbaga, and a method of surface enrichment known as *mise en couleur*. These are techniques of fundamental importance to advanced metallurgy. It is believed that they spread from Colombia to Peru in the Mochica period and to Panama and Costa Rica at the beginning of the Christian era, ultimately reaching Mexico about the end of the Classic period.

There are many gaps in our knowledge. We know almost nothing about the chronology of Colombian gold styles, and little can be said about the relative age of various types. A few Colombian pieces found in Panama may be contemporaneous with the early polychrome pottery. Many more radiocarbon dates are needed and metalwork must be correlated with other archaeological material. Terminology often is vague.

Two outstanding styles of Colombian metalwork are known to have flourished until the sixteenth century. One of these is assigned to the Chibchan tribes who lived in the vicinity of Bogotá at the time of the Conquest. These were the people who gave rise to the El Dorado legend and the many tales of "lost" cities of fantastic wealth which have persisted for centuries. There was in fact a Golden Man for, during one of their ceremonies, a chief was covered with gold dust, rafted to the center of a lake and swam to shore, thus washing off the gold dust. Chibchan chiefs lived ostentatiously in houses hung with gold plates and they traveled in gold-encased litters but they did not establish a stable political power.

A great deal of Chibchan metalwork is above ground today. For the most part it consists of flat gingerbread-like figures with details such as facial features, limbs, shields, weapons, etc., built up with threads of wax. Casting was in a single flow of metal and no attempt was made to smooth the rough surface left by the mold. These castings may have been children's toys. It is also thought that they may have been *ex votos* which did not call for burnished surfaces.

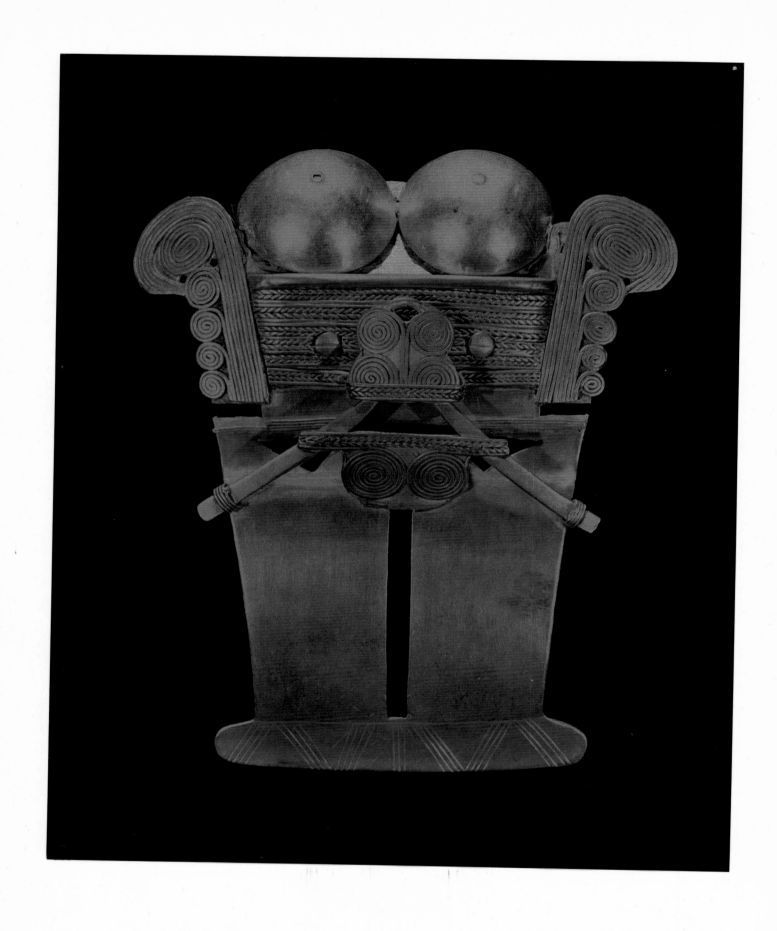

STYLIZED CAST GOLD PENDANT. PROVENANCE UNKNOWN. "DARIEN" STYLE. HEIGHT, 6⅝". WEIGHT, 293 GRAMS.
MUSEO DE ORO, BANCO DE LA REPÚBLICA, BOGOTÁ, COLOMBIA.

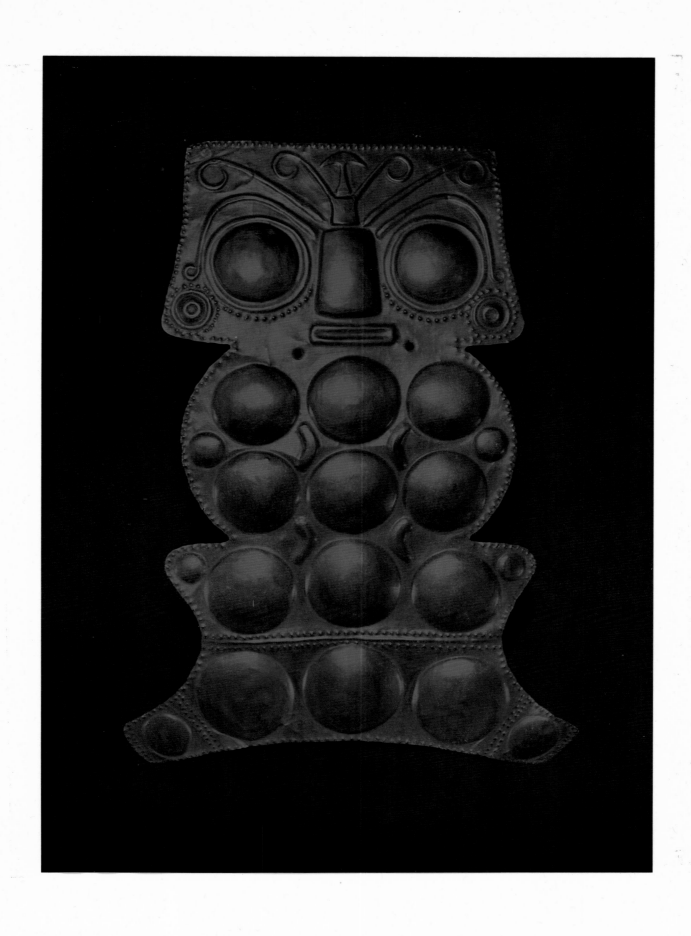

SHEET GOLD PECTORAL FROM THE HEADWATERS OF THE SINÚ RIVER. CALIMA STYLE (?). HEIGHT, 8⅝″. WEIGHT, 188 GRAMS.
MUSEO DE ORO, BANCO DE LA REPÚBLICA, BOGOTÁ, COLOMBIA.

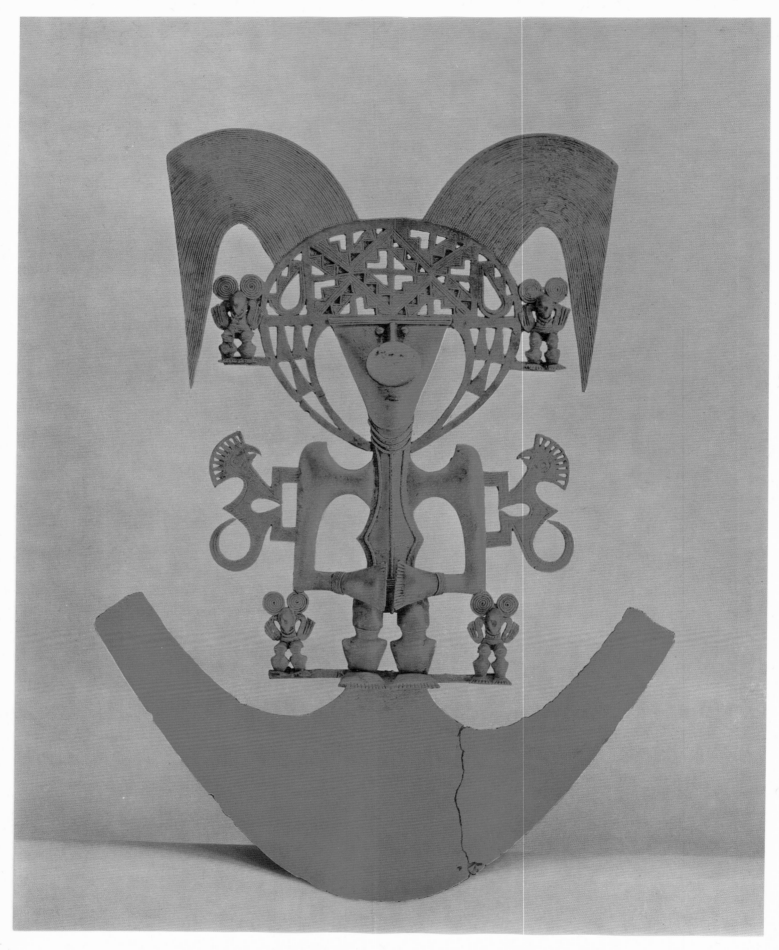

CAST TUMBAGA PENDANT FROM THE VICINITY OF POPOYAN, COLOMBIA. HEIGHT, 11″.
BRITISH MUSEUM, LONDON.

CAST TUMBAGA PECTORAL FROM HUACA DEL DRAGÓN, CALDAS, COLOMBIA. TOLIMA STYLE. HEIGHT, 9¼". WEIGHT, 315 GRAMS.
MUSEO DE ORO, BANCO DE LA REPÚBLICA, BOGOTÁ, COLOMBIA.

A second historic style is attributed to the Tairona who lived on the northeast coast and in the Sierra de Santa Marta. This style includes some of the finest false filigree casting in the New World.

The Quimbaya were the inhabitants of the present State of Antioquía where some of the most beautiful aboriginal objects of cast gold have been found. They had developed the technical ability to design internal bracing for molds with the result that hollow objects of unusual size were manufactured. Bottles of graceful shapes, delicately fluted or with human figures in relief, are truly works of art. Hollow statuettes, male and female, sitting and standing, may be seen in the museums. A particularly pleasing feature to European eyes is that, although obviously masters of intricate filigree casting, there is little emphasis on decorative details; the beauty of the burnished metal with its reflected highlights is unchallenged (p. 146).

Although found in Quimbaya territory, the pectoral on page 151 is considered an outstanding example of Tolima style. Many pendants in this style have heads with simple features combined with abstract bodies and limbs, which more often are curved than angular. In some cases, fringed edges suggest the feathers of a bird. The piece here illustrated apparently shows facial painting around the eyes. Slots and holes in the arms and legs form a simple pattern, a variant of which is seen in the headdress. No other example of Tolima style equals this pendant in vigor of design and flawless technique of casting.

A curious and not uncommon form of pendant is illustrated on page 148. The style used to be called Quimbaya and currently is known as Darien, referring not to the province in Panama but to the old name for the Atrato River in Colombia. The exact provenance in that country has not been determined but the type evidently was popular in aboriginal times, for examples have been found in the Panama Canal Zone and the Cenote of Sacrifice at Chichen Itza in Yucatan.

The subject is a stylized Bird god, always represented with two "mushrooms" on the head, which is framed by wings. Eyes characteristically are small like screw heads but nose and mouth are large and stand out from the face. The objects held in the hands are not flutes as has been surmised but some kind of staff or baton. In some cases they terminate in knobs and are held vertically.

The tumbaga pendant on page 150 has a base shaped like a Peruvian chopping knife. The figure surmounting it displays an elongated body on disproportionately short legs. Head and feet are flanked by small anthropomorphic figures and bird-headed monkeys are attached to the arms. A curious feature is the great number of toes and fingers.

Although Colombian metalwork is best known for casting techniques, magnificent hammered ornaments were produced. Pectorals in Calima style are noteworthy for their great size and intricate designs which characteristically include a multitude of attached danglers. The hammered pectoral on page 149 cannot readily be placed in any of the major stylistic groups in spite of the boldness with which the almost abstract design has been executed.

4

PERU

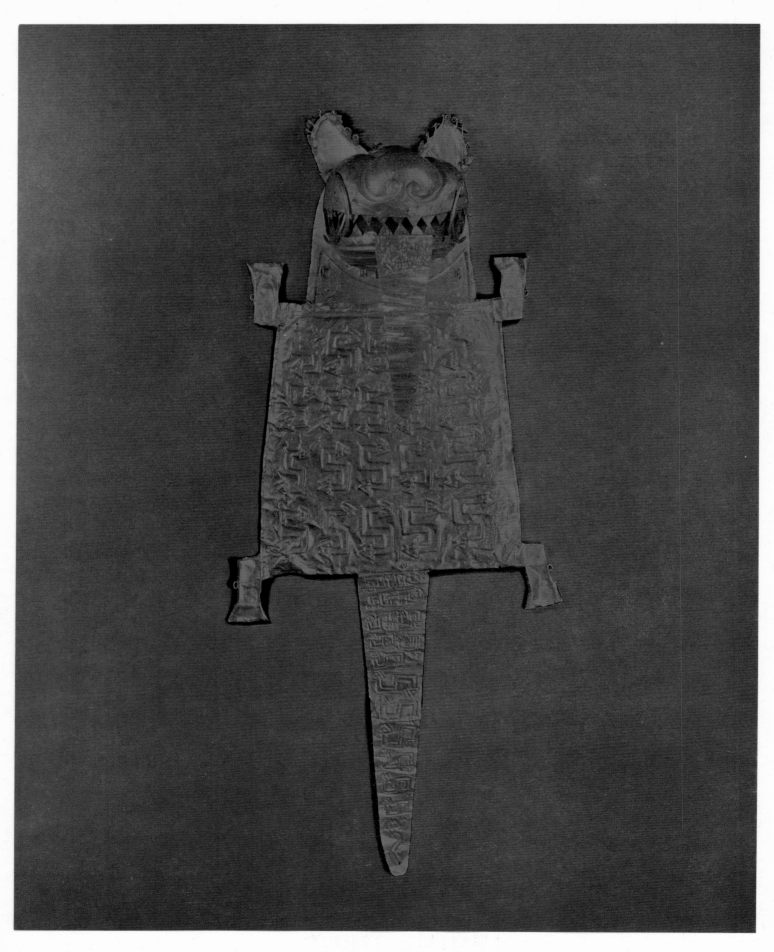

A PUMA HIDE OF HAMMERED GOLD. MOCHICA STYLE. FROM THE NORTH COAST OF PERU. LENGTH, CA. 40″. WEIGHT, 510 GRAMS.
COLLECTION MIGUEL MUJICA GALLO, LIMA, PERU.

PERU

The present Republic of Peru is a land of geographical contrasts. It is divided into three major zones, east and west, by the great mass of the Andes. Said to contain more peaks over 20,000 feet in height than any other range in the world, these mountains are rich in minerals, embrace fertile valleys and upland plateaus, and are the home of wool-bearing cameloids such as the alpaca, llama and vicuña. To the east are the tropical forests of the Amazon basin with rich and varied flora and fauna. To the west, facing the Pacific, approximately from the Equator to central Chile, is a band of coastal deserts, cut by rivers issuing from the mountains. Skilled use of irrigation has transformed these valleys into luxuriant gardens. At the same time, adjacent uncultivated lands are an archaeologist's paradise where normally perishable materials —wood, leather, cotton and wool fabrics brilliantly dyed, the feathers of tropical birds, etc.—have survived for many centuries in the arid soil. Even the bodies of the dead have become desiccated mummies and the food which was placed in the graves is often still preserved.

Peru, like other areas studied intensively, contains settlements which have been dated thousands of years in the past. Cultivation of maize became known along the coast before 1200 B.C., and, in succeeding centuries, the arts such as architecture, sculpture, pottery-making and metallurgy began to flourish.

It is interesting to note that the first known attempt at artistic expression on the north coast of Peru consists of a few fragments of incised and pyro-engraved gourds dated at approximately 1950 B.C. Of slightly later date are twined cotton textiles, some with elaborate designs. As all color has disappeared, it has been possible to recover these motifs only by use of a microscope laboriously to plot every shift in yarn. In addition to gourds and textiles, contemporary archaeological finds include stone, bone, shell, wood, basketry and bark cloth. No decoration has been detected on any of these materials.

The Peruvian past differs from other American aboriginal developments because it embraces three great eras of stylistic unity, usually referred to as pan-Peruvian horizons. Sandwiched between these are periods of local diversification. The three great Peruvian styles are known as Chavin, Tiahuanaco (or Huari) and Inca. This idyllic picture, which apparently provided a means for determining contemporary cultures in widely separated regions, has proved to be an oversimplification. True it is that these major artistic forces existed, but, in their spread, they developed local characteristics and, in certain communities, they lingered for centuries. Chavin, the oldest explosive style, is now believed to have persisted in small areas until the Mochica period. Tiahuanaco motifs have been detected from Chile to Costa Rica, again over a period of centuries. Only in the case of the Inca, whose expansion was cut short by the Spanish Conquest, do we find an art style of limited duration.

NORTHERN PERU

THE CHAVIN STYLES

The name comes from Chavin de Huántar, a small village in the high Andes (Cordillera Blanca) in north-central Peru. Here stands one of the oldest masonry edifices now known in the New World, surprisingly well preserved in spite of centuries of vandalism. Enlarged many times in rectangular units, the principal façade now measures about 600 feet in length and up to forty feet in height. The outer walls were adorned with gigantic grotesque heads, carved in the round and supported by tenons inserted in the massive masonry. Many fallen examples exist but only a single head is still in place. Flat panels carved with intricate symbolism also were set in the walls (p. 158) but all of these have fallen. Above was a wide cornice with major relief carvings on the lower side and, in some cases, on the outer edge. In ancient times, these great masonry blocks probably supported shrines of lighter materials. They appear to be solid but in fact are honeycombed by a windowless labyrinth of corridors, staircases and air ducts, all so complex that no adequate plan has yet been published. The oldest unit of the temple was U-shaped, a central mass with wings which enclosed a court. About a hundred feet behind the façade, corridors lead to the great idol in honor of which the temple was erected (p. 157). Popularly known as El Lanzon, this is a pointed shaft of white granite, some fifteen feet in height, irregular in shape, and not carved with a feeling for bone and flesh like the Olmec sculptures of Mexico. Rather it is a low relief carving, which follows the undulating surface of the stone to depict a long forgotten and, to our eyes, a monstrous deity—preserved owing to its isolation. John Rowe, most recent investigator, writes: "The scale of this Great Image and its setting in a dark passage give it an awe-inspiring quality which can be felt even by a present day unbeliever, but which photographs and drawings fail to communicate."

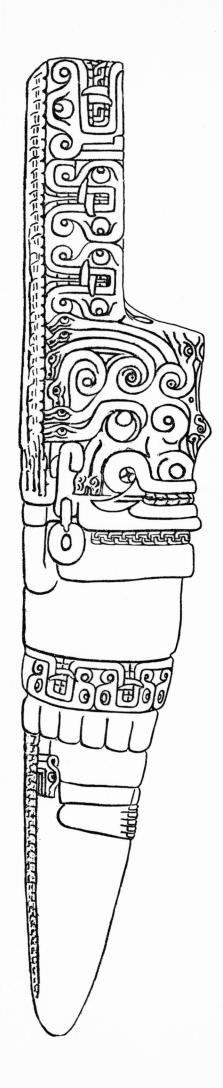

The central position of the Lanzon in the oldest part of the temple indicates that it is the oldest carving in Chavin style now known, but the intricacy and sophistication of the design, the strength and quality of the curving lines, in short, the entire concept indicate that we are far from the beginnings of an art which doubtless evolved in other media than megalithic sculpture.

A few local variants of Chavin-like carvings are known in Peru, but archaeology has still to reveal a center of development. Smaller artifacts in Chavin style have been found sporadically along the coast of Peru from Piura in the north to Yauca in the south, but the full range and penetration in the interior are still unknown.

At Cerro Sechin in the Casma valley the outer masonry wall of a temple consists of upright slabs up to seventeen feet high interspaced with two or three smaller blocks placed one on top of another. Over ninety of these stones have incised decoration. The tall columns show complete human figures, some cut in half at the waist, piled up skulls (suggesting the Mexican skull racks), rows of eyes and banners attached to a staff. The small blocks depict trophy heads. Chavin pottery has been found nearby but where the engraved stones fit in the Chavin picture is uncertain. Comparisons have been made, however, both in style and subject matter with the approximately contemporaneous *Danzantes* of Monte Alban in Mexico (p. 82).

EL LANZON, PROBABLY THE OLDEST MAJOR IDOL NOW KNOWN
IN THE NEW WORLD. HEIGHT, 15 FEET.
CHAVIN DE HUÁNTAR, PERU.

At Chavin de Huántar itself, where there is considerable rainfall, only broken pottery and major sculpture have been found. The first finds of Chavin style on the coast were in the Cupisnique valley north of Trujillo. Here the Larco Hoyle brothers opened graves with well preserved artifacts, chiefly pottery vessels but also delicate carvings of bone, some with turquoise insets.

Chavin pottery, once thought to be the oldest Peruvian style, is now known to have been preceded by other types. North coast examples for the most part are black as the result of firing in a reducing atmosphere. Stirrup-spout jars, probably mold made, are common, also bottles with tall tapering necks. Decoration of these monochrome vessels is surprisingly diversified. Incised designs which represent feline or reptilian motifs stand out boldly against stippled backgrounds. In the finest pieces the designs are carved in relief which is highly polished. An unusually elaborate example of this technique on page 159 displays large jaguar heads on opposite sides of the jar separated by elongated heads of snakes. Jaguar heads also appear on the curved shoulders of the spout and pairs of serpent heads are seen on both sides of the upright tube.

WALL PANELS FROM CHAVIN DE HUÁNTAR, PERU. LEFT, CONDOR MOTIF. RIGHT, ANTHROPOMORPHIC FELINE. NOTE THE CONSTANT PRESENCE OF SNAKES AS A DECORATIVE MOTIF.

BLACK WARE CARVED POTTERY JAR. CHAVIN STYLE. FROM CHONGOYAPE, LAMBAYEQUE VALLEY, PERU. HEIGHT, 8¾".
MUSEO NACIONAL DE ANTROPOLOGÍA Y ARQUEOLOGÍA, LIMA, PERU.

Effigy vessels, which dominate later ceramic styles, are not uncommon in this period. Some picture the heads of monstrous deities with huge fangs (p. 159). Others represent fruits or animals or a nursing mother. There is a suggestion of portraiture in the wrinkled head of an old woman on page 163.

With the introduction of fired colors on pottery, new techniques of decoration appear. Thus in the vessel on page 161 the modeled relief was outlined by incising the stippled brick-red background. Black and bright red pigments were then applied and firing took place, after which the body markings were incised in the hardened clay.

No figurines dating from this period have been reported in northern Peru, but in this area has been found the oldest known South American metalwork, stylistically comparable with the great Chavin sculptures. The techniques are chiefly hammering and annealing but, by joining sheets of metal, it became possible to create hollow figures in the round. Gold was the principal metal, in some cases with platinum as an impurity. Silver also was known (p. 162) and usually is found in bimetallic artifacts joined by a still undetermined process. Unknown were copper, tin, alloys, molds and casting, gilding and surface enrichment (*mise en couleur*), metal inlays and other advances in Peruvian metalworking characteristic of later centuries.

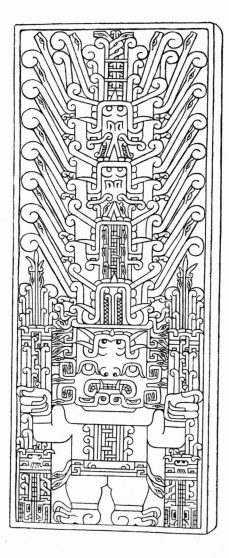

Chavin motifs extended southwards on the Peruvian coast where they blended with the polychrome decoration on Paracas pottery (p. 190). At Chavin de Huántar it had not been possible to arrange the sculpture in chronological sequence because much of it had been disociated from the architecture. A ceramic sequence, however, was established in the south by University of California scholars and then transferred to the monumental carvings which thus can be grouped in probable chronological order. The oldest is the great Lanzon (p. 157). The terminal phase is represented by the so-called Raimondi panel, which has obvious affinities with the Nazca pottery style which developed from the Paracas in southern Peru. The Raimondi carving was brought to Lima about ninety years ago, on mule back over a specially constructed road. It was the first object in Chavin style known to the outside world.

THE RAIMONDI WALL PANEL FROM CHAVIN DE HUÁNTAR, PERU. THE LAST PHASE OF CHAVIN SCULPTURE. MUSEO DE ANTROPOLOGÍA Y ARQUEOLOGÍA, LIMA, PERU.

PAINTED AND INCISED JAR ADORNED WITH PUMA-HEADED SNAKES. FROM SAUSAL, CHICAMA VALLEY, PERU. HEIGHT, 9½".
COLLECTION RAFAEL LARCO HOYLE, LIMA, PERU.

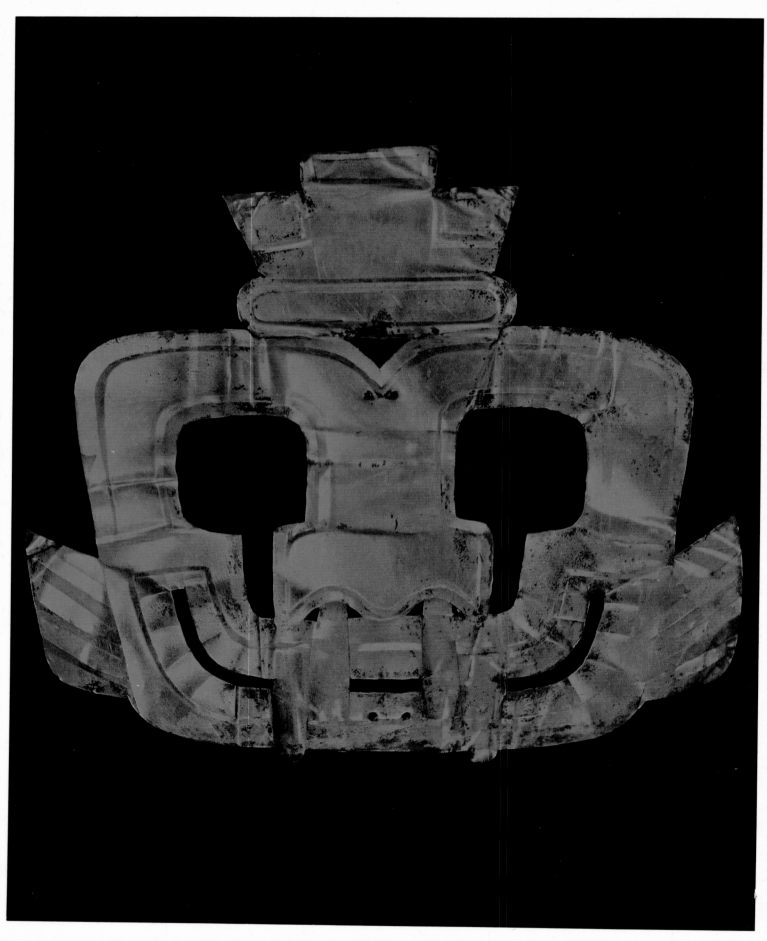

PUMA HEAD OF HAMMERED SILVER. FROM PACHACAMAC, PERU. HEIGHT, 8".
AMERICAN MUSEUM OF NATURAL HISTORY, NEW YORK.

PORTRAIT JAR REPRESENTING AN AGED WRINKLED FACE WITH SHRUNKEN JAWS. CUPISNIQUE STYLE. FROM THE CHICAMA VALLEY, PERU. COLLECTION RAFAEL LARCO HOYLE, LIMA, PERU.

The Chavin expansion is far from satisfactorily explained today and its elucidation will require much research. Current opinion is that it represents a cult rather than military conquest because it flourished at a period when communities were too small to overrun a vast area.

Dating is uncertain, but current opinion places the Cupisnique ceramic styles between 900 and 300 B.C. This allows time for the Salinar and Gallinazo developments (not discussed here) before the appearance of the great Mochica styles. Unexplained are the Chavin-inspired motifs on pottery in graves dating from the middle of the Mochica era.

MOCHICA

The culture and art styles known today as Mochica (formerly called Early Chimu) flourished on the north coast of Peru for several centuries at the beginning of the Christian era. The Mochica were master engineers who constructed great irrigation systems which still function in part today. The canal of La Cumbre penetrates seventy miles into the mountains to the head of the Chicama valley and brings water to the fields around Chanchan, once the greatest city of South America. Valleys and ravines were crossed by aqueducts. The Ascope aqueduct has a length of 4,500 feet, a maximum height of fifty feet, and its weight is estimated at over two million metric tons. This great ditch continued to function until 1925 when heavy rains—25 inches in a single month—caused a breach in its walls.

The Mochica material culture is based largely on clay to the exclusion of stone. They erected no great masonry structures like the temple at Chavin de Huántar nor did they develop a style of monumental stone carving. Both their temples and their dwellings were of adobe bricks. Their largest carvings were of wood. As the north coast of Peru is damper than the south, few of their textiles have survived. Few of the frescoes which adorned their buildings are now known.

Mochica claim to fame stems chiefly from the pottery, amazing in its quantity, variety and pictorial quality. A single private collection in Lima today contains nearly 40,000 examples. Effigy vessels represent men and deities, animals and birds, legumes and fruits. Figures modeled in the round were placed on top of jars and the walls were adorned with painted scenes or motifs in low relief. Mankind is shown in almost every conceivable contemporary activity from love-making to burial. As styles became more flamboyant and complex, animated scenes appear which depict many individuals involved in pageants of ritual and of war. In no other medium except perhaps some of the Classic Maya or Maya-Toltec frescoes do we have such an animated and comprehensive picture of aboriginal American life in the far past.

In spite of its vigor and scope, Mochica art is circumscribed by stylistic traditions, from which at times it tried to escape. Painted surfaces show all animals, birds and fish in full profile only. To be sure, some animals may be pictured looking backwards over the shoulder but the head is still in profile. Crabs are an exception, for they habitually are seen from above and the tail, which in life is clamped against the under side of the body, is shown in an extended position. This curious feature also is seen in the art of Panama and lower Central America. Centipedes and scorpions are occasional exceptions.

The human figure in painting normally is strictly conventionalized by dividing it into four sections, each pictured from its broadest aspect. Thus legs are represented from

RECTANGULAR JAR SURMOUNTED BY A SCULPTURED DRAGON HOLDING A HUMAN HEAD. MOCHICA STYLE. HEIGHT, 6¾″.
MUSEO DE AMÉRICA, MADRID.

the side in a striding position which suggests motion such as running or dancing, especially when one foot is on a higher level than the other. Bodies, on the contrary, are shown full face with the shoulders squared, a pose which may be emphasized by symmetrically placed patterns on the shirt. Heads, however, are in profile except the eye which is almond-shaped as seen from the front. There are a few exceptions to this pose, chiefly seated figures on thrones or in litters, who may be in full profile except for the eye. This manner of showing the human body, obviously not the product of direct perception, has been called a memory image or a conceptual representation. Perspective is not possible nor any meaningful use of light and shade. We may regard this as an archaic stage in style development. It is a widespread one, however, best known perhaps from similar conventions in Egyptian painting and reliefs throughout the long series of dynastic periods.

While sticking rigidly to their limiting conventions, the Mochica created scenes of great animation and activity, but the action normally is confined to a space no greater than the width of the human body. A crowd is represented as a procession of single individuals. The hands, however, may grasp such objects as a knife or the hair of a captive. An arm partly concealed by the body is on a slightly more distant plane.

BAS-RELIEF FROM A MOCHICA POTTERY JAR SHOWING A CHIEF CARRIED IN A LITTER.

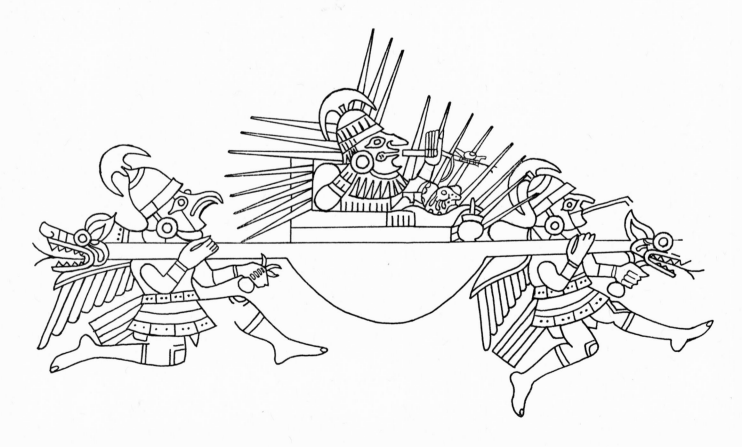

A GROUP OF TYPICAL MOCHICA WARRIORS ON A PAINTED POTTERY JAR.

There are several simple devices for indicating depth of scene such as so placing the nearest objects that they overlap and partially obscure the more distant. Although the Mochica might hold the human figures in a single plane, the nature of the land could be suggested by curving base lines with attached vegetation such as cactus. In some cases, distance is suggested by painted plant forms and birds or animals placed between or above the human bodies. Evidently a desire to depict depth existed but had only reached an embryonic stage of development.

Although Mochica vase painting developed in complexity in the course of centuries, its essential character and conventions did not change. On the other hand, when relief decoration on the walls of pottery vessels was introduced, a partial emancipation took place. This is indeed curious because the relief on pottery is so slight that any innovation might equally well have been depicted in paint. In relief, however, profile, full face and quartering views of the human body are found. In a few instances, violently contorted bodies suggest unusual creative ability of individual artists.

The Mochica also attempt to represent distance by a combination of modeling in relief and in the full round. Such vessels are not common and the subject matter is limited. In one of the best known types, the body of the vessels represents an island, indicated by shells around the base. Hills appear in relief and cactus is depicted. On top is an eagle boldly modeled in the round. It grasps in its talons either a snake or a shark,

"MOUNTAIN JAR" SHOWING THREE MAJOR PEAKS, LESSER HILLS AND VALLEYS. A SACRIFICE OR EXECUTION IS REPRESENTED. THE VICTIM APPEARS ON THE HIGHEST PEAK AND ALSO, DEAD AND DECAPITATED, ON THE LOWEST LEVEL. LATE MOCHICA STYLE. HEIGHT, 8¾". MUSEO NACIONAL DE ANTROPOLOGÍA Y ARQUEOLOGÍA, LIMA, PERU.

identified by the tail, pointed snout and semilunar mouth. Just what this combination —eagle, serpent, cactus and island—meant to the Mochica we cannot say. It is curious to note, however, that about a thousand years later in Mexico, the migrating Aztecs founded what is now Mexico City on a spot where they encountered the same association of symbols. Today the Republic of Mexico incorporates the eagle and the cactus in her coat of arms.

In addition to plastic models of limited areas, there is a small group of Mochica jars which endeavors to indicate considerable heights and distances. In concept if not in style they recall the so-called mountain jars of the Han dynasty in China, for in each case an attempt was made to depict massive topography by small scale modeling.

The Peruvian vessels have flat bases with vertical or outsloping walls rising to about half the total height. The ground level may be indicated by an undulating painted line. Hill crests may be shown at the half height by modeling or painting. Behind these there often is a plateau which merges at the back with higher flat mountain peaks modeled in the round. To us today this may seem a crude and ineffective attempt to represent a landscape in depth, yet there is an element in common with our concept of geometrical perspective which shows more distant objects decreased in scale.

The topography of Mochica mountain jars is not an end in itself but a background for scenes which may be painted or sculptured. The subjects represented are esoteric and are not easily interpreted. By far the commonest motif portrays the death of an individual by throwing him over a cliff (p. 168). In some cases the scene is dominated by a fanged deity seated beside the mountain and a religious sacrifice is implied. In other instances, the principal personage seems to be entirely secular and the scene may portray an execution, perhaps even a well-known historical event. The victim usually is represented twice. First he is shown perched on the highest mountain peak, bent forward with hair hanging downward. Then he is shown crushed on the valley floor below. On some vessels the lifeless body has been decapitated. In addition to the victim, small human figures appear on the mountain slopes, sometimes accompanied by a dog. Often they seem to be dancing.

Portrait jars call for a word of comment. The oldest head effigy vessels from Peru date from the Chavin and Salinar periods and exhibit little modeling. Mochica jars, however, represent a number of distinct physical types. Individuals can be detected by their characteristic features, the way their faces are painted and, in some cases, by scars or other peculiarities. The importance and popularity of certain individuals is indicated by the number of vessels which represent them. In most portrait vessels the head is thrown backward and the face points diagonally upward. This probably is not an attempt to indicate a dignified bearing but is the result of absence of tables among the Mochica. Portrait jars thus were kept on the ground and viewed from above.

Portraiture, the picturing of individuals so that they can be recognized, is not a characteristic of New World art. It requires a society governed by personages of such importance that the recording of their appearance for posterity becomes desirable. In regions such as Mexico and the Maya area where writing existed, individuals were identified by name both in sculpture and in frescoes but it is questionable whether artists were trained to reproduce the features of the Great Man. His identity was made evident to the illiterate by his paraphernalia and accoutrements, but the physical types were idealized.

The so-called portrait jars of the Mochica fall in a different category. They represent a variety of physical types, some of which may be idealized, but definite individuals obviously are portrayed in some cases doubly identified by personal peculiarities such as scars or other blemishes. In the finest pieces the artist evidently has rendered a faithful likeness and has successfully captured the aristocratic bearing, the arrogance and forceful personalities of rulers both young and old, whose names and exploits are unknown today (p. 171).

In addition to deities, the Mochica portrayed various mythical beasts which correspond to the European concept of a dragon, for they combine the characteristics of two or more animals. The example on page 165 exhibits the head of a jaguar with a second and smaller head attached to the tail. The claws and spotted feet evidently belong to the same animal. Both the scales projecting from the back and the body markings, however, are those of a crocodile. The snakes painted on the rectangular body of the vessel have the heads and ears of a jaguar or puma.

Over half the Mochica jars have globular bodies rising from a flat base. On top is a device known as a stirrup spout. This consists of a tube shaped like an inverted U with a single spout projecting from the top of the curve. This is a very practical combination of a handle and a tube for drinking. If the U-shaped element is held vertically, liquid can be drunk through the lower arm while air enters above. In later times with other forms of narrow spouts, it was necessary to pierce a hole in the walls of the jar to allow air to replace the liquid.

A majority of Mochica vessels were pressed to shape in molds. A master image first was made over which a clay cover was fitted, and, when partially dry, was cut in half vertically and fired. Copies could be made by pressing clay against the molds and jointing the two halves together when partially dry. Stirrup spouts were shaped in the same fashion and then luted to the body of the jar with wet clay. Finally a disk was inserted to close the base which had been left open in order to facilitate the preceding operations. Smoothing, tooling of details and painting preceded firing. Several vessels could be made from the same mold but the sharpness of the impression decreased with use.

MOCHICA PORTRAIT JAR WITH STIRRUP SPOUT, PROBABLY REPRESENTING A DEFINITE INDIVIDUAL.
MUSEO NACIONAL DE ANTROPOLOGÍA Y ARQUEOLOGÍA, LIMA, PERU.

Over the course of centuries, Mochica pottery went through various stylistic modifications and it is now customary to divide it into three or five phases, based on the use of colors and on alterations in shapes. In general, painted motifs are in red on a white or cream background. The oldest group may have the colors separated by incised lines and the most recent may have touches of yellow and black as added colors. In portrait jars and vessels modeled to represent the human figure, flesh tones are indicated by a beige or tan pigment. A rare type of early date, always with geometric designs, is dark brown and black separated by incised outlines. Also there is a highly burnished black ware with the color produced in the firing, a type derived from Chavin which became almost universal during the Chimu period several centuries later.

It has long been held that the Mochica ceramic styles first appeared in the Chicama and Moche valleys and spread southward as far as Casma and to the north as far as Pacasmayo, forming a unified state extending 300 miles along the coast. During a recent visit to Lima, we saw several dozen Mochica vessels of the earliest known types which had come from nearly 300 miles further north, beyond the Chira River. The chronological and historical relationship of this group to the well-known finds further south is an unsolved problem but the possibility exists that the style was brought to the Chicama-Moche area from the far northwestern part of Peru.

Not much metalwork of Mochica style is found in existing collections but the quality is outstanding. Gold, silver and copper, together with their alloys, were the chief metals in use. Metal tools and weapons made their appearance and became progressively more common and complex in type, facilitated by the introduction of *cire perdue* casting. Outstanding are the portrait heads of hammered metal, comparable in size to the pottery types. They may be partly of gold and partly of silver. Several great gold breastplates and head ornaments have been found (p. 177). Smaller articles of jewelry include rings, necklaces and nose pendants. Some of the ear ornaments are of superb workmanship, especially the gold disks inlaid with shell and turquoise (p. 176).

Many Mochica vessels represent either men or women with mutilated faces or limbs. Some of these portray the ravages of various diseases the nature of which is obvious to a physician. Others, however, with cut-off noses or lips and with amputated hands or feet, evidently portray deliberate and cruel mutilations. Formerly it was assumed that such butchery was inflicted as a punishment for crimes. It has been noted that the severed hands and feet in themselves were of ceremonial significance, for not infrequently pottery vessels were shaped to represent them and sometimes they were modeled in hammered gold. The Frontispiece in this volume illustrates a pair of life-size golden hands. Current opinion is that the mutilations may have been a religious offering, commemorated by replicas of the sacrificed limbs.

The seated cripple on page 173 is unusual in several ways. One foot has been replaced by a rounded stump and he carries a massive staff. Various details were added by fine-line incising. What appears to be a mustache is a profile view of some long-tailed animal; two other animals are shown flanking the eyes. The pupils of the eyes are incised and also the locks of hair in front of the ears and on the back of the head and neck. The skull cap and the shirt with sleeves extending to the wrists are not characteristic Mochica style.

EFFIGY VESSEL REPRESENTING A SEATED CRIPPLE WITH A STAFF. LATE MOCHICA STYLE. HEIGHT, 10½″.
COLLECTION RAFAEL LARCO HOYLE, LIMA, PERU.

EFFIGY VESSEL REPRESENTING A CAPTIVE DEER-MAN. MOCHICA III. HEIGHT, 9¾".
COLLECTION RAFAEL LARCO HOYLE, LIMA, PERU.

BIRD EFFIGY JAR FROM HUANCACO, PERU. MOCHICA STYLE. HEIGHT, 13¼". LENGTH, 12¾".
MUSEO RAFAEL LARCO HERRERA, LIMA, PERU.

Although a large part of Mochica art was devoted to religion and its symbolism or to secular scenes with the pageantry of warfare and ceremonies, Mochica potters took delight in modeling the animals and birds which were a part of their daily life. To western eyes this aspect of Mochica style is particularly pleasing because the artist was not bound by conventions and obviously worked from direct observation of nature.

A unique and powerful piece of this kind is illustrated above. It portrays a long-necked bird with head turned backwards and gracefully arched over the body. Head, beak and eyes are modeled in detail and there is a suggestion of muscular strength in the neck and shoulders. The large plump body forms a harmonious setting for the head but is a complete abstraction.

The unusual effigy jar on page 174 represents a captive deer-man. Human characteristics include the body and genitals, the arms and hands, the crossed legs but not the feet which are replaced by hoofs. Among the animal features are the head, ears and antlers, the tongue, hide, hoofs and a white tail.

EAR DISKS ADORNED WITH BIRD-HEADED WARRIORS CARRYING SHIELDS, SPEARS AND SLINGS. TURQUOISE, GOLD AND SHELL. MOCHICA STYLE. DIAMETER, 4″. MUSEO RAFAEL LARCO HERRERA, LIMA, PERU.

In many cases the manner in which Mochica jewelry was worn is pictured in the modeled pottery, especially the portrait heads (p. 171). In other instances the function may be far from clear. The great gold puma hide on page 154 is a unique piece of unknown use. Approximately 40 inches long, it is decorated from throat to tail tip with two-headed serpents. Back and front are separate sheets of metal, and it has been suggested that it once was a container for coca leaves.

Historical accounts suggest that the Mochica made much greater use of metals than is indicated by recorded archaeological finds. In the year 1602, a "mining" company was formed to divert the Moche River against the big adobe terrace and pyramid known as the Huaca del Sol. The terrace measured 750 by 450 feet and was 60 feet in height. On one end was a terraced pyramid 340 feet square on the base and 75 feet high. Nearly half of this edifice was carried away by the water. Gold including a large statue was collected to the amount of 800,000 ducats—at least such was the value declared

HEAD ORNAMENT OF REPOUSSÉ GOLD REPRESENTING A PLUMED FELINE DEITY. MOCHICA STYLE. WIDTH, 14½″.
MUSEO RAFAEL LARCO HERRERA, LIMA, PERU.

for taxes paid to the Spanish crown. We hesitate to place a value on this sum as Spanish coinage varied with time and place. In the sixteenth century the ducat was 23½ carats fine and weighed 3.485 grams. At present there are 28.716 grams to the ounce.

RECUAY   Recuay is a style of pottery and stone carving found principally in the inter-Andean valley known as the Callejón de Huaylas. This is the only valley between major ranges of the Andes which drains into the Pacific. Recuay pottery therefore occurs on the coastal plains in the area known as the Santa Valley where Mochica styles also flourished. Their chronological relationship has not been exactly determined but they seem to have been partly contemporaneous.

Recuay houses and temples were constructed of stone slabs which were split but not dressed. There are surface constructions which may be two or three stories high and are roofed with stone. Also there are subterranean buildings which may extend two or three stories underground. Entrances are small; today they are indeed dark and dismal, and, on account of the altitude, extremely cold. Sculpture consists of seated human figures carved in the round with incised designs also found on the pottery. In addition there are stone lintels with pumas carved in relief.

Recuay pottery exhibits variety in shape and there are many modeled forms, which, however, are distinctly inferior to Mochica workmanship. Recuay potters frequently made use of an exceedingly fine-grained clay which remained pure white after firing. With this clay it was possible to construct vessels with extraordinarily thin walls, rivaling the Nazca pieces which have justifiably been described as "egg-shell." Painted decoration characteristically was applied in a two- or three-color negative technique. Crested dragons shown in profile are frequently represented.

The Recuay vessel on page 179 represents a seated deity or chief with his wives and servants. Ten modeled figures occupy a circular area only 8 inches in diameter. The chief is sitting on a low rectangular bench or throne. Close beside him are a pair of women facing backwards. Flanking them on either side are two women who face forwards. A fifth woman—a spout projects from the back of her head—is facing the chief, who presumably is getting drunk as all the women are holding cups.

At the corners of the throne stand four men with arms upraised to support a mat or awning. All wear ponchos which flare at the waist and those in front are decorated. They all have long hair divided in the back but looped up so that the ends meet on top of their heads.

Mochica and Recuay styles were submerged by the pan-Peruvian spread of Tiahuanaco art forms, discussed in connection with southern Peru. Hence here we continue with developments on the north coast.

A CHIEF OR DEITY SEATED ON A LOW THRONE. FOUR MEN SUPPORT A CANOPY OVER HIS HEAD AND FIVE WOMEN ARE PRESENTING DRINKING CUPS.
RECUAY STYLE. PROVENANCE UNKNOWN. HEIGHT, 8¾". COLLECTION RAFAEL LARCO HOYLE, LIMA, PERU.

CHIMU

The dominant culture of northern Peru after recession of Tiahuanaco influences until the Inca conquest is known as Chimu. This "kingdom" was a militaristic state which dominated the coast from Túmbez in the north nearly to Lima. It apparently was a time of increasing population which called for additional crops and irrigated land. As a result the canal systems of adjacent valleys were consolidated so that water could be shifted from one to another. The economy fostered the growth of large cities.

Chanchan, the Chimu capital, is in the Moche valley near Trujillo. Existing remains cover about eight square miles. The foundation date is not known but it is probable that most of the construction took place during the fourteenth and fifteenth centuries. Within the city were ten or more "palaces," walled rectangular areas. One measures 1600 by 1100 feet and the walls today are over 30 feet high. These units contain houses, streets, storerooms, reservoirs, irrigated gardens, pyramids with temples for worship and cemeteries for the dead.

It is curious but unfortunate that there is no written description of this metropolis when the Spaniards first occupied it. It must have been spectacular with many house walls adorned with relief motifs or brilliantly painted. Prior to the Spanish occupation, as Pizarro marched towards the Inca capital, his men found ten slabs of silver, each 20 feet long, one foot wide, and variously stated to be one, two, or three fingers thick. "These slabs, the Indians told (us), were (being) carried to Trujillo in order to build there a house for their idol who was called Chimo. The gateway of this (idol's house) was found later, and was worth ninety thousand castellanos."

Chimu pottery is a revival of Mochica but of a much inferior quality. Most vessels are of the stirrup-spout type with pressed designs. An identifying feature is a small animal, usually a monkey, placed in the angle where the curved and vertical portions of the spout are joined. The standard color is black and painted decoration is rare.

Most of the existing pieces of Peruvian metalwork are in Chimu style. In the sixteenth century, objects valued at nearly a million pesos were extracted from a single temple substructure in Chanchan. Chimu graves have been ransacked ever since but still continue to yield large quantities of precious metal. Chimu jewelers were masters of annealing and hammering, often over molds. They excelled at covering the largest possible surface with a minimum amount of metal.

The big breastplate on page 181 is a typical example of Chimu workmanship. It is two feet in width. The decoration consists of seven rows of identical figures shown in profile. This piece is a single sheet of metal. Gorgets of this type usually were of five to seven wedge-shape units which were strung together.

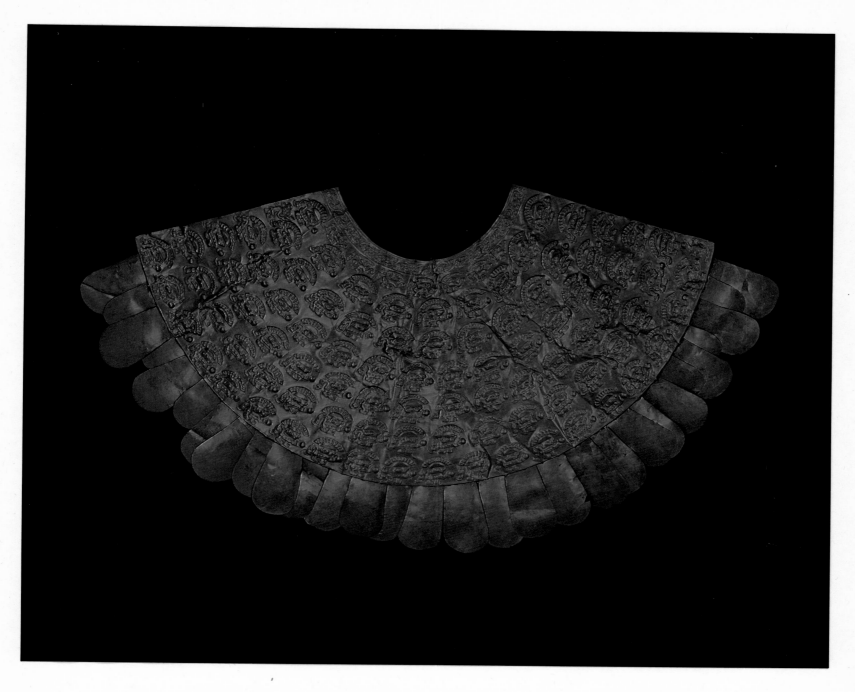

REPOUSSÉ GOLD BREASTPLATE ADORNED WITH BIRDS AND SEVEN ROWS OF HUMAN FIGURES. WIDTH, 24″. CHIMU STYLE.
COLLECTION RAFAEL LARCO HOYLE, LIMA, PERU.

Chimu chopping knives usually are of copper or bronze but there was a type in gold with a handle in the form of a standing human figure (p. 183). These have been built up from both cast and hammered units and have turquoise inlays. Occasionally portions of the gold were plated with silver. As these knives may be as much as a foot and a half high, it is probable that they were for ceremonial use.

Spanish inventories of huge vessels and statues sent to Spain after sacking the Inca capital list the individual objects by weight rather than size. It is recorded, however, that there were "two large pots, one of gold and the other of silver, each of which was capable of containing a cow cut in pieces." The silver jar seen on page 184, however, is of comparable dimensions for it is five and a half feet in circumference.

This great vessel was fashioned in three sections. Each half of the body was hammered to shape separately and there seems to have been difficulty in joining the central seam. The cylindrical neck has a flat lip which is thicker than the rest of the vessel. The scene in relief, repeated four times, pictures a pair of towering demons with a small victim between them. There are four animals at the base and a pair of badly eroded figures on the shoulders.

The history of this jar is as follows. It is said to have been one of eleven silver vessels found at Chanchan, not in a grave but in an underground storeroom, together with a large number of textiles. Three silver beakers from this hoard known to the writer are all small, less than a foot high. The big jar eventually was given to President Leguía. When his regime fell and the presidential palace was looted, the late Dr Julio C. Tello watched for it to be carried out and purchased it for one Sol. Several years later he presented it to the museum in Lima.

The small silver bowl on page 185 is unusual because it has double walls. The exterior surface which is illustrated is completely covered with small birds in relief. A solitary bird in the center is surrounded by six concentric circles of birds alternately facing to the right and left. The inner wall combines the interior curve of the vessel and a flat lip half an inch wide which has been clinched over the decorated exterior. So expertly are the two fitted together that there is no solder. The flat lip is decorated with a line of birds. To facilitate drinking, there is a small section where the width is reduced by more than half, somewhat like a mustache cup.

The cutting up of living individuals, apparently as a sacrificial ritual, extended far into the Peruvian past. Mochica painted vessels show completely butchered bodies; modeled jars depict individuals with missing noses and lips or amputated arms and legs. Sometimes pottery jars were fashioned in the shape of missing legs and feet or arms and hands, represented either singly or in pairs. Occasionally such replicas were made of hammered gold. Evidently the severed limbs had some esoteric value and their reproduction in clay or in metal persisted along the north coast of Peru until the Spanish conquest.

It has been suggested that golden hands such as are seen in the Frontispiece were actually worn by the dead. This we doubt because in at least one instance, the opening in the forearm has been closed by a metal cap and there is a depression in the palm of

CEREMONIAL CHOPPING KNIFE OF COPPER WITH A GOLDEN HANDLE REPRESENTING A STANDING HUMAN FIGURE. THE INSETS ARE OF TURQUOISE. FROM ILLIMA, DEPARTMENT OF LAMBAYEQUE, PERU. CHIMU STYLE. HEIGHT, 16″. COLLECTION MIGUEL MUJICA GALLO, LIMA, PERU.

LARGE JAR OF HAMMERED SILVER. CHIMU STYLE. FOUND IN A STOREROOM AT CHANCHAN, PERU. HEIGHT, 27¼". CIRCUMFERENCE, 67".
MUSEO NACIONAL DE ANTROPOLOGÍA Y ARQUEOLOGÍA, LIMA, PERU.

184

the hand, intended perhaps to hold incense or some ceremonial offering. The decoration on the back of the hands and the forearms undoubtedly represents tattooing, which often is seen on mummified bodies.

Chimu textiles are technically excellent and, owing to their comparatively recent date, often are well preserved and retain their brilliant colors. Feathers survive surprisingly well in the arid coastal plains of Peru. It is not unusual to find feathers retaining their original color and elasticity with pottery that has crumbled owing to the absorption and crystallization of salts.

THE BASE OF A BOWL OF BEATEN SILVER ADORNED WITH SMALL BIRDS. CHIMU STYLE. DIAMETER, 6⅞".
COLLECTION RAFAEL LARCO HOYLE, LIMA, PERU.

PONCHO WITH FEATHER DECORATION CONSISTING OF BIRDS, PUMAS AND FISH SURROUNDED BY A GEOMETRIC BORDER.
CHIMU STYLE. PROVENANCE UNKNOWN. HEIGHT, 31". THE ART INSTITUTE OF CHICAGO.

FEATHER HEADDRESS AND PONCHO DECORATED WITH STYLIZED OWLS. FROM THE COAST OF PERU. HEIGHT, 51″. WIDTH, 26″.
UNIVERSITY MUSEUM OF ARCHAEOLOGY AND ETHNOLOGY, CAMBRIDGE, ENGLAND.

GORGET MADE OF BEADS OF COLORED SHELL. CHIMU STYLE. FROM CHANCHAN ON THE NORTH COAST OF PERU. HEIGHT, 17″.
AMERICAN MUSEUM OF NATURAL HISTORY, NEW YORK.

Feathers were extensively used for head ornaments of various kinds. They also were attached to woven fabrics, chiefly ponchos, in such fashion as to form decorative designs (pp. 186-187). The technique employed was to bend the ends of the quills into a loop and to attach them individually to a cord which was then stitched to the base cloth so that the feathers overlapped like shingles. The Mexican technique of cutting up feathers and gluing them in a mosaic was not understood in Peru.

SOUTHERN PERU

The southern portion of Peru is of great artistic importance. The coastal climate here is even drier than in the north, with the result that the finest textiles of all periods usually have been found in this region. Furthermore, the southern highlands fostered the growth and spread of two great pan-Peruvian cultures, Tiahuanaco and Inca. Southern Peru is noted for the exuberant use of color, both in textiles and in pottery. Megalithic carvings of several styles were developed. In metallurgy, however, both in techniques and quantity, the south did not equal the rest of the country until the Inca period.

Pre-ceramic sites have been discovered along the south Peruvian coast and radiocarbon dates indicate that it has been settled for at least 5000 years. Early ceramic types have been announced but the first outstanding style we can discuss is Paracas.

PARACAS

Paracas is the name of a large rocky peninsula a few miles south of the port of Pisco. As an archaeological term it must be qualified owing to the fact that it covers two distinct archaeological types. *Paracas Cavernas* is applied to the oldest known polychrome pottery from southern Peru, found with very simple textiles. *Paracas Necropolis* designates a fantastically complex and colorful group of textiles and a very simple type of pottery. The chronological position of the two styles is not too firmly fixed and it is quite possible that they are partly contemporaneous.

Paracas Cavernas pottery is of many shapes including open bowls (p. 190), globular jars with a projecting head and spout joined by a flat handle, also effigy vessels of eccentric shapes. Decoration is by incising, black on black burnished designs, negative painting and by polychrome with incised outlines. In large part the polychrome pigments were applied after firing with some kind of a lacquer base, but the techniques of permanent fired colors were developed within the life of the style, which terminated around 100 A.D.

Decorative motifs may be purely of local significance or they may be ancestral to the subsequent Nazca styles. In many cases, however, they are in the lithic style of Chavin (p. 190). The Paracas Cavernas pottery has been divided into four chronological phases, which have made it possible to place the Chavin sculpture of northern Peru in a similar chronological sequence.

The Paracas Necropolis textiles were wrapped around the seated body of the dead, forming a conical bundle as much as five feet wide and five feet high. There are belts, turbans, ponchos and shawls. Some are miniatures and symbolic. Often garments such as ponchos and shawls have matching designs. These bundles were built up in layers

Chavin stylistic influences are particularly noticeable in the Paracas remains from the Ocucaje section of the Ica Valley. Changes in these phases have been placed in a chronological sequence which has been extended to cover the monolithic sculptures in Northern Peru. The bowl here illustrated has four decorated panels, three with bird motifs and one with a jaguar head. The angular quality of line and the division into parallel bands are considered late Chavin characteristics. The jaguar head is unusual. The mouth with four large canine teeth evidently is pictured from the front but the upper part of the head with a single eye is shown in profile.

BOWL DECORATED WITH A JAGUAR HEAD AND BIRD MOTIFS. PARACAS CAVERNAS STYLE.
FROM OCUCAJE, ICA VALLEY, PERU. MUSEO NACIONAL DE ANTROPOLOGÍA Y ARQUEOLOGÍA, LIMA, PERU.

and, as they increased in size, the individual garments became larger until they were too large to wear. The outer wrappings were of plain cloth. Single fabrics have been found measuring as much as eighty feet in length by nearly twenty in breadth. We doubt that hand looms of such size have ever existed elsewhere in the world. Obviously they could have been manipulated only by a team of women, but it staggers the imagination to think of the task involved in setting up the warps and controlling them to insert the wefts. The decorated garments, whether of outsized ceremonial types or intended for daily use are of cotton or camel-hair wool. The latter suggests contacts with the interior mountains, which has yet to be proved archaeologically.

Peruvian weaving is believed to combine more techniques than any other area in the world, but the Paracas Necropolis weavers greatly favored embroidery. Typical are large rectangular shawls or mantles with solid bands of embroidered design on the long sides, which make an angled turn at the corners but do not form a solid border on the short sides. The central field becomes a checkerboard covered with dozens of small embroidered figures, usually facing alternately in opposite directions.

To give an idea of Paracas Necropolis funeral furnishings, we list the articles placed with a personage now known as Mummy 49. Top quality decorated garments included 11 big mantles, 20 ponchos and shirts, 11 skirts, 6 turbans and 5 belts. Many of the mantles, ponchos and skirts were embroidered with matching designs and colors. In addition there were 26 plain textiles. The largest, a single loom product, was 87½ feet long and 11¼ feet wide. It contains an estimated 100 miles of two-ply yarn. Also there were 12 pieces of sheet gold, a shell necklace, a fox skin, a fan, a wooden baton, a stone-headed club, a wooden knife handle and a sling.

Paracas mantles normally were made by joining three separately woven textiles of exactly the same length. As the ends were not tailored, this in itself was quite a feat, dependent on uniformity of spinning, uniformity of tension on the warp threads and uniformity of beating in the weft threads.

The wide central section normally was woven of alpaca wool and the narrower side panels were of cotton. All were adorned with embroidered motifs, essentially similar but with variations in color and minor details such as facial adornment. In the central portion, these motifs were usually placed in checkerboard fashion; in the side panels they were placed end to end and the background was filled in with solid wool embroidery. We have counted 320 embroidered figures in the center of a single mantle with 36 larger repeats of the same theme in the two borders. No doubt more elaborate examples exist. The use of cotton in the border fabrics was indeed unfortunate as, after centuries underground, the cotton may have completely rotted away, "leaving nothing but a tangled mass of wool embroidery—disheartening and depressing," whereas the central wool panel has survived with little damage.

To return to Mummy 49, one of the mantles with this nobleman is described in Bird and Bellinger's classical analysis of Paracas Necropolis fabrics as "a perfect example of complete simplicity: solid, monochrome wool embroidery in a medium dark green on a rose-red cotton field." The borders, of standard width, were divided transversely by pairs of heavy embroidered stripes. The central area had thirteen pairs of four-centimeter wide embroidered cross bars which are estimated to contain more than one million, two hundred thousand stitches. The borders probably represent about eight hundred thousand stitches more. We cannot estimate the time a woman devoted to her household in the far past and how much was available for weaving. There can be little doubt, however, that most Paracas textiles represent the work of months and many may have taken years to complete.

A MYTHOLOGICAL DEMON CARRYING A TROPHY HEAD. PARACAS NECROPOLIS EMBROIDERY. FROM THE PARACAS PENINSULA, PERU. HEIGHT, 9″.
MUSEO NACIONAL DE ANTROPOLOGÍA Y ARQUEOLOGÍA, LIMA, PERU.

EMBROIDERED MYTHOLOGICAL BIRD. PARACAS NECROPOLIS STYLE. FROM THE PARACAS PENINSULA, PERU. HEIGHT, 8½".
MUSEO NACIONAL DE ANTROPOLOGÍA Y ARQUEOLOGÍA, LIMA, PERU.

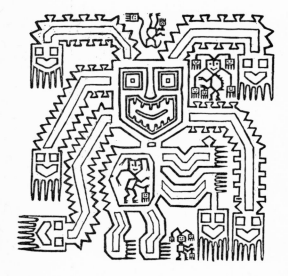

BASIC STYLES OF TEXTILE DECORATION. PARACAS NECROPOLIS.

Most major motifs on Paracas Necropolis textiles either are embroidered in two distinct styles or are painted. A typical geometric embroidery (above, left) consists entirely of straight lines and angles with smaller versions of the major motif used to fill blank spaces. Curvilinear embroidery (above, center) is unrestricted in subject but the units of design are repeated with minor variations. Only two great painted fabrics are known to the writer. There are no repeated motifs; each and every figure is a unique and exotic creation.

Paracas Necropolis embroidered patterns can be divided into two major groups. Geometrical or linear designs represent such subjects as jaguars, birds and snakes, always with angular outlines. Blank spaces are filled in, usually with smaller versions of the major motif. Curvilinear patterns are the type we illustrate. There is a seemingly limitless range of subject matter and its manner of presentation: dancers, warriors, animals, serpents, birds and fish. Usually several elements are combined in a single figure to form dragon-like monsters or partly human demons. What these represented to their designers we cannot say. It is noteworthy, however, that many symbolic devices, such as double tongues, serpent tongues (p. 193), mouth masks and belts with serpent tassels (p. 196), apparently had their origin in this style but survived in modified forms in later periods in other areas.

EMBROIDERED FIGURE OF A DANCER CARRYING A BATON AND FAN. PARACAS NECROPOLIS STYLE. FROM THE PARACAS PENINSULA, PERU. HEIGHT, 9″.
MUSEO NACIONAL DE ANTROPOLOGÍA Y ARQUEOLOGÍA, LIMA, PERU.

AN EMBROIDERED MYTHOLOGICAL FIGURE WITH SERPENT TONGUES AND BELT AND WITH CLAWED FEET. PARACAS NECROPOLIS STYLE.
FROM THE PARACAS PENINSULA, PERU. HEIGHT, 9¼″. MUSEO NACIONAL DE ANTROPOLOGÍA Y ARQUEOLOGÍA, LIMA, PERU.

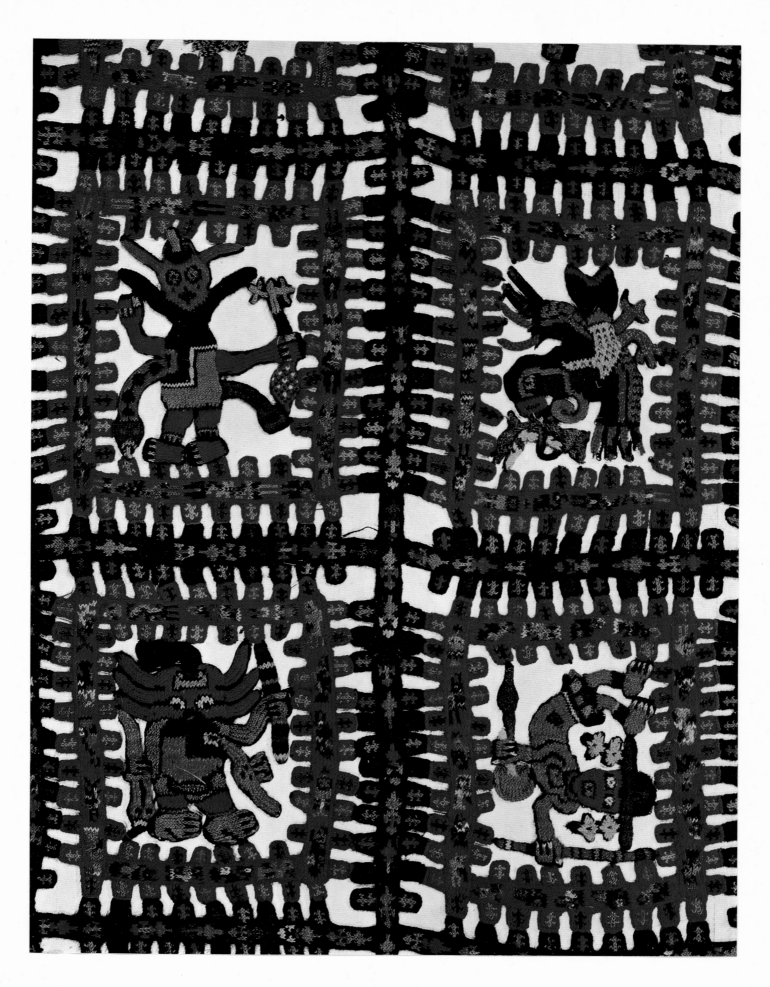

DETAIL OF TEXTILE COMPOSED OF KNITTED FIGURES. PARACAS NECROPOLIS STYLE. ETNOGRAFISKA MUSEET, GÖTEBORG, SWEDEN.

FABULOUS TEXTILE COMPOSED ENTIRELY OF KNITTED FIGURES. THIS TECHNIQUE, WHICH
THIS IS THE ONLY KNOWN COMPLETE EXAMPLE. PARACAS NECROPOLIS STYLE.

HAS BEEN DESCRIBED AS THREE-DIMENSIONAL LACE, IS USUALLY USED FOR BORDERS.
HEIGHT, 20½″. WIDTH, 41″. ETNOGRAFISKA MUSEET, GÖTEBORG, SWEDEN.

We have discussed the manner of representing the human figure on Mochica painted vessels. In Paracas Necropolis art the legs normally appear in profile but both the bodies and heads are shown from in front. The heads of birds are an exception for they may be presented in profile both in the geometrical and curvilinear styles.

The Necropolis tendency to combine seemingly unrelated forms is illustrated on page 193. At first glance this appears to picture an owl with wings and tail. The face, however, has whiskers suggesting a cat. Upraised serpent-like arms grasp a pair of small dancing human figures. Inside the bird body there is a jaguar with twin tongues and in its belly a smaller version of the same animal. Embroidered figures who seem to be dancing appear on pages 192 and 195. The first, which has the feet replaced by claws and a tremendous tongue, must be a mythological concept. The other dancer, who wears a belt and skirt, carries a rod and a fan, probably symbols of authority.

One of the more complex Necropolis designs appears on page 196. The only garment worn is a small apron with a belt to which are attached streamers in the form of swirling serpents. These are balanced by a serpent tongue running over the head, from which issues a second serpent tongue. Small animals on either side of the face have been identified as foxes. This specimen is from one of the best known Necropolis grave lots. Each fabric has its own basic type of decoration with variations in color. The faces of the chief characters are distinctly individual. Over sixty have been published in color without repetition of any pattern.

Paracas Necropolis textiles are often bordered with fringes which were fashioned by various technical processes. Garments of this and the subsequent Nazca period sometimes have the outer margins, as well as neck and arm openings, outlined by tabs or by small figures which are in the round. The technique, known as knit-stem stitch or needle knitting, produces what has been described as a three-dimensional lace.

A remarkable small mantle in the Göteborg Etnografiska Museet, illustrated on pages 197-199, not only has the outer edges fringed by rounded figures but the entire interior, divided into square panels, is filled by an infinite variety of images fashioned in the round. This must be an epitome of the supernatural world as conceived by Paracas weavers some two thousand years ago.

Several thousand Paracas Necropolis textiles are above ground today. Individual fabrics, especially the large embroidered shawls, must have required not months but years to weave. There is no way of estimating the time required for gathering the raw cotton and wool, spinning and dyeing. The valleys of southern Peru are not large and the population has been limited by the amount of water available for irrigation. The Necropolis weavers must have devoted a large part of their lives preparing garments to be placed in the graves of their relatives.

The Nazca period is best known through the polychrome pottery, regarded as the most colorful ware developed in South America. Its inception may have been due to the adaptation of the post-fired Chavinoid motifs to the techniques of fired colors, the assimilation of Paracas Necropolis designs, and to the appearance of a new and naturalistic manner of representing animals, birds, fish and fruits. New deities, such as the Cat demon (visible on the headdress on page 203) or Jagged-staff demon (p. 202, left), were introduced or perhaps the older gods were pictured in new guises.

Nazca pottery currently is assigned to nine sequent phases and is dated between 100 and 800 A.D. The geographical range in coastal valleys varied with period. At the beginning, Nazca pottery was produced chiefly in the adjacent Pisco, Ica and Rio Grande de Nazca valleys but ultimately extended from Asia in the north to Acari in the south. Late aspects of Nazca style penetrated the Southern highlands.

The shapes of Nazca vessels include open bowls, cups, several types of jars and bottles with twin spouts joined by a bridge (p. 202). Surfaces to be painted (slips) appear in at least six different colors, any or all of which might be applied to various parts of a single vessel. The number of colors used for decoration depends partly on how one defines them. Those commonly seen include white, beige, tan, brown, red, maroon, purple, gray and black. Decoration sometimes is in free-line style; more commonly, however, zones are outlined in black or white and filled with color—at least in theory. In practice, as close examination shows, the base colors were applied first, then the filling colors and lastly the outlines. This sequence demanded a detailed memory of complex motifs but it produced the quality of line which typifies the style.

As for the designs themselves, several dozen can be identified by name. The earlier types tend towards natural forms and restraint. In later centuries, the decoration is flamboyant. An added complication is that what may be called standard presentation of a deity often acquired multiple associations. Thus the Cat demon is pictured with at least fifteen extraneous attributes, including cactus and other plants, birds, mice, snakes, and fish, trophy heads, and various emblems usually associated with other deities. Such combinations seem complex and obscure to us but in Nazca times they probably were commonplace and generally understood. Comparison can be made with the multiple functions of individual saints in the Catholic church. These we comprehend through literary and oral tradition, but many aspects would be lost were our knowledge derived solely from art forms and symbols.

The older vessels often are decorated with a single motif which may or may not be repeated. Later styles usually exhibit a variety of subjects. Thus the typical late jar on page 202 has a row of trophy heads at the top. Below are a pair of Cactus demons, each with a triple headdress adorned with fleur de lys. Next is a band of interlocking step frets. At the bottom is a trophy head. The sex is indicated by a mustache and the lips are sealed with bloody thorns. The spouted jar shown below has two lines of identical faces with a row of trophy heads between them. On top is a figure of the Jagged-staff demon.

Nazca textiles are of fine quality but do not occur in great bundles as was common during Paracas Necropolis times. Embroidery continued to be fashionable but other techniques such as tapestry, brocade, warp and weft stripes, gauze and painted cloth appear more frequently. Three-dimensional borders were still manufactured. New designs allied to contemporary pottery appeared.

Nazca pottery is noted for its color rather than its modeling, but some effigy vessels occur. Usually they are small, but in the Lima museum there are several great polychrome effigy jars. The example illustrated on page 203 is over two feet high although the base is missing. Modeling is largely limited to the head which shows how the

JAR WITH TWIN SPOUTS AND A BRIDGE HANDLE (LEFT) AND CYLINDRICAL JAR (RIGHT). LATE NAZCA STYLE. HEIGHT, 6½″ AND 7″. MUSEO NACIONAL DE ANTROPOLOGÍA Y ARQUEOLOGÍA, LIMA, PERU.

CEREMONIAL EFFIGY JAR ADORNED WITH MYTHOLOGICAL FIGURES AND TROPHY HEADS. NAZCA STYLE. HEIGHT, 25″.
MUSEO NACIONAL DE ANTROPOLOGÍA Y ARQUEOLOGÍA, LIMA, PERU.

so-called mouth masks of gold were worn with tips curled against the nose. Two small human figures are clasped in the arms. Trophy heads surround the base, back and front, and others are attached to a band at the back of the neck. Two big star-studded bosses on the shoulders are hollow and open into the vessel.

The purpose served by such a big effigy is not self evident. No large sculptures in wood or stone are known from the Nazca area. This and other large pottery figures are impressive enough to have been worshipped as idols. The example here considered, however, has an orifice five inches wide concealed by the head and evidently could function as a container.

During the Nazca period comparatively little use was made of metals. Sheet gold mouth masks such as is shown on page 203 frequently are pictured on pottery but few examples have been found. Hammered plaques of gold at times were sewn on shirts. These may repeat the motifs found on pottery and thus can be placed in the ceramic sequence. Characteristically the edges were trimmed to outline the embossed designs. No technical advances were made until near the end when a few small copper objects such as pegs for spear throwers were cast.

Nazca culture seems to have run its course for centuries and then collapsed internally. The vigor and spirit of the earliest phases gave way to flamboyant and over-ornate diffuseness, followed by technical and stylistic degeneration. When Tiahuanaco motifs reached the south coast of Peru, the Nazca tradition disappeared for good. After the Tiahuanaco tide receded, new ceramic styles such as Ica or Chincha appeared. These exhibit nothing in common with the older art forms except a predilection for polychrome decoration.

TIAHUANACO

The famous ruins of this name are on the Bolivian side of Lake Titicaca at an elevation of over 12,500 feet. This is above the tree line and far too high for the development of an important economy. Hence Tiahuanaco is regarded as a ceremonial center constructed by pilgrims. Abandoned before the Spanish Conquest, it has served as a quarry for later builders.

CLASSIC PERIOD The largest construction at Tiahuanaco was a stepped pyramid, 690 feet square and 50 feet high. This was once faced with stone. On top there are house foundations and a reservoir. Another unit, known as Calasasaya today, looks like an enclosure measuring 445 by 425 feet but originally it was a stone-faced platform. The masonry technique called for large upright slabs at intervals with the space between them filled with smaller stones which have since been carted away. Stone blocks were carefully fitted

Although larger than others, this is a typical Tiahuanaco statue in the Classical style. These pillar-like statues carved in the round give less attention to anatomical detail than others supposedly of earlier date. Major outlines of head, body and limbs are either vertical or horizontal and there is little attempt to show rotundity or musculature. The incised and low relief designs indicate body painting of textile motifs.

THE BENNETT STELA, FROM TIAHUANACO, BOLIVIA. HEIGHT, NEARLY 24 FEET. NOW IN LA PAZ, BOLIVIA.

THE GATE OF THE SUN AT TIAHUANACO, BOLIVIA. HEIGHT, 10 FEET. WIDTH, 12½ FEET.

and sometimes bound together by I-shape copper cramps set in notches. The famed monolithic Gate of the Sun formed part of this unit. The masonry at Tiahuanaco is the finest in the Americas and even surpasses Inca masonry in exactness and precision. Some of the blocks are very large and weigh as much as a hundred tons.

Tiahuanaco art styles fall into two groups. One is called Classic or Bolivian; the other is termed Coastal or Peruvian. At Tiahuanaco itself there are two schools of sculpture. One produced massive seated or kneeling figures with a definite attempt at realism. The other, regarded as Classical, fashioned tall standing statues, also lintels and monolithic gateways, adorned in low relief with designs apparently borrowed from textiles. This is the style which became pan-Peruvian.

Standing statues may be up to 24 feet high. Head, arms and legs are roughly blocked out with no attempt at realism. The whole effect is angular, as if the corners of a square column had been rounded but the sides left flat. The angularity of the head is emphasized by a horizontal turban which is exactly parallel to the forearms, belt and feet. The hands always hold a pair of objects vertically, often ceremonial staffs or beakers. The entire surface of these statues is carved in low relief with textile patterns.

The monolithic Gate of the Sun is a block of stone measuring twelve and a half by ten feet with a doorway cut through it. Over the entrance is the standing figure of a deity carved in high relief. He holds staffs topped with condor heads. The face is framed by rays which terminate in disks and puma heads. On each side of this figure is a frieze in low relief which shows in profile three rows of runners, some with condor masks. Their cloaks flare behind them. At the bottom are angular frets enclosing a series of faces similar to the head of the central deity.

Classic Tiahuanaco polychrome pottery has designs in black, gray, yellow and white on a red slip. The subjects represented, human figures and faces, condors and pumas, are also found in stone but the quality of line is quite different. No Classic Tiahuanaco textiles have survived. Metalwork is not common but includes objects of gold, silver, copper and bronze, which may have been a local invention.

The expansion of Classic Tiahuanaco cannot be fully explained. It has been suggested   COASTAL PERIOD
that the climate of Tiahuanaco rules out the area as a center of stylistic innovations and that the great habitation site at Huari in the Peruvian highlands was the true center of development. This seems unlikely because both local and Nazca-influenced pottery styles occur at Huari and the Tiahuanaco forms may well be intrusive. Furthermore, the total Tiahuanaco culture never did reach Huari, only its religious symbols. Typical masonry and stone carvings are not found either at Huari or on the coast.

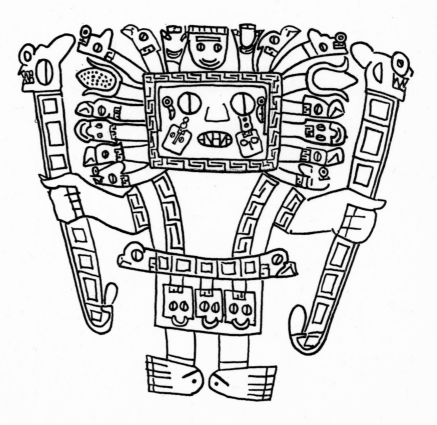

THE SUN GOD OF TIAHUANACO AS PICTURED ON THE PERUVIAN COAST. MUSEO NACIONAL DE ANTROPOLOGÍA Y ARQUEOLOGÍA, LIMA, PERU.

Some of the Classic Tiahuanaco designs appear on the Peruvian coast in only slightly modified form. The deity here depicted is carved in relief on the Gate of the Sun at Tiahuanaco. This version is one of several painted on large flaring jars from Fundo Pacheco, Rio Grande de Nazca, Peru.

It is highly probable that religion played an important part in the dispersal of a Bolivian art style. Military conquest and occupation is suggested by the total elimination of all previous styles on most of the Peruvian coast. Only Mochica survived—in the modified form known as Chimu. Neither conquest nor religion, however, will explain the appearance of Tiahuanacoid symbols as far away as Costa Rica and Chile, and we can suggest only that they had aesthetic appeal. One new factor appeared on the Peruvian coast during the era of Tiahuanaco dominance. For the first time, *guaras* or centerboards were buried with the dead. This shows that sails had been invented and ocean travel was facilitated. Centerboards can only function in combination with sails.

The most direct ceramic link between the Bolivian highlands and coastal Peru is a series of large thick flaring jars found at Fundo Pacheco in the valley of the Rio Grande de Nazca. They are painted inside and out with standing figures which might well have been copied from the Gate of the Sun (p. 207). They have angled heads framed by rays tipped with puma and condor heads. The weeping eyes show tears incorporating small heads. They wear kilts supported by shoulder braces and a belt adorned with tabs, and carry ceremonial staffs with animal heads. Only two new features have been added in the coastal presentation. The mouth with N-shaped canine teeth is not found in Bolivia but is typical on the coast. Also, the vertically divided bichrome eye is a coastal characteristic.

A simplified version of the Classic Tiahuanaco head is shown on page 209. The face is still angular but lacks the surrounding rays. The eyes have tears which end in heads and the same motif is repeated on the bridge of the nose. The checkerboard painted below the face suggests a poncho. Around the rim is a band of plant forms which have been pictured with attempted realism.

The effigy jar on page 210 also exhibits the angular Tiahuanacoid face elaborately painted or tattooed. The square cap is of a well-known type which usually is made of pile cloth and has small upright tabs at the corners. Apart from the face, modeling is confined to the hands and the tips of the toes. The body of the vessel represents a patchwork poncho adorned with tie-dyed rings.

Some twenty years ago, a workman dug into an ancient mound to secure clay to make adobe bricks. He brought to light eight large pottery vessels, each containing a dozen large feather-decorated mantles. Nearby were found fine textiles, pottery and various articles of silver, which definitely were of Inca style. This fortuitous find probably was not a burial but a hoard of equipment for a temple, concealed perhaps at the time of the Spanish Conquest. The feathered mantles, all decorated with alternating yellow and blue rectangles, were obviously not garments to be worn. Attached tie strings indicated they were to be displayed horizontally, presumably on temple walls.

ONE OF A PAIR OF POLYCHROME JARS. COASTAL TIAHUANACO STYLE. FROM CAHUACHI, RIO GRANDE DE NAZCA, PERU. HEIGHT, 25″.
MUSEO NACIONAL DE ANTROPOLOGÍA Y ARQUEOLOGÍA, LIMA, PERU.

EFFIGY JAR, ONE OF A GROUP OF ELEVEN. THE SHIRT IS TIE-DYED PATCHWORK. COASTAL TIAHUANACO STYLE. FROM FUNDO PACHECO, RIO GRANDE DE NAZCA, PERU. HEIGHT, 19½″. MUSEO NACIONAL DE ANTROPOLOGÍA Y ARQUEOLOGÍA, LIMA, PERU.

CEREMONIAL POLYCHROME JAR, ONE OF EIGHT USED TO STORE FEATHER-DECORATED TEMPLE WALL HANGINGS. RUKANA STYLE. FROM LA VICTORIA, CHURUNGA, CUENCA DE OCOÑA. HEIGHT, 37″. CIRCUMFERENCE, 74″. MUSEO NACIONAL DE ANTROPOLOGÍA Y ARQUEOLOGÍA, LIMA, PERU.

EFFIGY VESSEL REPRESENTING A MALE LLAMA. FROM FUNDO PACHECO, RIO GRANDE DE NAZCA, PERU. COASTAL TIAHUANACO STYLE, HEIGHT, 29″.
MUSEO NACIONAL DE ANTROPOLOGÍA Y ARQUEOLOGÍA, LIMA, PERU.

The exact number of mantles is rumored to have been ninety-six, over fifty of which reached the museum in Lima. There are some twenty examples in the United States. Brought together in a loan exhibition, they formed a spectacular wall decoration.

Six of the eight polychrome jars are now in the Lima museum. They all are face-collar jars with designs painted on the body of the vessel. No two are alike, but none of them can be considered Inca. The example we illustrate (p. 211) has three trophy heads in a central panel. On either side are pumas seen in profile, holding a snake which has a human head. The neck of the jar evidently represents a headband. In the center of this is a degenerate form of the well-known Nazca fleur-de-lys motif shown on page 202. We do not find it strange that ceremonial vessels for temple use should be treasured for years and ultimately be found with articles of a much later period. Another jar was decorated with an elongated type of monkey which appears only on late Nazca pottery. On various vessels we noted Coastal Tiahuanaco traits such as profile puma and condor heads, vertically divided bichrome eyes, three-fingered hands, N-shaped canine teeth and weeping eyes.

Peruvian camels, including the domesticated alpaca and llama, thrive in the cooler climate of the mountains but have been used as well on the coast. They are pictured in the styles of Mochica, Chimu, Nazca and Paracas. They also appear as effigy vessels of Coastal Tiahuanaco date. A great variety of positions is represented, standing, lying down, grazing and scratching. One vessel is shaped like a llama skull, modeled with obvious anatomical accuracy. The standing male llama on page 212, alert and graceful, is one of the largest of these figures. It must resemble the gold and silver "sheep" mentioned in the Spanish inventories of Inca treasure.

The basis of good weaving is good spinning, for the excellence of the yarn is the truest guide to the quality of the cloth. Textile experts agree that the perfect thread is not to seek; it was made in Peru long ago. In regularity of twist and evenness of diameter the Peruvian women were in advance of the best machine spinning of today. The modern power loom improves the rate of production but not the quality of the fabric. Coastal Tiahuanaco tapestries are famed for their harmonious colors and the excellence of the weaving. They are fashioned with cotton warps and wefts of vicuña wool, the finest known animal fibre, with a count of 2500 to the inch. A Gobelin tapestry made several centuries ago will average twenty warps and eighty-five wefts per inch. Coastal Tiahuanaco tapestries have been analyzed which contain forty to fifty warps per inch and 200 to 300 wefts. In small areas an incredible 500 wefts per inch have been counted. Inca tapestries differ in designs but are of equally fine quality. In comparing the workmanship of the two continents we should point out that New World fibres could be manipulated with greater ease and that technological developments in other industries, notably the production of metal cutting tools and weapons, were far more advanced in the Old World.

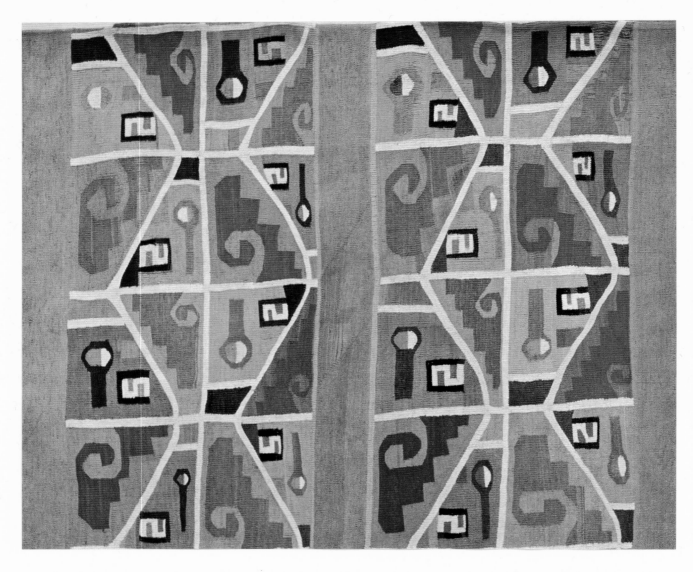

DETAIL OF TAPESTRY PONCHO. COASTAL TIAHUANACO STYLE. THE ART INSTITUTE OF CHICAGO.

The designs found on Coastal Tiahuanaco textiles are based on the Classical Bolivian sculpture, but, more often than not, only an expert will realize that they are anything but pure abstractions. The tapestry illustrated above contains in each square an epitome of the well-known puma motif. Whatever the importance of the symbolism of this animal, its essence is still preserved by a bichrome divided eye which weeps, by an angular S-shaped element which represents the mouth and teeth and, cut off by a diagonal line, a terraced scroll which indicates the body and tail.

Archaeologists divide the Coastal Tiahuanaco art period into two or more phases. It is probable that the beginning took place rapidly. The ultimate fading out and amalgamation with new local art schools must be worked out for each coastal valley. No dates are yet known. We can summarize the entire Tiahuanaco phenomenon by stating that no other influence in art reached such proportions in the New World. How, when and why remains an archaeological problem which perhaps never can be fully solved.

INCA

The Inca were a dynasty of petty chiefs who for many years had struggled to maintain themselves in the vicinity of Cuzco. A century before the Spaniards reached Peru the Inca began to leave permanent garrisons wherever their troops won victories. Within four generations, they had established an empire which extended from Colombia to south-central Chile and northwestern Argentina. Furthermore, they had imposed a social system and set up means of communication which enabled them to govern a vast polyglot area, which never before or since has been a political unit.

The Inca expansion was not achieved without hard fighting, but this was accompanied by astute diplomacy. Many tribes, beset by enemies or of inferior culture, could appreciate the economic advantages and military security offered by the Inca and submitted voluntarily. The Inca had one great military advantage over the highly developed coastal valleys because they could attack from the rear and divert the vital irrigation waters.

Our picture of Inca rule is largely derived from Spanish sources whose major interest lay in the military and political power which had been overcome. We know very little about the people who, either voluntarily or by force, had been incorporated in the Inca realm. It is evident, however, that many revolts occurred of which we lack the details. When Pizarro arrived, a successful revolution had just taken place. The legitimate ruler Huáscar had been defeated and captured by his half-brother Atahualpa.

Inca sovereignty in theory was based on their divine descent from the Sun and Moon. In fact their power was derived from advanced economic and governmental organization and from the development of a system of rapid communications which facilitated normal administration and permitted the rapid concentration of military force when needed. This was the only true empire ever developed in aboriginal America, designed to incorporate permanently within its framework the peoples who were conquered.

At the head of the system was the ruling Inca whose power was absolute and who was worshipped as divine during his lifetime. His queen in the later reigns was his sister, to maintain the complete purity of Inca blood, but he had many secondary wives whose children formed a new royal clan or *ayllu*, a nobility by inheritance. High officials were of pure Inca birth and functionaries of lesser rank came from the royal clans. The empire expanded so rapidly that to obtain a sufficient number of officials a hereditary class of Incas by privilege was created from the chiefs who had submitted voluntarily.

The population was divided into groups of families numbering from 10,000 to 100, each governed by an Inca noble. Smaller units of 10 or 50 families were placed under non-hereditary officers. The general population also was divided into age groups, each with appropriate tasks and duties. Thus each individual was given an occupation: farming, public works, mining, etc., and specialists were developed such as metal workers or weavers.

This system worked well as it provided for the individual, governmental officers and the temples. To keep it functioning, a method of accounting became necessary which was accomplished with a device known as a *quipu*. This consisted of a base cord to which knotted strings of various colors and thickness were attached. The meaning of each string presumably was a matter of individual memory, for *quipus* often were buried with the dead. The knots, however, formed a numerical system, based on decimals and place notation. The knots were what we call a "hangman's knot" and the numbers from 1 to 9 were indicated by the number of turns in any given knot. Higher units, tens, hundreds, thousands, etc., were determined by the position of a knot in relation to the extended fingers, hand and arm. This numerical system is not vigesimal such as was employed by the Maya and other Middle American peoples. It contained no visual method of expressing zero but nevertheless very large numbers could be recorded.

The Inca presumably used some unit of linear measurement but it has not been detected. Peru was the only region in the New World where balance scales were employed. They consist of finely carved small beams of wood, bone or metal with nets or small pans suspended from either end. A system of weights has been tentatively identified which was altered after the Conquest to conform with Spanish monetary units in which tribute was paid.

Maintenance of the Inca empire depended on the roads, many of earlier date, which were consolidated into two great parallel systems running north and south, linked by numerous cross-roads. No great width was necessary as there was no wheeled traffic. Construction on the coast presented few problems, but in many places they were built up above the ground level, especially in the vicinity of ceremonial centers such as Pachacamac. The principal mountain road, running from the Ecuador-Colombia frontier through Quito and Cuzco to Lake Titicaca where it branched into Argentina and Chile, was a formidable engineering problem. Mountains had to be passed, at times by cutting tunnels and stairs in the living rock. Torrential streams called for bridges. Some were of beams or stone slabs built up on the principle of the corbel vault used by the Maya. Others were suspension bridges with wooden floors supported by great fibre cables with others serving as rails. Maintenance was a serious problem as the cables tended to rot and had to be renewed frequently. Nothing better was developed in Colonial times and the famous Inca bridge over the Apurimac gorge was in use less than a century ago. Several such suspension bridges of similar type still function, for instance in Costa Rica. Crossing them is a dubious pleasure, for they quiver and shake at every step and they also sway both up and down and sideways.

Travel was limited to government business but the roads were highly organized. At frequent intervals a pair of houses were built on either side of the road where runners called *chasqui* waited to forward messages. Every few miles there were inns which also served as store houses. High officials and the Inca traveled in litters. Completely furnished palaces were established in every province for the accommodation of the ruler. In one of these there was a circular swimming pool filled with salt water carried from the ocean in jars.

As a matter of policy, the Inca often allowed the conquered peoples to continue to live much as they had done before and to worship their own gods. As a state religion, however, Sun temples were erected in all important centers and were richly endowed with gold.

The Inca rulers became masters of everything produced in their domain, but among their subjects were many fine craftsmen who worked in the local styles of Cuzco. Wherever the Inca troops had marched and especially where garrisons had been established, artifacts in Inca style may be expected to turn up. Although the Inca occupation was brief, assimilation and blending with local types had begun.

The Inca rulers worshipped the Sun and Moon whom they claimed as ancestors. Hence they demanded as tribute the entire gold and silver production of their realm, symbolic of this divine pair. It was this concentration and control of wealth which made possible the great treasure secured by the Spaniards from the ransom of the captured Emperor Atahualpa and the loot of Cuzco. When an emperor died, the rooms where he had slept in his palace in Cuzco were sealed with all their precious furnishings. His mummified body was placed in the Temple of the Sun. His golden statue, however, remained in his palace and was served as if alive by a numerous retinue. When these attendants died, their offspring replaced them, and were maintained by revenue set aside for their support. The new ruler had to build a new palace for himself in Cuzco and accumulate the treasure for its furnishings. The Emperor Huáscar, at the time of his death, had ruled for five years but had not completed a palace. It is said that he threatened to bury his ancestors and seize their possessions because the dead had all that was best in his kingdom.

After the conquest of Mexico, not only were gold and silver sent to Spain but many artifacts exemplifying the technical skills and artistic standards of the country. Apparently only gold and silver were sent from Peru but there is an inventory of the King's fifth which gives a slight idea of its nature. There were thirty gold jars with an average weight of forty-five pounds each and there were twenty-eight gold statues of men, women and "sheep" (i.e. llamas) with an average weight of forty pounds. The silver, said to have been more artistically wrought than the gold, included three "sheep" and a shepherd, twelve women and twenty-nine two-handled silver jars.

INCA SILVER DOLL FROM CERRO PLOMO, CHILE. HEIGHT, 7″. MUSEO NACIONAL DE HISTORIA NATURAL, SANTIAGO DE CHILE.

INCA SILVER LLAMA WITH GOLD APPLIQUÉ. HEIGHT, 9⅛". AMERICAN MUSEUM OF NATURAL HISTORY, NEW YORK.

INCA VASE OF STANDARD ARYBALLOS SHAPE. HEIGHT, 44″. UNIVERSITY MUSEUM, PHILADELPHIA.

Eight of these great silver vessels reached the court, and, like everything else, were reduced to bullion. There is no known description of them and it is possible that Charles V never looked at them. A signed receipt shows that the King was more interested that day in the simultaneous arrival of an unfortunate individual for his prison than in the silver from Peru.

Surviving examples of Inca workmanship in gold or silver are not numerous nor are they outstanding in size and artistry. The concentration of precious metals in the hands of the royal family was without precedent and enabled the Spaniards to seize much treasure. It also facilitated the transportation and successful hiding of the wealth amassed from temples and palaces, which probably included much of what the natives considered to be of outstanding artistic and technical merit.

On page 218 we illustrate a silver doll dressed in a mantle especially woven to size. It was placed with the child of an Inca official who had been sacrificed by exposure on a mountain top in central Chile. It is of interest that this hollow silver figure was fashioned by joining hammered thin sheets of metal. This was a technique developed by Chavin craftsmen before the Christian era. That it continued in use for probably 2600 years is characteristic of the conservatism found in this and other aspects of Peruvian art.

The silver llama on page 219 is a massive casting. In spite of the conventionalized cylindrical body, the alert pose characteristic of this animal (also seen on page 212) has been captured. The artist carved his wax model so that most of the blanket covering the back as well as the girth was sunken and could be color-filled, but silver diamonds projected above the surface to form a pattern. The sides of this coverlet were outlined by a narrow inlaid zigzag band of gold. A final touch of technical virtuosity are the tiny toenails of gold. The size of the statues and vessels of gold and silver shipped to Spain is reflected in the great silver jar on page 184; this small figurine must exhibit some of the qualities which induced an unimaginative compiler of the official inventory to state that the silver especially was "artistically wrought."

Inca pottery is of high quality, well fired and hard. The principal shapes are small plates (p. 222) and jars with tall flaring necks and a conical base (p. 220). Inca textiles, especially tapestry shirts, rank with the finest weaving (p. 223). A technical advance in metallurgy was the inlaying of one metal in another. More important perhaps was the spread of the use of bronze and knowledge of the proper copper-tin alloys for producing both tools with sharp cutting edges and clean castings for ornaments.

The Inca did not produce major stone or wooden statuary, perhaps because they preferred large images of precious metals, but they carved small objects such as bowls of stone, figures of llamas, star-shaped club heads. They were, however, excellent

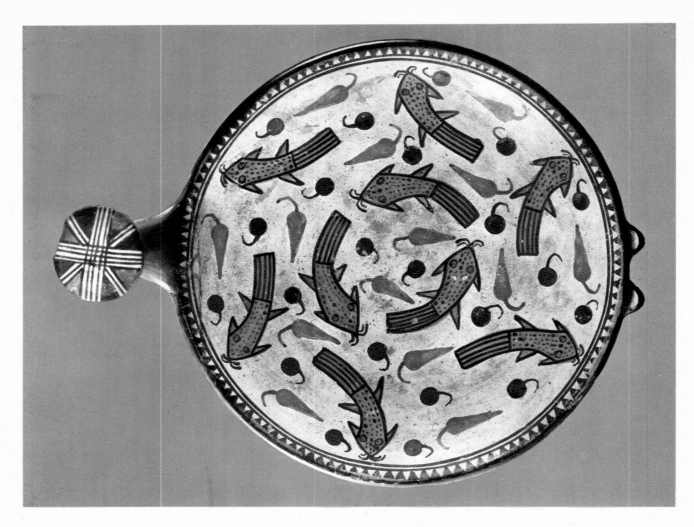

INCA PLATE. DIAMETER, 9⅜″. THE ART INSTITUTE OF CHICAGO.

masons and stone cutters. We have already mentioned their great road system. In addition they constructed agricultural terraces and water systems both for irrigation and domestic use. They also erected an amazing number of government and public buildings such as palaces, temples and fortresses. These were of adobe in the coastal valleys but, in the mountain regions from Ecuador to Argentina, they were of cut stone.

The fame of Inca masonry is fully justified because, with the exception of Classical Tiahuanaco, it was unexcelled in the New World. There are several styles which formerly were thought to be sequent but now are accepted as contemporaneous. Carefully dressed blocks of stone were laid in courses, sometimes with a smooth exterior surface—sometimes with a slight bulge on the exterior which gives a pleasing effect of light and shade. Polygonal masonry has angular blocks of individual shapes, each one of which had to be ground to fit its appointed place. This type of masonry appears in house walls but more often it consists of large blocks in terrace and foundation walls. Sacsahuaman, the great triple-tiered Inca fortress on the outskirts of Cuzco, is famous for its polygonal masonry, and some of the stones are as much as twenty feet in height.

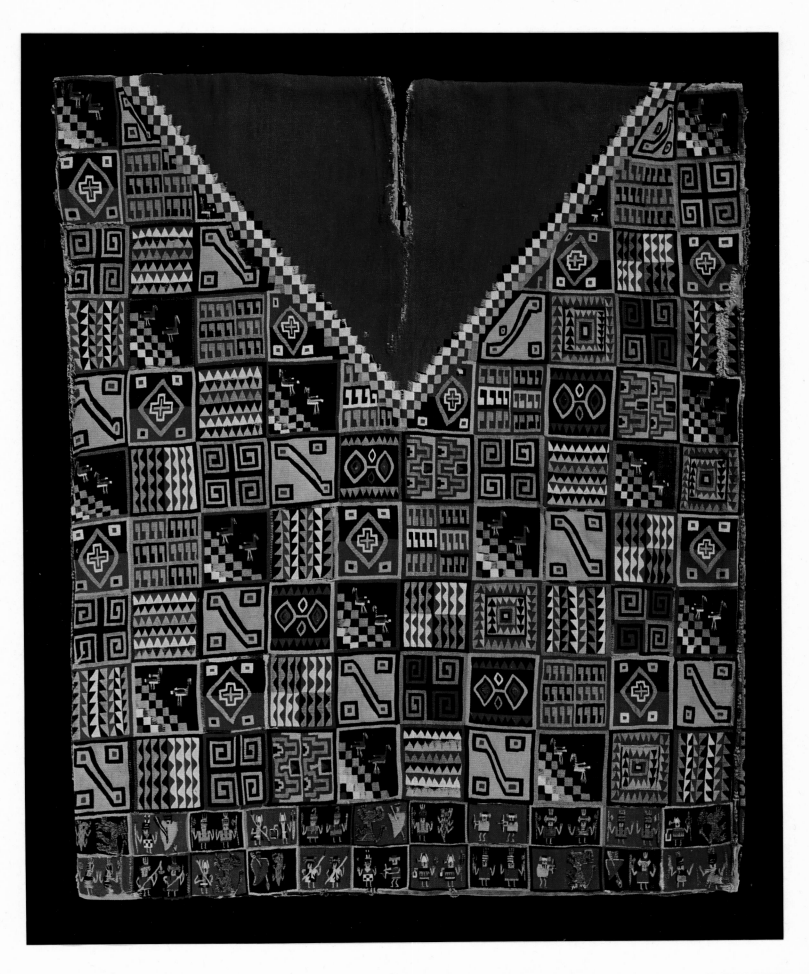

INCA PONCHO FROM THE ISLAND OF TITICACA, BOLIVIA. HEIGHT, 38″. WIDTH, 30″. AMERICAN MUSEUM OF NATURAL HISTORY, NEW YORK.

We have very little information about the appearance and interior arrangement of the major Inca buildings. The walls were as much as 15 to 20 feet in height and the gabled roofs were supported by great wooden beams covered with thatch several feet in thickness. Trapezoidal doorways and niches were the chief architectural feature. The Sun Temple at Cuzco, known as *Coricancha,* the Court of Gold, had a band of gold two palms wide encircling the outer walls and a wider band around the inner court. These were replaced with plaster after the Conquest. Parts of this building today are incorporated in a Dominican church. Apparently it consisted of a series of chapels and contained no large rooms but some of the palaces are said to have included halls measuring up to 60 by 200 paces. It is clear that the Spaniards found no use for such buildings. Cuzco streets today often are lined by exterior Inca walls but the interiors have been demolished. In several cases when Inca buildings were granted as residences to the victorious Spaniards, they were so large that several individuals were assigned to each.

As one would expect, the most imposing Inca buildings were in Cuzco, the ancient capital, and its vicinity. In spite of the fact that this area was soon settled by Europeans who used the Inca constructions chiefly as quarries, much may be seen today. Half a century ago a surprising archaeological discovery was an abandoned Inca city now known as Machu Picchu. It straddles a mile-high mountain ridge encircled on three sides by the Urubamba river and it commands a majestic view of the surrounding mountains. This city was completely unknown to the Spaniards. Its walls are of the finest Inca masonry; excavation has brought to light various artifacts of pure Inca style but no treasure of precious metal. The size and arrangement of houses and rooms suggest neither a garrison post nor a royal residence.

Machu Picchu is an archaeological jewel but it remains an enigma. There is no evidence that it was ever conquered and looted. There is nothing to indicate why or when the inhabitants packed their household goods and departed. Large areas in the Peruvian Andes are completely unknown today. When explored, it is to be hoped that they will disclose unknown and unsuspected vistas of life in the past.

CONCLUSION

One cannot but wonder what the future held for the Aztec and Inca, the major American political powers of the sixteenth century, had not the armies of Spain dominated them. Both had reached a flood tide of conquest; both nourished the seeds of self destruction. The Inca had created a great empire and the mechanism to rule it, but a civil war had disrupted the continuity of government, and the immediate future was unpredictable. The Aztecs apparently were about to consolidate their conquests by posting garrisons but had yet to devise a unified system of government. Hostile neighbors were a menace. Would an aboriginal leader have united them to overwhelm the Aztecs or would they have yielded one by one to the Aztec armies?

Looking further into the past, archaeological finds reveal the rise and fall of distinctive art styles, but those of major significance, both in geographical distribution and chronological longevity, stemmed from Mexico, Peru and adjacent areas. We cannot explain what forces led to the appearance, apparently without antecedents, of styles like Chavin and Olmec. In some cases, such as Teotihuacan, destruction by fire and sword is indicated. In others, such as Nazca, internal collapse and degeneration may have paved the way for the succeeding Tiahuanaco styles. What caused the termination of many cultures, including Classic Maya, is purely speculative. The prospects of Aztec or Inca survival are not enhanced by the repeated elimination of older cultures.

A comparison of the arts from the Old World and the New is scarcely justified because the function, symbolism and ideals of beauty are so far apart. Something, however, can be said about technical skills. Aboriginal Americans normally built civic or ceremonial centers rather than true cities with concentrated housing. Tenochtitlan, the Aztec capital, however, is said to have had 300,000 inhabitants with aqueducts supplying fresh water and an adequate sanitary system. Peruvian hydraulic engineers employed the principle of the inverted siphon to bring water to houses, temples and forts. Peruvian and Bolivian masonry is unsurpassed, individual stones weighing up to a hundred tons. Maya edifices of lime mortar covered with a veneer of cut stone have survived for centuries in tropic jungles. New World sculpture, from the Lanzon of Chavin to the Aztec Coatlicue, symbolizes the gods, mysterious, monstrous but awe-inspiring. To European eyes, however, minor sculpture, picturing the contemporary world, has definite charm. Maya figurines, small Aztec carvings, Mochica portraits and animal figures are outstanding. Painting is confined to murals and pottery vessels. At Teotihuacan, religious motifs are seen on both. Maya painting does not indicate distance by perspective nor contours by shading but can picture the body in any position which can be outlined in silhouette. Quartering views and the suggestion of motion thus become possible. Mochica potters evidently desired similar effects but lacked the skill to achieve them.

Certain arts of the Americas reached distinguished heights. Textiles even today are unsurpassed in spinning, tightness of weave, variety of techniques and brilliance of color. Metallurgy was in skilled hands. Outstanding workmanship included bimetallic castings of gold and silver, also a technique for working platinum several centuries before it was achieved in Europe. Lapidaries, especially in Mexico, produced exquisite carvings in jade, emerald, crystal, onyx and other semi-precious stones. A unique skill, now forgotten, was the employment of feathers as pigment in Mexico. Copies of European paintings, a few of which may still be seen in Madrid, reveal a scarcely believable virtuosity. In contrast, the American Indians lacked commonplace aspects of contemporary European culture. Animals for domestication such as the horse, ox or sheep did not exist. There was no wheeled transportation. Most important perhaps, the entire complex of iron and steel was unknown. Alloys of comparable hardness such as bronze (copper-tin) and tumbaga (copper-gold) had been manufactured for centuries but their use in tools and weapons never was fully developed. The New World eagerly received the products of the Old and they spread with remarkable rapidity.

On the other hand, Europeans had little interest in the Americas, apart from immediate sources of wealth. Two Italians and a German left written appreciations of the Mexican artifacts which reached Spain. Two of Cortez' treasure ships were captured by the French but we know nothing about their cargoes except for one item: the great pyramidal emerald of Montezuma, as large as the palm of the hand. This became part of the crown jewels and disappeared during the French revolution.

European artists first recognized the skills of other continents, followed by a constantly growing public. Other lands were recognized before the Americas. The Boston Museum of Fine Arts, less than half a century ago, was the first institution to display an art exhibition, thus named, of New World artifacts, followed a few years later by the Burlington Fine Arts Club of London. From these two displays have stemmed the constantly growing general interest in the craftsmanship, skills and exotic ideals of beauty which make possible the publication of this volume.

INDEX OF NAMES AND PLACES

Acari, Peru 201.
Acatlan de Pérez Figueroa, Oaxaca 28.
Ahuitzotl 52, 66, 67.
Alaska 5.
Altar de Sacrificios, Guatemala 120, 122, 123.
Amazon River 155.
Andes Mountains 155, 156, 178, 224.
Anghiera, Peter Martyr d' 4.
Antioquía State, Colombia 151.
Apurimac Gorge, Peru 216.
Arctic Ocean 5.
Argentina 215, 216, 222.
Ascope Aqueduct, Peru 164.
Asia 5.
Asia, Peru 201.
Atahualpa 215, 217.
Atrato River, Colombia 152.
Austria 4.
Axayacatl 52, 57.
Azcapotzalco, Valley of Mexico 49, 50.
Aztec civilization 3, 4, 9, 19, 24, 27, 29, 39, 40, 44, 46, 47, 50, 51-69, 72, 74, 75, 86, 87, 89, 95, 113, 126, 133, 134, 169, 225, 226.

Baja Vera Paz Department, Guatemala 121.
Balser, Charles, Collection, San José, Costa Rica 136.
Barbachano Ponce Collection, Mexico City 108.
Basel, Museum für Völkerkunde 61.
Behring Straits 5.
Bellinger 192.
Bennett Stela 205.
Bird, Junius B. 192.
Bogotá 147-149, 151.
Bolivia 3, 147, 204, 208, 214, 223, 226.
Bonampak, Mexico 62, 107, 110.
Bonampak murals 107, 110-112, 120, 126, 127.
Boston Museum of Fine Arts 226.
British Honduras 83, 94.
Brooklyn Museum 35.

Burlington Fine Arts Club, London 226.

Cadiz 3.
Cahuachi, Rio Grande de Nazca 209.
Calendar Stone 56-58.
California Indians 63.
Calima style 149, 152.
Callejon de Huaylas Basin, Peru 178.
Cambridge, England, University Museum of Archaeology and Ethnology 187.
Campeche, Mexico 107, 108.
Carnegie Institution, Washington 16.
Carnegie Museum, Pittsburg 138.
Carthage 9.
Casma, Peru 172.
Casma Valley, Peru 157.
Caso, Dr Alfonso 89.
Cativé, Panama 145.
Cellini, Benvenuto 4.
Cenote of Sacrifice, Chichen Itza 113, 152.
Centeotl 62.
Cerro Montoso style 36-38.
Cerro Plomo, Chile 218.
Cerro Sechin, Peru 82, 157.
Chacmool figures 127.
Chalchihuitlicue 56.
Chamelecon Valley, Honduras 133.
Chanchan, Peru 164, 180, 182, 184, 188.
Chapultepec, Mexico 51, 63.
Charles V of Spain 4, 221.
Chavin style 15, 36, 147, 156-160, 163, 169, 172, 190, 201, 221, 225, 226.
Chavin de Huántar, Peru 156-158, 160, 164.
Chiapas State, Mexico 76, 80, 83, 92, 93, 96, 100, 107, 114, 115.
Chibchan tribe, Colombia 147.
Chicago, Art Institute 186, 214, 222.
Chicama Valley, Peru 161, 163, 164, 172.
Chichen Itza, Yucatan 31, 34, 49, 50, 52, 58, 62, 113, 124-128.
Chichimec period 50, 69.

Chile 156, 208, 215, 216, 221.
Chimo 180.
Chimu style 2, 164, 172, 180-189, 208, 213.
China 133, 169.
Chincha style 204.
Chira River, Peru 172.
Chiriqui Province, Panama 134, 138.
Cholula, Mexico 83, 97.
Cholula ware 69, 83.
Chongoyape, Peru 159.
Chou Dynasty, China 133.
Chupícuaro, Mexico 10, 71.
Churunga, Peru 211.
Cihuacoatl 29.
Coatlicue 56, 58, 59, 226.
Cocijo 76.
Coclé style 138, 139, 142-145.
Coixtlahuaca, Oaxaca 86.
Colima style 72, 73, 75.
Colombia 36, 75, 83, 131, 147-152, 215, 216.
Columbus, Christopher 3, 142.
Comalcalco, Mexico 98, 99.
Comayagua Valley, Honduras 133.
Copador style 133.
Copan, Honduras 95, 98, 103-105, 133.
Cortez, Hernando 4, 9, 52, 54, 56, 64, 66, 226.
Costa Rica 16, 20, 53, 83, 130, 131, 134-141, 147, 156, 208, 216.
Covarrubias Collection 33, 43.
Covarrubias, Miguel 62, 66.
Coyolxauhqui 58.
Cuenca de Ocoña, Peru 211.
Cuicuilco, Valley of Mexico 13-15, 39.
Culebra Bay, Costa Rica 136.
Culhuacan, Valley of Mexico 49, 50.
Cupisnique, Peru 158, 160, 163.
Cuzco, Peru 147, 215-217, 224.

Dada, Juan, Collection, San José, Costa Rica 135.
Darien style 148, 152.
Diaz del Castillo, Bernal 53, 54, 56, 69.
Diquis Delta, Costa Rica 138.

Dresden 124.
Dürer, Albrecht 4.

Eagle Knights 29.
Ecuador 75, 131, 216, 222.
Eecatl 29.
Egyptian art 166.
El Arbolillo, Valley of Mexico 13.
El Dorado 147.
El Lanzon 4, 156, 157, 160, 226.
El Opeño, Mexico 71.
El Peten, Guatemala 94, 96, 97, 101,
    102, 106, 112, 115, 117, 124.
El Salvador 13, 16, 19, 31, 39, 41,
    60, 93, 120, 133.
England 69.
Equator 155.
Escorial 4.

Florence, Museo Archeologico 45.
Fonseca Bay, El Salvador 60.
Fundo Pacheco, Peru 207, 208, 210,
    212.

Gallegos, Roberto 87.
Gallinazo style 160, 163.
Gobelin tapestries 213.
Göteborg, Etnografiska Museet, 197-
    200.
Great Lakes, United States 147.
Grijalva, Juan de 69.
Guanajuato State, Mexico 71.
Guápiles, Costa Rica 134, 137, 138.
Guatemala 11, 16, 19, 34, 39, 41, 52,
    71, 80, 93, 94, 96, 97, 101, 103, 104,
    105, 107, 112, 115-120, 124, 128,
    133.
Guatemala City, Museo de Arqueo-
    logía y Etnología de Guatemala 101,
    103, 106, 116, 119, 121-123.
Guerrero State, Mexico 16, 43, 71, 73.
Gulf of Mexico 15, 16, 19, 20, 31, 34,
    36, 49, 58, 80.

Han Dynasty, China 169.
Harvard 120, 123, 143.
Hawaii 63.
Hidalgo, Mexico 48.
Hochob, Mexico 98.
Holmul, Guatemala 94, 124.
Honduras 13, 16, 31, 95, 105, 120,
    132-134.
Huaca del Dragón, Colombia 151.
Huaca del Sol, Peru 176.
Huari, Peru 207.
Huari style 156.
Huascar 215, 217.
Huastec 34-37, 62.
Huehueteotl 29.
Huitzilopochtli 54, 58, 60.

Ica style 204.
Ica Valley, Peru 190, 201.
Illima, Lambayeque, Peru 183.
Inca civilization 3, 4, 131, 156, 180,
    182, 189, 206, 208, 213, 215-225.
Intermediate Area 129-152.
Isla de Sacrificios, Vera Cruz 36, 68,
    69.
Isthmian art 138.
Italy 4.
Itza 124.
Itzcoatl 51.

Jaina style 107-109.
Jalapa, Mexico 17, 18, 25-27, 32.

Kaminaljuyú, Guatemala 44, 96, 119,
    120, 124.
Kukulcan 29, 125, 126.
Kunz, Dr G. F. 20.
Kunz Axe 20, 21.

La Cumbre Canal, Peru 164.
Lambayeque Valley, Peru 159, 183.
Landa, Bishop Diego de 124.
Lanzon, see El Lanzon.
La Paz, Bolivia 205.
Larco Herrera Museum, Lima 175-
    177.
Larco Hoyle Collection, Lima 161,
    163, 173, 174, 179, 181, 185.
La Vaca, Punta Burica, Costa Rica
    130, 139, 141.
La Venta, Vera Cruz 19, 22.
La Ventilla, Mexico 41, 42.
La Victoria, Peru 211.
Las Bocas, Mexico 12, 13, 158.
Las Huacas, Nicoya Peninsula 138.
Leguía, Augusto Bernardino 182.
Lenca tribes, Nicaragua 133.
Leyden, Rijksmuseum 112.
Leyden Plaque 102, 103, 112.
Lima, Peru 2, 154, 160, 164, 172, 180,
    182, 202, 213;
    Museo Nacional de Antropología y
    Arqueología 159, 160, 168, 171, 184,
    190, 192, 193, 195, 196, 202, 203,
    207, 209-212.
London, British Museum 64, 100, 150.
Los Cerros, Vera Cruz 26, 27.
Lubaantun region 107.
Luna ware, Costa Rica and Nicaragua
    134.

Machu Picchu, Peru 224.
Macuilxochitl 89.
Madrid 124, 226; Escorial 4; Museo
    de América 165.
Magellan, Straits of 5.
Mampox, Colombia 147.
Maya civilization 5, 14, 20, 29, 44,
    47, 49, 62, 71, 73, 80, 83, 91-128,
    131, 170, 216, 226.
Mayapan, Yucatan 16.
Mérida, Yucatan 16.
Mexico 3-5, 9-89, 92, 99, 108, 109,
    114, 115, 126, 127, 131, 133, 134,
    137, 147, 156, 157, 169, 170, 189,
    217, 225, 226.
Mexico City 5, 8, 10, 51, 56, 125,
    169;
    Diego Rivera Museum 47, 70;
    Museo Nacional de Antropología
    15, 22, 28, 33, 37, 41-44, 48, 55, 57-
    59, 63, 68, 72, 73, 77, 79, 81, 85,
    86, 92, 99, 109, 114, 115;
    Museo Nacional de Mexico 41, 63.
Mezcala carvings 71.
Michoacan State, Mexico 71, 72.
Mictlantecutli 27, 84, 87.
Mihuatlan, Oaxaca 88.
Mitla, Mexico 4, 82.
Mixcoatl 49.
Mixtec 27, 44, 50, 62, 65, 66, 69, 76,
    82-89, 113.
Mixteca-Puebla style 69, 82.

Moche River and Valley, Peru 172,
    176, 180.
Mochica style 27, 82, 147, 156, 160,
    163-179, 180, 182, 200, 208, 213,
    226.
Monagrillo ware, Panama 131.
Monte Alban, Mexico 34, 76-82, 84,
    87, 157.
Montezuma I 51.
Montezuma II 4, 52-54, 60, 64, 69,
    83, 226.
Mujica Gallo Collection, Lima 2, 154,
    183.

Nacasola, Costa Rica 135.
Nahua 34, 82.
Nayarit, Mexico 70, 74, 75.
Nazca style, Peru 160, 178, 190, 200,
    201-204, 207, 213, 225.
Nebaj, Guatemala 116.
New York, American Museum of
    Natural History 21, 88, 162, 188,
    219, 223;
    Museum of Primitive Art 29.
Nicaragua 13, 53, 60, 133, 134-141.
Nicarao 134.
Nicoya, Costa Rica 83, 134-138.

Oaxaca, Mexico 21, 24, 28, 29, 52,
    69, 77, 79, 81, 82, 84-87, 89;
    Museo Regional de Oaxaca 84.
Ocucaje, Peru 190.
Olmec style 14, 16-23, 24, 43, 52, 71,
    73, 76, 80, 96, 106, 137, 156, 225.
Olmeda de Olvera Collection, Mexico
    City 78.
Osa Peninsula, Costa Rica 149.
Otates, Vera Cruz 37.

Pacasmayo, Peru 172.
Pachacamac, Peru 162, 216.
Pacific Ocean 5, 83, 93, 134, 138, 155,
    178.
Palenque, Mexico 80, 92, 94, 98, 102,
    113-115, 120, 125.
Paleo-Indians 5, 11, 39.
Paleolithic Age 5.
Panama 16, 75, 83, 131, 138, 142-146,
    147, 152, 164.
Panama Canal Zone 152.
Panama City, Museo Nacional de
    Panama 144, 145.
Paracas Cavernas style 160, 189-200,
    213.
Paracas Necropolis style 160, 189-
    202, 213.
Paracas Peninsula, Peru 189-200.
Paraguay 29.
Paris 124.
Pennsylvania, University of 102.
Peru 3-5, 14, 15, 19, 27, 36, 63, 72,
    82, 131, 142, 147, 152, 153-226.
Philadelphia, University Museum
    132, 143, 146, 220.
Philip II of Spain 4.
Piedras Negras, Guatemala 101, 103,
    113, 115, 125.
Pisco, Peru 189.
Pisco Valley 201.
Pitao Cozobi 80.
Pittsburg, Carnegie Museum 138.
Piura, Peru 157.
Pizarro, Francisco 180, 215.

228

Pleistocene Age 5.
Polynesia 63.
Popoyan, Colombia 147, 150.
Portuguese 53.
Puebla State, Mexico 12, 43, 66, 69, 82.
Puerto Barrios, Guatemala 112.
Puerto Jiménez, Costa Rica 140.
Punta Burica, Costa Rica 130, 138, 139, 141.
Purulhá, Guatemala 121.
Pyramid of the Moon, Teotihuacan 15, 39, 40.
Pyramid of the Sun, Teotihuacan 15, 39, 40.

Quetzalcoatl 29, 40, 49, 124.
Quiché District, Guatemala 71, 116.
Quimbaya style 46, 151, 152.
Quirigua, Guatemala 103, 104.
Quito, Ecuador 216.

Raimondi Panel 160.
Recuay style 178, 179.
Remojadas style 24-29, 60.
Rio Grande de Nazca Valley, Peru 201, 207-210, 212.
Rio Tonalá, Mexico 19.
Rome, Museo Preistorico 65.
Rowe, John 156.
Rukana style 211.
Ruz Tomb, Palenque, Mexico 113-115.

Sacsahuaman, Cuzco 222.
Salamanca 54.
Salinar style 160, 163, 169.
San Andres Tuxtla, Vera Cruz 33.
San José, Banco Central de Costa Rica 130, 139, 140, 141; Museo Nacional de Costa Rica 135.
San Lorenzo, Mexico 18, 19.
San Luis Potosí, Mexico 34, 35.
San Vicente Tancuayalab, Mexico 35.
Santa Marta River, Colombia 147.
Santa Rita, British Honduras 83.
Santa Valley, Peru 178.
Santiago de Chile, Museo Nacional de Historia Natural 218.
Sausal, Chicama Valley, Peru 161.
Sayil, Yucatan 125.
Sayula, Vera Cruz 17.
Seville 3.
Shang Dynasty, China 133.
Siberia 5.
Sierra de Santa Marta 151.
Sinaloa, Mexico 71, 83.
Sitio Conte, Panama 143.
Sologuren Collection 78.

Spain and the Spanish 4, 56, 60, 63, 66, 69, 72, 138, 142, 147, 178, 180, 182, 213, 215-217, 221, 224-226.
Spanish Conquest 3-5, 9, 15, 24, 34, 40, 54, 58, 63, 66, 69, 76, 82, 83, 124, 147, 156, 182, 204, 208, 216, 224.
Spanish Royal Historians 3, 4.

Tabasco, Mexico 16, 34, 99.
Tairona tribe, Colombia 151.
Tajin style 29, 34, 58.
Tamaulipas, Mexico 34.
Tarascans 72, 74, 83.
Tehuantepec, Mexico 52.
Tello, Dr Julio C. 182.
Temple of the Cross, Palenque 92.
Temple of Huitzilopochtli, Tlateloco 54.
Temple of the Inscriptions, Palenque 114, 115.
Temple of Quetzalcoatl, Teotihuacan 38.
Temple of Tezcatlipoca, Tlateloco 54.
Temple of the Warriors, Chichen Itza 127.
Tenayuca, Valley of Mexico 47, 50, 69.
Tenochtitlan, Valley of Mexico 51-53, 56, 58, 66, 69, 225.
Teotihuacan, Valley of Mexico 5, 9, 15, 20, 34, 38-47, 49, 50, 52, 56, 60, 62, 69, 71, 73, 76, 80, 87, 97, 102, 113, 120, 124, 127, 225, 226.
Tepantitla murals 42.
Tequixquiac, Mexico 5.
Tetitla, Teotihuacan 46.
Texcoco, Valley of Mexico 41, 50, 51, 54, 61.
Tezcatlipoca 49, 54, 56, 60.
Tiahuanaco, Bolivia 156, 178, 180, 189, 204-214, 225.
Ticoman, Valley of Mexico 13.
Tierra Blanca, Vera Cruz 26, 27.
Tikal, Guatemala 94, 97, 98, 101-103, 112, 115, 117, 118, 120, 124.
Titicaca Basin, Bolivia-Peru 147.
Titicaca, Lake, Bolivia-Peru 204, 216, 223.
Tizoc 52.
Tlacolulan, Vera Cruz 32.
Tlacopan, Mexico 51.
Tlalixcoyan, Vera Cruz 25.
Tlaloc 29, 40, 46.
Tlalocan 127.
Tlaltecuhtli 60.
Tlateloco, Mexico 51-55, 60, 69.
Tlatilco, Mexico 8, 10 13, 15, 24, 36.
Tlaxtli 29.
Tlazolteotl 61.

Tolima style 151, 152.
Toltec 24, 31, 34, 41, 48-50, 52, 58, 62, 83, 124-128.
Tonatiuh 56, 67.
Topiltzin 49.
Totonac 24, 29-34, 36, 74.
Tres Zapotes, Vera Cruz 19.
Trujillo, Peru 158, 180.
Tula, Valley of Mexico 9, 34, 41, 48-50, 52, 124.
Tulum, Yucatan 83, 125.
Túmbez, Peru 180.
Tzinzuntzan, Mexico 72.

Uaxactun, Guatemala 94, 96, 106, 124.
Ulua Valley, Honduras 132, 133.
United States 29, 98, 147, 213.
Urubamba River, Peru 224.
Usumacintla Basin, Guatemala 94, 101, 107, 113, 115, 125.
Uxmal, Yucatan 98.

Venezuela 131.
Ventilla Stela, Teotihuacan 42.
Vera Cruz, Mexico 16, 19, 24, 27, 29-34, 36, 42, 52, 68, 133; Museo de Antropología, Vera Cruz University 17, 18, 25-27, 32.
Veraguas Province, Panama 134, 138, 139, 145.
Vienna, Museum für Völkerkunde 67.

Washington, D.C., United States National Museum 138.
West Indies 29.
Worcester, Mass., Art Museum 74.

Xipe 60, 61, 86, 87, 134.
Xipe Totec 60, 61.
Xitle Volcano, Mexico 14.
Xochimilco District, Valley of Mexico 51.
Xochipilli 47.
Xochiquetzal 62.

Yauca, Peru 157.
Yaxchilan, Mexico 100, 101.
Yojoa style 133.
Yope 76.
Yucatan, Mexico 5, 16, 34, 49, 83, 94, 96, 98, 112, 124-128, 152.

Zaachila, Mexico 85, 87.
Zacatenco, Valley of Mexico 13.
Zacualpa, Salvador 124.
Zapotec 16, 20, 24, 60, 62, 76-82, 83, 87, 113, 115, 117.
Zoomorph P, Quirigua, Guatemala 104.

THIS BOOK WAS DESIGNED AND PRODUCED BY THE TECHNICAL STAFF OF ÉDITIONS D'ART ALBERT SKIRA. TEXT AND COLOR PLATES WERE PRINTED BY THE

COLOR STUDIOS
IMPRIMERIES RÉUNIES, LAUSANNE.

FINISHED THE THIRTIETH DAY OF JUNE NINETEEN HUNDRED AND SIXTY-FOUR.

BLACK AND WHITE PLATES ENGRAVED BY ROTO-SADAG S.A., GENEVA.

COLOR PLATES ENGRAVED BY GUEZELLE & RENOUARD, PARIS.

All the photographs in this book, both in color and in black and white, are by

LEE BOLTIN, NEW YORK

except those on the following pages: page 61 (Maurice Babey, Basel), page 165 (by J. Dominguez Garcia, Madrid), page 42 (Fotos Irmgard Groth Kimball, Mexico City), page 67 (Foto Meyer, Vienna), pages 45, 65 (Scala, Florence), pages 197, 198-199 (Folke D. Sörvik, Göteborg), pages 2, 154, 183 (Ralph Tietgens, New York), pages 64, 150, 187 (Zoltan Wegner, London), page 100 (British Museum, London), pages 186, 214, 222 (Art Institute of Chicago), pages 97, 132, 220 (University Museum, Philadelphia), page 206 (Peabody Museum, Harvard University), pages 30, 104 (American Museum of Natural History, New York), and page 35 (Brooklyn Museum). The sources of the line drawings are as follows: page 40 (by J. A. Gomez Rubio, from "Arquitectura Prehispánica" by Ignacio Marquina, Instituto Nacional de Antropología e Historia, Mexico City, 1951); pages 41, 57, 110, 111, 122, 166 (by Antonio Tejeda); pages 62, 66, 127 (by Miguel Covarrubias, from "Indian Art of Mexico and Central America" by Miguel Covarrubias, Alfred A. Knopf, Inc., New York, 1957); page 95 (by Abel Mendoza, from "Palenque, una ciudad maya" by Laurette Séjourné, Fondo de Cultura Económica, Mexico City, 1952); page 103 (from "Native American Art" by G. B. Gordon, The Museum Journal, University Museum Philadelphia, March, 1918); page 126 (by Miguel Angel Fernández, from "Arquitectura Prehispánica" by Ignacio Marquina, Instituto Nacional de Antropología e Historia, Mexico City, 1951); page 138 (by Miss Symme Burnstein); pages 157, 158, 160, 167 (by Pablo Carrera); page 194 (from "Chaski," Organo de la Asociación Peruana de Arqueología, Vol. I, No. 1, January-February, 1940); page 207 (by Lauro Venturi).

PRINTED IN SWITZERLAND